PN 3171 .H334 1987
Creative drama resource book
Heinig, Ruth Beall

2272

DATE DUE

Creative Drama
Resource Book
for Grades 4–6

Creative Drama Resource Book for Grades 4–6

Ruth Beall Heinig
Western Michigan University

Prentice-Hall, Englewood Cliffs, New Jersey 07632

Library of Congress Cataloging-in-Publication Data

HEINIG, RUTH BEALL
    Creative drama resource book for grades 4-6.

    Bibliography: p.
    1. Drama in education. I. Title.
PN3171.H334 1987   372.6'6   85-31242
ISBN 0-13-189333-5

Editorial/production supervision and
    interior design: Dee Amir Josephson
Cover Photo: Ann Hagen Griffiths
Manufacturing buyer: Harry P. Baisley

Printed in the United States of America

10 9 8 7 6 5 4

ISBN 0-13-189333-5   01

Prentice-Hall International (UK) Limited, *London*
Prentice-Hall of Australia Pty. Limited, *Sydney*
Prentice-Hall of Canada Inc., *Toronto*
Prentice-Hall Hispanoamericana, S.A., *Mexico*
Prentice-Hall of India Private Limited, *New Delhi*
Prentice-Hall of Japan, Inc., *Tokyo*
Prentice-Hall of Southeast Asia Pte. Ltd., *Singapore*
Editora Prentice-Hall do Brasil, Ltda., *Rio de Janeiro*
Whitehall Books Limited, *Wellington, New Zealand*

To all the teachers at Columbia Elementary School in Rochester, Indiana, during the years 1942 to 1950, who first opened the world of drama to me.

Contents

1

2

4

5

Nov. 95
missing
article →

Preface

This resource guide has been written for you—the elementary teacher who wants to begin teaching theatre arts and creative drama in your classroom. I have assumed that most of you have had little or no previous drama training.

The material grows out of and expands upon my earlier text (*Creative Drama for the Classroom Teacher,* 2nd ed., by Ruth Beall Heinig and Lyda Stillwell. Englewood Cliffs, NJ: Prentice-Hall, 1981). Essentially the same format, principles, and philosophy in that text remain throughout this new one. However, much material has been revised and significantly expanded. New chapters on puppetry, masks, and theatre attendance have been added; story dramatization now covers two chapters; over twenty sample lesson plans have been included; all bibliographies have been increased and updated, and many new photos have been added.

I realize that for some of you the thought of teaching creative drama and theatre arts is overwhelming. But I know you are thoroughly capable of the task. As an elementary teacher, you are already highly skilled in knowing about children's educational and psychological needs. You already know how children think and what they like. And, just as this knowledge is vital in teaching other curricular areas, so, too, is it in teaching drama. So you need not be intimidated by any of this material. In fact, I hope it sounds as if it is "right down your alley."

I have tried to demystify drama by leading you through activities from the most simple to the more complex, slowly and gradually, using methods I have developed during my twenty five years' experience in elementary and college classrooms. As much as possible, I have tried to build skills for you, chapter by chapter. In addition, within many of the chapters, the activities begin with the simpler ones and progress toward those that are more advanced. The masks in the margins highlight specific drama activities for easy reference. Numbers in parentheses throughout the text refer to correspondingly numbered anthologies and children's novels listed in Chapter 15.

Chapter 1 gives you an overview, particularly of creative drama since that is the major theatre arts activity for elementary children. Chapter 2 explains many of the guidelines you will find useful before beginning any drama activities. Chapter 3 launches you with simple and often well-known games to begin on, as does Chapter 4, which also introduces some suggestions in expanding playing space. Both chapters present sample lesson plans. Narrative pantomime, one of the most useful activities for beginners as well as those who are more advanced, is covered in Chapters 5 and 6. Extensive bibliographies of children's literature specifically selected for narrative pantomime work are included in both chapters. Three sample lesson plans are at the end of Chapter 6.

With Chapter 7 the focus moves to the many variations of pantomimes for guessing, while Chapter 8 explores the many variations of verbal activities. Both chapters present many games, ideas for incorporating curricular topics, as well as bibliographies of children's literature you can use. Chapter 9 gives special attention to creative work and ways to help children build their own plots and stories. Two sample lesson plans are included. Chapters 10 and 11 cover two methods for story dramatization that I call "circle stories" and "segmented stories" and include lesson plans for sixteen popular stories and books as well as an additional bibliography. Chapter 12 covers extended lesson planning, giving three sample extended lessons as well as a lesson plan reference chart. In Chapter 13 you will learn how to construct puppets and masks and how to use them in dramatization. Bibliographies of children's literature specifically suited to puppetry and masks are included. Chapter 14 addresses theatre attendance and theatre etiquette and includes a selected bibliography of theatre-related children's literature. A final bibliography of children's books and a glossary of terms completes the text.

I think it would be helpful for you to read through the material first in the order it is presented. After that, you need not feel bound to implement the book in lock-step fashion. Begin where you feel most comfortable and let that exploration lead you to your next attempts. Some may wish to begin with puppetry or story dramatization before trying material in the earlier chapters, for example. I believe I have given you more ideas than you can possibly use in a year's time so that you will have numerous choices and options. Feel free to experiment and to enjoy these activities with your students.

I wish to thank the following people for making this book possible: Coleman A. Jennings, Chairman, Drama Department, The University of Texas at Austin;

Kim Wheetley, Fine Arts Department, Texas Education Agency; the people at Prentice-Hall including editor, Steve Dalphin and production editor, Dee Josephson; special friends Robin Nott, Renée Rossman, Elaine Sievers, Andy, Anna, Ben, Brian, Brianna, Melanie, Lee, Ravi, and Ryan; and most especially my dear husband, Ed, who helps me keep my sanity and humor even during the darkest days.

Introduction

1

WHAT IS CREATIVE DRAMA?

If you were to look in on several upper elementary classrooms during a creative drama lesson, you might see a variety of activities. In one classroom, students might be exploring the mechanical movements of robots performing a variety of tasks; in another classroom they might be pantomiming a variety of occupations while their classmates guess; and in a third classroom, students might be dramatizing a favorite story, making up the dialogue as they go along.

Creative drama is known by a variety of names. Some have called it "informal drama," "creative play acting," "developmental drama," "educational drama," and "improvisational drama," to name only a few of the other terms.

The American Association of Theatre for Youth, a national organization of child drama professionals in this country, prefers the term "creative drama" and defines it, in part, as

> an improvisational, nonexhibitional, process-centered form of drama in which participants are guided by a leader to imagine, enact, and reflect upon human experiences.[1]

[1] Jed H. Davis and Tom Behm, "Terminology of Drama/Theatre with and for Children: A Redefinition," *Children's Theatre Review*, 27, no. 1 (1978), 10–11.

The definition further explains:

> The creative drama process is dynamic. The leader guides the group to explore, develop, express and communicate ideas, concepts, and feelings through dramatic enactment. In creative drama the group improvises action and dialogue appropriate to the content it is exploring, using elements of drama to give form and meaning to the experience.[2]

WHAT ARE THE GOALS OF CREATIVE DRAMA?

In that same definition it is stated that participation in creative drama has the potential to aid children in such areas as language and communication abilities, problem-solving skills, and creativity. Participation in creative drama can also enhance self-concept, social awareness, empathy, and understanding of the art of theatre.[3]

Many of these goals overlap one another, but several deserve a closer look.

LANGUAGE AND COMMUNICATION

In the last twenty years, there has been an increasing emphasis on the importance of both verbal and nonverbal communication in the language arts curriculum. In the child's development, oral language naturally precedes written language. Therefore, it is reasoned, children need to develop their oral and nonverbal language skills, including abilities to focus attention and listen, in order to successfully undertake reading and writing tasks.

One well-known language arts educator claims that "drama is nothing less than the 'basic skill' that is the foundation of all language development."[4] A past president of the National Council of Teachers of English, John Warren Stewig, emphasizes in numerous writings the importance of creative drama as a means to foster reading, the study of literature, oral language and vocabulary development, nonverbal communication, listening abilities, and creative writing.[5]

Creative drama offers a variety of communication experiences to children. The emphasis on self-expression helps them to form their self-concepts, expand their self-confidence, and increase their ability to communicate their thoughts and feelings both verbally and physically. Their increased ability in self-expression leads to better interpersonal communication skills in informing and questioning, organizing and sharing ideas, and in enjoying the companionship and group interaction processes with others.

[2]*Ibid*, p. 10

[3]*Ibid*, p. 10.

[4]Betty Jane Wagner, "Educational Drama and Language Development," in *Educational Drama for Today's Schools*, ed. R. Baird Shuman (Metuchen, N.J.: Scarecrow, 1978), p. 95.

[5]See especially John Warren Stewig, *Informal Drama in the Elementary Language Arts Program*. (New York: Teachers College Press, 1983).

Creative drama emphasizes process and the personal development of the players rather than the production of an elaborately staged formal play for an audience. (*The Prince and the Pauper,* Terre Haute, Indiana, circa 1905.)

In fact, children use oral communication in creative drama constantly as they respond to and discuss ideas, share personal observations, organize and plan their drama activities. Even in the characters they play, they will be communicating orally, working through the characters' dramatic situations, and interacting with other characters. Enacting the dramatic scene or story itself encourages them to become more effective in their use of language.

When students improvise drama, they observe and participate in language spontaneously, the way situations are met in everyday life where we have no script to tell us what to say. They can experiment with various alternatives, learning first hand which alternative is most effective. And, they do not have to suffer any real life consequences for mistakes they may make. As a result, they are able to increase their communication options and to experience the self-confidence that comes as a result of rehearsing some of life's situations before meeting them.

POSITIVE SELF-CONCEPT

In order to grow into well-developed persons, children need to have faith in and to value themselves. Only when they feel secure in who they are can they be confident enough to explore and take risks.

It will be important in creative drama, as in all learning, for you to foster a climate in which children can grow to their maximum potential. Children who are afraid of themselves and of others around them cannot fulfill their maximum potential.

Creative-drama leaders have often noted that one of the most dramatic changes children experience in drama classes is the development of a more positive self-concept. Sometimes it is because they have played a role they have never experienced before—a powerful king, a hero, or a brave person. They see themselves in a new light, with a strength they never knew they had within them. Sometimes they dis-

Drama can help develop a more positive self-concept.

cover talents they never had a chance to express before. Perhaps it is the offering of a new idea, or leadership in a group, or a creative suggestion they have made to a drama project. Thus, they suddenly find themselves further along the road to their own self-development.

Even when the goals of a particular creative drama lesson are educational (stressing curricular information) or aesthetic (encouraging imagination), the growth of the children is also being fostered in other ways. Many educators and specialists have found creative drama useful in helping to resolve reading problems, speech and language disorders, and socialization difficulties, to cite only a few examples.[6] It is this drawing out of the person that one educator speaks of when he claims, "Just to be—really *be*—another person in an undistinguished play is to make one immeasurably free forever."[7]

CREATIVITY

Being creative, according to one writer, means continually evolving into one's own unique self, responding to life and its experiences to the fullest.[8] Because our educational system recognizes the importance of creativity and independent thinking in our society, it is generally a goal in almost all curricular areas.

Most researchers and writers on the subject of creativity believe that everyone has creative potential. In looking at people who are labeled particularly creative, characteristics such as fluency, flexibility, innovativeness and curiosity emerge. They may even be constructively discontented, upredictable, and a bit different. A spirit of playfulness is another frequently mentioned characteristic. In a complex society such as ours, one that is bursting with technology and sweeping changes constantly, it is the creative ones who will be able to tackle the problems and find the solutions necessary for us all. Their personal lives will also be richer for the flexibility and risk-taking qualities they possess.

As a teacher you foster the inherent creative abilities in children by providing the nurturing environment in which they can feel free to try and fail, to take risks and explore or when you encourage the spirit of curiosity, of playing with ideas, and of testing and rethinking. When you present problem-solving tasks, you also stimulate creative thinking.

Creative drama encourages creativity when it encourages spontaneity, imaginative thinking, brainstorming for solutions, and provides opportunities for visualizing possibilities. A reasonable "anything is possible" attitude on your part gives

---

[6]Ann M. Shaw and C. J. Stevens, eds., *Drama, Theatre, and the Handicapped* (Washington, D.C.: American Theatre Association, 1979). See particularly the review of literature and annotated bibliography by Linaya Leaf.

[7]Hughes Mearns, *Creative Power* (New York: Dover Publications, 1958), p. 96.

[8]Clark E. Moustakas, *Creative Life* (New York: D. Van Nostrand, 1977). This theme is stressed throughout the book.

Everyone has the potential to be creative.

meaning to children's realization that there is always a place for their ideas and their contributions.

PROBLEM-SOLVING SKILLS

Drama can stimulate the development of problem-solving skills. When students are presented with problems, they are encouraged to imagine, to hypothesize, to test options, and perhaps even to redefine the problem.

Problem-solving is frequently apparent in the stories the children enact. What solutions will they suggest for helping a princess learn to cry? How will they pretend to be stupid in order to outwit a tyrant? How will they find a compromising solution in order to appease two groups holding differing viewpoints?

Students can experience group problem-solving in other drama activities as well. What machine will a group decide to create with their own bodies, and how will they demonstrate its working parts? How will they choose to stage their puppet play, and how will they handle the scenery and lighting? How will they decide in a group skit to demonstrate what a particular proverb means?

In all of these experiences students are encouraged to seek answers, push for new ideas, explore solutions, synthesize information, and exercise imagination. This is all a part of the problem-solving process which drama can stimulate.

EMPATHY AND SOCIAL AWARENESS

Empathy is the ability to see life from another person's perspective and to "feel with" that person. In drama, children have the opportunity to see the world from another point of view and to look at the inner attitudes of another. They can, as the Native American proverb encourages, "walk a mile in another's moccasins."

Drama can be a rehearsal of life itself. By reliving the experiences of others—the people from the pages of a history text, a reading book, or anyone else they find interesting and significant—students can identify and empathize with others. They can find out what it is like to play a different societal role—a community helper, a parent, a political leader—learning of their concerns and problems, finding appropriate solutions, and experiencing their difficulties as well as their successes.

Drama also provides experiences in social and group process. In many ways drama is a group art. Plays focus on social interaction; the theatre requires the talents and skills of numerous artists. So, too, as students engage in drama, they must plan together, enact their ideas together, organize and create the appropriate playing space, as well as experience the plays' social interaction. Often it is obvious to even the youngest child that effective socialization is required and that there are rewards for cooperative group behaviors. Truly, drama is an experience in cooperating.

AN UNDERSTANDING OF THE ART OF THEATRE

In creative drama, children learn about the theatre in a way best suited to their developing talents and skills. Rather than focusing on the memorization of scripts and the elaborate production of a play, children are encouraged to improvise dramatic materials. An emphasis is placed on discussing and internalizing information and then playing it out, using self-expression rather than prescribed materials.

At the same time, children are gaining insights into the important elements of theatre such as action, conflict, plot, mood, characterization, and spectacle. They will be exposed to plot structure and to the themes of stories. They will begin to understand characters, not only how they appear on the outside but also how they think and feel on the inside. They will be more attuned to the characters' motivations for their behaviors. Their own interpretation of the characters will give them experiences in expression through movement and voice.

The drama corner of this classroom features a display of puppets, a reproduction of Shakespeare's Globe Theatre, and a Hamlet poster.

Students will also have the opportunity to experience the aspects of theatrical staging and, in modified forms, all the related spectacle of setting, props, lights, costumes, music, and dance. In bringing all of the various art forms of the theatre together, students will learn the importance of working together to create a unified, artistic whole.

The study of theatre, along with the other arts, has been too frequently neglected in our children's education. A significant panel report, *Coming To Our Senses: The Significance of the Arts for American Education*, documents how we have been remiss as a nation in acknowledging and appreciating the arts as an integral part of our cultural heritage.[9] The arts have traditionally provided a way for nations and cultures to develop and communicate, as well as preserve, their identity.

The report further documents the many interrelationships of the arts to the traditional disciplines of learning. Because the arts also develop intellectual and social skills, they are, in a very real sense, as basic to the curriculum as the three R's. These relationships will be outlined in the next section.

[9]David Rockefeller, Jr., Chairman, *Coming To Our Senses: The Significance of the Arts for American Education, A Panel Report* (New York: McGraw-Hill, 1977).

CREATIVE DRAMA AS AN EDUCATIONAL MEDIUM

Drama in many ways has served as a method of teaching for centuries. The great dramas, both tragedy and comedy, though their primary purpose has been theatrical entertainment, have shown us our human faults and foibles. By showing us a slice of life, theatre gives us the opportunity to study people's interaction with each other in a given dramatic situation. We identify with the characters as they deal with their problems and suffer or rejoice with them depending on the outcome.

Creative drama, while it can be considered as an art form by itself, is also a way of teaching. As we know in watching children at play, they naturally dramatize. Most educators now realize that this dramatic play is a child's way of understanding life. In using creative drama in the classroom, you are actually capitalizing on something children already know how to do.

When children dramatize, they are using information in a more concrete and meaningful way. They experience the information kinesthetically, which deepens their understanding and their emotional involvement. They become an integral part of the ideas and concepts, internalizing information and increasing the likelihood of its being remembered. For some children this learning style is mandatory.

Creative drama activities can interrelate with language arts, science, social studies, mathematics, physical education, or the fine arts. In history, for example, students may enact the discovery of America; in literature, they may enact and bring to life one of their favorite books, such as *A Wrinkle in Time*; in music, they might dramatize a folk song such as "I Know an Old Lady Who Swallowed a Fly;" for a science lesson, they might conduct a character panel discussion on the topic of ecology; in mathematics, they may enact a biography of a famous mathematician.

Curricular topics can be previewed or extended through creative drama. You will soon discover that you can check students' understanding of facts and concepts by playing them in creative drama. Do they understand, for example, the construction of simple machines as they enact pantomimes of them? Have they understood the character interactions in a piece of literature as they dramatize an important scene? You will be able to see where the correction of misunderstandings needs to be made. Often students are motivated to explore new or more detailed subject areas in order to play an activity with greater accuracy.

And, finally, though not unimportantly, creative drama is usually fun for all. Learning is made more enjoyable when it can be dramatized. Often students who have difficulty with other classroom tasks find success and a place for themselves in drama, a discovery that gives them a renewed interest in learning. Enjoyment and success together lead to self-confidence, a prime requisite for becoming a thinking, feeling, and creative person able to face life's challenges.

For some teachers creative drama may be a totally new experience. For others, it may be an activity you have wanted to try but did not know how to begin. And for still others, creative drama may be something you have done throughout your teaching career.

This resource guide has been prepared with all of you in mind. It is hoped that there will be something for everyone to choose from. Begin where you feel most comfortable, but challenge yourself to move on to the new ideas as well. As an educator, you know the importance of trying new things, of experimentation and the right to fail and try again. You allow this of students. Be sure to allow yourself the right to try something new, to fail, and to try again, too. And enjoy yourself!

SELECTED BIBLIOGRAPHY

Bolton, Gavin, *Towards a Theory of Drama in Education*. New York: Longman, 1979. Using classroom examples to illustrate, a British drama educator presents his theories and outlines a drama approach which combines children's play and elements of theatre.

Cottrell, June, *Teaching with Creative Dramatics*. Skokie, Ill.: National Textbook Company, 1975. Presents a basic overview of creative drama with chapters on play, sensory awareness, pantomime, dialogue, drama in curriculum, and storytelling.

Heinig, Ruth Beall and Lyda Stillwell, *Creative Drama for the Classroom Teacher*, 2nd edition. Englewood Cliffs, N.J.: Prentice-Hall, Inc., 1981. This text is the source of many of the techniques and activities contained in this resource guide.

McCaslin, Nellie, *Creative Drama in the Classroom*, 4th edition. New York: Longman, Inc., 1984. An introductory text presenting theory and practical application. Includes exercises in sensory awareness, pantomime, and improvisation. Story dramatization, puppetry, and formal production are also covered.

Shuman, R. Baird (ed.), *Educational Drama for Today's Schools*. Metuchen, N.J.: Scarecrow, 1978. Presents a variety of essays on some of the uses of drama by several authors and drama specialists. Extensive annotated bibliography.

Stewig, John Warren, *Informal Drama in the Language Arts Program*. New York: Teachers College Press, 1983. A well-known language-arts educator presents his rationale for the incorporation of creative drama into the language arts curriculum. Many language arts activities and references to children's literature are made throughout.

Wagner, Betty Jane, *Dorothy Heathcote: Drama as a Learning Medium*. Washington, D.C.: National Education Association, 1976. A detailed explanation of the techniques used in drama by a British educator, whose work has become familiar in this country in recent years.

Ward, Winifred, *Playmaking with Children*. New York: Appleton-Century-Crofts, 1957. The text that first introduced creative drama in this country. Discusses drama in elementary and junior high school. Emphasis is on story dramatization.

Way, Brian, *Development Through Drama*. Atlantic Highlands, N.J.: Humanities Press, 1967. Well-known British drama teacher presents his philosophy, focusing on development of the whole person. Practical exercises and activities in sensory awareness, imagination, speech, and improvisation.

2 The Drama Process

In creative drama the focus is more on the creative process of drama than on some finished product such as a well-mounted play. In this chapter we will look at some of the considerations important to that process and at your role in helping them happen. As a teacher you are probably familiar with some of them.

DRAMA GOALS AND GUIDELINES

In planning drama instruction, as with many other curricular areas, there are multiple goals that can be identified. Generally, in creative drama we emphasize:

1. drama goals (e.g., pantomime, improvisation)
2. personal development goals (e.g., creativity, group work)
3. additional curricular or other subject matter goals (e.g. career education, health and safety).

Each of these goals, by itself, can be a justifiable reason for undertaking a creative drama activity. So, at times you might focus mainly on one; often you will consider all three equally.

In addition to the major goals, you need to consider the level of difficulty in selecting appropriate activities. All the variables in the left-hand column *generally* precede their more advanced counterparts in the right-hand column.

EASIER	to more	ADVANCED
1. Desk area		Larger areas of space
2. Teacher direction		Creative or independent thinking
3. Pantomime		Verbal activities
4. Solo playing		Pair and group playing
5. Run-through playing		In-depth playing for greater involvement
6. Humorous or "light" material		Highly dramatic or "serious" material
7. Minimal informational content		High data content
8. Unison playing for one's own satisfaction		Playing to share/communicate with observers

This resource guide is designed to help you move from the easier activities to the more difficult. But it will still be helpful for you to consider the above variables for any given drama activity you choose to do with your class. (Further discussion of this point is covered in Chapter 12).

GUIDING CREATIVE DRAMA

CHILDREN'S PARTICIPATION

There is a natural tendency for many teachers to feel that children should participate immediately in all drama activities. Some may even feel that if children are not playing they are not benefitting from the activity or even having fun.

But students participate in drama in several ways. They may participate as observers, discussants, analyzers, or as players. Their participation varies according to their interest in the topic, their mood, their confidence, and their awareness of their own needs. They also need to know that their efforts will be accepted and encouraged rather than judged or perhaps be made fun of.

It is best to invite students to play and allow them to make their own decisions. Sometimes reticent students like to watch their classmates first. As they see you continue to give support they will gain the courage to participate freely. Resist the temptation even to cajole shy students into participation against their will. More often than not, when they see an activity being fun, within their capabilities, and guaranteeing their anonymity, they will enter in.

But, there are also those students who are confident and secure and who want to play all activities. Some may have difficulty watching their classmates or being able to wait for their turn. And some may even need more reminding of rules and limitations in their exuberance to be involved constantly.

When you have a classroom of eager participants, it becomes important to involve as many students in the activities as possible while still maintaining order. Often you will have the students work in unison. An entire class can work individually, in pairs, or even in groups in unison. This gives more children the opportunity to participate. It also encourages the shy students since there is no undue attention placed on anyone.

Involvement means believing what you are doing.

USE OF SPACE

Contrary to many other writers on creative drama, I do not encourage a beginning drama leader to use a lot of space. To me, most classrooms are preferable to large, open rooms or gymnasiums. I also prefer the desks, tables, or carpeted areas to the more expansive, less well-defined space. To me it is easier to concentrate on guiding the activity itself when you do not have to worry about keeping thirty active students organized in space.

There are also psychological advantages of using desk/table areas or a circle arrangement on a carpeted floor. These are familiar spaces for children that give a sense of security to the shy child and speak of order for the overly active one.

In this guide we will begin with seat activities and move to the use of more space gradually.

SELECTING MATERIALS

Be sure you like the material you are using and sense its importance. And, equally important, from what you know of your class, they should also find it appealing and worthwhile.

In my own experience, humorous material is easier to begin with than the more dramatic material. Humor relaxes most people and helps build group rapport. Students do not have to feel as much tension in playing humorous material because there is less concern about making a mistake. Dramatic material with a serious mood may take a little more work, as we shall discuss later in this chapter.

PRESENTING MATERIALS

Be prepared with all your materials, props, pictures, records, or whatever you use. Arrange them carefully so you will have exactly what you want when you want it.

Know the piece of literature you are using. Be able to read it well so that you can look up from time to time and check the students' reactions. If you are telling a story, be sure to go over it beforehand or have a brief outline on hand so you can tell it smoothly and accurately.

Create the appropriate mood with the material—is it eerie, exciting, serene, happy? Are you creating that mood with your voice and body? Are you asking your questions in a curious, stimulating manner? Are you aware of your vocal quality, pitch, timing, or loudness as you speak? Can your voice become soft when it describes a rabbit's fur, or be warm when speaking of a glowing fire, or moan like

the wind, or boom like thunder? There is no need to overdramatize or sound phoney. Just be aware of the voice as a human musical instrument that has potential
many of us never tap.

UNDERSTANDING MATERIALS

Students cannot play or enact material they do not understand. Are there pictures
or visual aids that can assist? For some students the experiences may be totally new.
What can you give them firsthand that will help them?

Are the words and events understandable to them and within their experience?

"In this poem, 'Foul Shot,' the basketball player is said to be 'squeezed by silence.' He also 'measures the waiting net.' What do you suppose that means?
Have you ever been 'squeezed by silence'? And, how would you 'measure a
waiting net'?"

"This is a story about maple sugaring. Who knows what that is? Have you ever
seen it being done?"

Perhaps an analogy is needed:

"In Maia Wojciechowska's *Shadow of a Bull* there is one scene when all the
boys jump from a wagon of hay. All except Manolo; he's too afraid. Have you
ever been afraid of doing something the way Manolo is afraid of jumping off
the wagon?"

ANALYZING CHARACTERS

In drama, students will be playing many different characters. A character is any person, animal, or being in literature with distinguishing
physical, mental, and attitudinal attributes. Students will need to develop their understanding of character in order for the playing to be
meaningful.

Some characters are very simply drawn in the literature. They
may even be stereotypes as "a wily fox," "a curious child," "a cruel
king." Folk-tale characters are usually quite simple. There may be a
young man or woman off on an adventure—"a clever, handsome
fellow," or "a witty, comely lass." A villain may be "an old witch,"
or "an evil servant." Because of their simple characters, folk tales
are the easiest stories to begin with and the reason so many are included in this resource guide.

Generally, the more complex the literature, the more developed
the characters. More discussion and more playing time is required
for stories whose characters are not one-dimensional but unique.

These characters usually appear in longer stories or book-length literature. It may take the author that length of time to show us the many facets of the character. By the time we reach the end of the book, we have the many sides of the character revealed. And, thus we can say more about the characters and can have many more discussions about them. Charlotte the spider in *Charlotte's Web* or Johnny in *Johnny Tremain* are unique characters and ones we are not likely to forget.

In playing characters, however, we are also looking at how they are both similar to and different from us. Much of this information is revealed in the events that happen to them and how they feel about those events and how they react to them. Discussions are often necessary in order to examine characterization. And so is playing time. So, we discuss, play, discuss some more, and play some more, and eventually arrive at a better understanding of the literature.

The following discussion questions are examples of the sort of probing you will want to do to help your students.

> "The 'Star-Bellied Sneetches' don't play with the Sneetches that don't have stars. Why do you suppose they don't? How do you think the 'plain-bellied' Sneetches feel about that?"
>
> "How do you think Johnny Tremain felt when Isannah screamed that his scarred hand was 'dreadful'?"
>
> "James Huston describes a very dramatic moment when the Eskimo *Tiktaliktak* gives up hope for living and builds himself a coffin. Why does he do that? What do you think his thoughts are as he arranges his weapons by his side? Why does he want his relatives to understand the reason for his death?"

While these questions are probably no different from those you would ask in a literature class discussion, they are doubly important in a drama lesson since the students will need to do this sort of exploring together in order both to understand and to play the characters with depth and meaning.

PLAYING THE MATERIAL

One of the most frequently asked questions from teachers is, "How do you keep the kids from acting silly in creative drama?" Most of the time, in my experience, students act silly because they either do not know what to do or because they are being asked to do something too difficult or something they have not been fully prepared for. The silliness simply comes from embarrassment. Without understanding this, you can often find yourself losing patience, and this will just add to, rather than solve, the problem.

HUMOROUS MATERIAL

As was stated earlier, beginning with simpler materials and with humorous materials should keep silliness at a minimum. If the characters are funny, there is less pressure on students to play the part in a formal or polished way. And, even if there is a bit of silliness with humorous material, it does not destroy the mood. You can all have a laugh together and then continue.

DRAMATIC MATERIAL

Yet, playing material rich in dramatic tension or conflict is often the most rewarding experience students can have. Once you have been successful with it, you will discover that it is worth the time and effort it may take to experience it. Sometimes it is also surprising to find that the students who are the typical class clowns often show another side of their abilities when challenged with more dramatic material and serious moods. Since you will want to move eventually to these materials, you will want to know how to handle it. Following are some suggestions.

1. Clarify the Nature of the Material and the Expectations You Have

Sometimes we think students will automatically understand that certain material is serious and highly dramatic and that they will respond appropriately. But often students simply will not know. Telling them at the outset can save later difficulties.

> "We've been studying about the difficulty of surviving in an extremely cold climate. Today's story is about an Eskimo child who is alone on a hunt, becomes lost, and must fight for his life. We've never worked on a serious story like this before, so it will probably take a little more effort."

2. At First, Play Briefly

It is much easier for students to sustain a serious mood if they know they will not have to be involved for long periods of time. This fact can help them be less anxious and less embarrassed.

A brief playing will also help you become accustomed to creating a strong, dramatic mood. Your chances of success will be increased and that should give you and the students confidence to try such material further.

3. Create the Appropriate Mood

Your voice can do a great deal in conveying the mood of any material. The way you introduce it, discuss it, and the side-coaching you do can make a great difference in conveying and sustaining the appropriate mood.

As in the theatre, the use of music, lights, and sound effects can also help create the mood for the students and can provide appropriate background for your voice as well. Pretending to be young plants growing may be easier for you to narrate and side-coach and the students to enact if you play a musical selection like Grieg's "Morning" from *Peer Gynt*. Or, an experience of visiting a bustling city might be encouraged by Herb Alpert's "Tijuana Taxi."

Just flicking the classroom lights off and on can help students envision lightning, the flashing of photographers' cameras, and the glittering lights of outer space. A darkened room can help create a cave, an underwater world, or a haunted house.

Sound effects, whether made by students' voices or by other means, can also build and sustain mood. Carefully made and orchestrated sounds of a jungle, drums beating ominously, or a storm arising at sea, can lend atmosphere for all.

4. Help Create a Good Working Climate by Limiting Distractions

Separating students from each other can lessen distractions and aid concentration. Dimmed lights can, in addition to providing a mood, help students focus on their own work.

Another aid is having students close their eyes. (Obviously this works best when students are playing individually and in a limited space.) Not only does this help block out distractions, it helps the students focus on the images needed to visualize the experience.

Ask students what aids and what distracts them. Even young children usually know what interferes with their concentration and will frequently list such things as: "having other kids too near me, especially touching me;" "my best friend making faces at me;" or "I don't like it if anyone watches me." This information can be helpful to you in making working conditions more favorable to individual students as well as to the whole class.

Talk with students after they have concentrated particularly well

Keeping your eyes closed can help focus your thinking.

in a certain story or exercise. Have them reconstruct for you and for themselves the description of how they felt during the playing.

"When I was being one of those explorers on the *Kon-Tiki*, I remembered what it was like when my Dad and I were in a canoe and it capsized. If we had been closer to the rapids, we might not have made it. I wasn't scared then, but I was afterwards when I thought about it."

"When I was playing at being blind, I was trying to think of this lady who lives in my neighborhood. You wouldn't know she was blind unless you watched real close, so I tried to make myself look like her."

5. Select Volunteers for Initial Playings

Although you want to have as many students as possible play an activity, it is often wise to select for first playings those few who can be the most easily involved. This is particularly useful when trying out new material and you cannot anticipate the class' response to it. The players can be a model for subsequent replayings. It is also easier to build on the mood set by the first players.

You might also ask for volunteers "who can really concentrate on the material and play it believably." Sometimes children who already have their hands raised for volunteering will think again about this requirement and sit out the first playing. This gives them a chance to self-select and avoid what they think they are not ready to handle. Using this technique, I have often been amazed at students' awareness of their own limitations and their willingness to approach a task with determined seriousness.

SIDE–COACHING

Side-coaching is a technique in creative drama in which the leader give suggestions or comments from the sidelines to heighten and advance as well as control the playing. It is literally "talking the children through" an experience and is an indispensable aid to encouraging concentration and involvement. Side-coaching can also fill in awkward silences, giving security to those who are unsure and guidance to those who might need calming down.

"You're looking in a crystal ball. . . . " Leader narrates, side-coaches, and plays along to encourage involvement and concentration.

You should always be prepared to side-coach, although you will probably never know exactly how much and what kind of side-coaching will be necessary until the playing begins. Side-coaching is a skill that will grow with experience and with your own sensitivity to your students' needs.

LEADER'S PARTICIPATION

In many drama activities your own participation will be helpful and sometimes even necessary. You may simply pantomime along with the students as you side-coach. You may take your own turn at a sequence game or play a role in a group narrative pantomime. You may even play a role in order to give students a character or situation to respond to.

By playing with the students, you are demonstrating a willingness to accept the challenge the activity presents. Your participation can also set the scene, create the mood, and highlight the dramatic tension. It can also be a lot of fun!

STRENGTHENING CONCENTRATION AND INVOLVEMENT

Even the beginning teacher knows when students are engrossed in their classroom work. You can see the furrowed brow of concentration, the oblivious attitude to disruptions, and the look of pleasure and satisfaction that acknowledges a job well done.

The same is true in drama. There are moments in drama, observable even to the novice, when the players/actors are truly concentrating and being involved in their activities and their art. They may be so absorbed and engrossed that they are unaware of anyone observing them. There is an attention to detail, the imagination at work creating believability, and a revitalization of energy with each repeated playing.

When students are not absorbed, there may be showing-off behaviors. These, in reality, are the result of being embarrassed because others are watching or simply being too concerned about what others think. Being shy or insecure can also stand in the way of concentration and involvement. These are the students who may giggle with embarrassment, crowd against others in an attempt to hide or disappear in the masses, or hesitantly look at other classmates to see what they are doing.

All of the techniques discussed in this chapter will play a great role in helping you lead children to greater involvement in their playing over time. Sometimes you will be amazed at how easily it happens. At other times, you will be disappointed because you will not get the response you expected immediately. But when students have once experienced in-depth involvement in drama work, they will often not be satisfied with superficial playing again. They may still need assistance in arriving at that goal. But with all working toward it, many more enriching experiences will be possible.

EVALUATION

When you and the students evaluate the playing together, there is increased possibility for further involvement in subsequent playings. When students are asked to say what they liked about their playing, they are verbally reinforcing themselves.

When you evaluate what the students have done, be sure to be as specific as possible. Saying "good," while it is nice to hear, does not really tell the students what you are referring to. However, if you say, "Good ideas! I saw so many different animals," or "Good control. You stayed right with the music," then students understand your judgment better and also know what to repeat in further playings.

Believability is also important. "Good pantomiming; I could really see some zoo animals that time," or "Your robots were so believable, I almost wondered for a minute if my fourth graders had disappeared!" These comments place a premium on the look of reality, achieved only by controlled, imaginative thinking.

Without students' self-evaluation and the leader's evaluative guidance, drama work will probably only be superficial in the long run. Only when careful attention is given to all aspects of the playing will the best results occur.

REPLAYING

If a drama exercise or story is worth playing once, it is usually worth taking some time to replay it. Seldom is the best creative thinking and the deepest understanding forthcoming in a first playing, even if you and the students are experienced in drama work.

You may need to play an idea three times, even in one session. The first playing might be a run-through in order to get a total picture. A second playing gives the opportunity to add new ideas, to drop out less effective ones, and to do further refining and polishing. A third playing can become a final synthesis of ideas.

It is helpful to you and to the students to remember that the best work is not achieved immediately. Taking an experimental viewpoint is comforting to anxious students and will allay your own fears of not knowing what to expect. But, not only is it important to remember, it is important to *verbalize* for your own sake as well as the students'.

"We've never done this before. Let's just try it and see what happens."

"I thought we did well for our first time with this story. What did you think was particularly good—and where might we make some changes for the next time?"

GROUP PROCESS

Working with children in creative drama is an experience in group management. Effective group work will depend on each unique individual in the classroom, including you. There must be a positive climate for all to work in for maximum growth. In a positive climate, the students and the teacher have a mutual trust and respect for each other. This climate is set mainly by leaders who show acceptance of themselves as well as their students.

ACCEPTANCE

Conveying acceptance is one of the most important factors in fostering a positive climate in the classroom.

Acceptance of Self
It is very difficult to accept another person if we have trouble accepting ourselves. To accept ourselves, we need to recognize our own

Creative drama is an experience in group management.

humanness, including our frailties as well as our strengths. If you expect perfection from yourself and from your students, you may have many frustrating experiences. If you are unaccepting, the result will be negativism.

When we are aware of our feelings, we can more easily express them in so-called "I-statements." For example, if you say, "I get really upset when I hear so much talking," rather than, "You're the noisiest bunch of kids I've ever had," you have expressed your own feelings and taken responsibility for them. The point is that the same amount of noise might not be interpreted the same by another teacher, so the feelings lie in you. The "You-statement" frequently places blame and negative judgment on the other person. "You-statements" cause guilt and resentment rather than the change of behavior you probably want. So, by learning to make "I-statements," you can get in touch with your own feelings and values and make them clear to others as well. You can also be more objective about your own needs, "Hey, this noise may not bother anyone else, but it's driving me crazy. Please hold it down."

Acceptance of Ideas

Acceptance is shown both nonverbally and verbally. A warm smile, an encouraging touch, a nodding head can indicate acceptance. Verbal statements can also indicate acceptance.

"Good idea."

"Um, I never thought about it that way before."

Acceptance of Feelings

Acceptance of feelings is important in creative drama because there will be so much discussion of character and dramatic situations based on daily living. Through creative drama you can help children understand what emotions are, how they are expressed, why people behave as they do, and how emotional responses differ. Since these topics are a part of other curricular areas such as social studies, literature, and health it is important to be aware of several considerations.

Although we think of feelings as good (happy, excited, loving) and bad (angry, lonely, unhappy) because of the effect they have on us, having a particular feeling is neither good nor bad by itself. It used to be thought (and some people still think) that we should be able to keep ourselves from having "bad" feelings. That's why many people will say, "Don't be unhappy," or "You shouldn't be afraid," or even "You must never hate anyone." But all feelings are normal and just *are*. We cannot keep ourselves from having them. It is what we do with our feelings that makes a difference.

When students talk about people and situations and emotions, they will often draw upon their own experiences. You need to be aware and accepting of these comments without showing judgments so that students will know they and the feelings they experience are normal.

STUDENT: I hate his guts!

TEACHER: You're really angry with him.

STUDENT: My sister's dumb.

TEACHER: Your sister did something you think is stupid.

Children readily identify with certain characters. Often these are the ones they choose to play, and through those characters they have the opportunity to release important feelings. They often feel safe under the guise of the character to express feelings they may not feel are allowed them otherwise.

Many creative drama leaders have noted shy students suddenly becoming assertive in a particular character role or an aggressive one becoming subdued. I remember distinctly the very feminine youngster who surprised her classmates and me by playing Tom Sawyer with great believability. I also remember the rather aggressive boy who was a class clown but who asked to play a wish-granting sprite in a story we were dramatizing. I threw caution to the winds and allowed him to do it and was amazed to find a caring and kind personality emerge in the playing. Both these students apparently felt safe in expressing their emotions through the characters they chose to play.

Acceptance of Mistakes

Accepting mistakes is often difficult for leaders and children who are perfectionists. Many people interpret mistakes as failure, and since failure must be rejected, so must the mistakes. But if I am afraid of making a mistake, then I will never try anything new and may restrict my own growth as a result.

If as a leader you can accept your own mistakes, students will soon learn that mistakes are tolerable. And, if you can do this verbally, you will demonstrate to the students and verify to yourself (That is equally important!) that neither you nor they will disintegrate if a mistake is made.

"Wow, I goofed that time! Let's try it again."

"You don't seem pleased with what you did. Would you like to try it again?"

Acceptance of Imitation

Sometimes in creative drama we are so concerned about encouraging creativity that we expect immediate and outstanding results. Often I have heard a beginning teacher say, "Now be as creative as you can," or "Give me a creative answer," or even "I thought you'd be more creative than that."

But most ideas are rather ordinary at first until we have had a chance to experiment and probe deeper. And the amount of creativity we get from students is often in direct proportion to the creative planning we have done beforehand or the creative stimulation we have given while working with the children.

Frequently in creative drama activities, students will imitate each other. How often have you praised one response or idea from a student only to have another student say or do something very similar? They want praise, too. Usually they really are not even aware that they are repeating what someone else has done. The desire to be accepted is so strong that they simply absorb the praised answer and assume it to be theirs.

To imitate is normal and natural. Indeed, imitation is the basic mode of learning. Yet some adults and students think of imitation as cheating and even say so.

"Janice is copying my idea!"

"Bob's cheating! He's doing what I'm doing!"

In response, you can communicate an acceptance of imitation in a way that protects the imitator and reassures the originator.

"Sometimes when people see an idea they like, they want to try it themselves. Bob must have liked your idea."

REJECTION

Rejecting Behavior

Even though you are an accepting person, you also have a responsibility to set limits on inappropriate behaviors. Sometimes ignoring a behavior will be sufficient to make it stop if it is a bid for attention. At other times, one must take action. Students need to learn, for example, that even if they are allowed to be angry, that anger cannot be turned on others around them.

At the same time, it is helpful to reject the behavior without rejecting the person. Notice in the two statements below that the feeling is accepted, but the behavior is not.

> "I know you're angry that I won't let you play this time. But you know the rules. You punched Joey and that means you sit this one out."

> "I can tell you're all excited, but we can't start playing until you settle down."

Sometimes students' behaviors become disruptive to the rest of the class. When this happens, rules for participating should be reinforced as objectively as possible. When reprimanding individual students, it is also helpful to speak to them privately so they are able to "save face."

> "Please sit down. When you feel that you can follow the rules to remain by yourself and not disturb others, you may rejoin the group."

> "I'm sorry. I know you are disappointed. But I can't allow you to bother other people who are trying to do their work. Perhaps it will be easier for you to follow the rules tomorrow."

GROUP INVOLVEMENT

Creative drama also encourages group interaction. Organization, cooperation, group problem solving, and decision making become integral parts of the group experience.

A group, even though composed of various individuals, also has its own personality—as if it were one huge person embodying separate individuals. Teachers note this phenomenon of group behavior when they say such things as: "My class this year is so silly all the time," or "My class would never like that story."

A group can also grow and change—just as individuals can. And, when a group is given the opportunity of working on its own, it can begin to have a life of its own. It may also take on a power that can be scary, especially if a leader feels his or her own control or influence is being usurped.

Some students have no trouble integrating themselves into a

The need to belong to a group is strong.

group. These are usually the children who are outgoing, friendly, and secure with themselves. Other children will have many difficulties. Some are fearful of a group and avoid interaction. Some demand constant attention from a group and have difficulties compromising and cooperating.

But the group is a microcosm of society, and the need to belong is strong. Often this need can be counted on to motivate students to integrate themselves with the group.

As much as possible, you will want to prevent cliques from forming. Although there are times when you let the class form its own subgroups for activities, you will also want to vary subgroups so that children learn to interact with all members. Counting off and placing 1's together, 2's together, and so forth is a common way to mix the group. Vary these methods of grouping, too. If students know you expect them to work together, they will begin to accept this procedure automatically. The procedure will prevent petty squabbling over who plays with whom. It also gets to the fun of the activity more quickly.

Some teachers find that it is helpful to establish ground rules with the group. Usually children can help formulate these rules with you. One class listed the following:

I like to have people listen to me; I will listen to others.
I don't like it when someone says my ideas are stupid or dumb; I won't say that about anyone else's.

I don't want anyone to make fun of the way I feel; I won't make fun of anyone else's feelings.

I can enact my own ideas as long as I don't bother anyone else.

If I don't like an idea the group has, I don't have to play; but I shouldn't bother anyone.

I don't like being disturbed; I won't disturb others.

I want people to be a good audience for me; I will be a good audience for them.

I don't like being left out of a group; I will accept others into my group.

Throughout all experiences in creative drama, you will be helping students understand and empathize with others. You will want them to discover their common bond of humanness with others, whether those others are classmates, people in literature, or real life persons. This understanding and awareness is the essence of drama, which is, in fact, the study of life. And it is the basic goal of education in a society in which the quality of life will depend on the quality of human relationships.

Creating a group idea requires careful planning and social cooperation.

RESOURCE MATERIALS TO USE WITH STUDENTS

The following materials are a selection of the many that are available, dealing with interactions. You will find them interesting just for students to read on their own or to use for reading and discussion with the entire class. Many will also provide material for creative drama lessons.

Adoff, Arnold, *Outside/Inside Poems*. New York: Lothrop, Lee & Shepard, 1981. Description of feelings on the inside which do not often appear on the outside.

Aliki, *Feelings*. New York: Greenwillow, 1984. Brief stories and sketches of childhood feelings.

Berger, Terry, *I Have Feelings*. New York: Behavioral Publications, 1971. Situations and black and white photos covering seventeen different feelings, giving a brief story for each and followed by an explanation of each.

Estes, Eleanor, *The Hundred Dresses*. New York: Harcourt Brace, Jovanovich, 1944. Wanda, the daughter of a poor immigrant family, is rejected by her classmates. Her escape is to talk about her many dresses, which turn out to be beautiful drawings. In spite of its age, this book has stood the test of time in evoking readers' concern for Wanda's plight.

Feelings, Tom, and Nikki Grimes, *Something On My Mind*. New York: Dial Press, 1978. Descriptions of many inner emotions that are not often expressed.

Rosenbaum, Jean, and Lutie McAuliffe, *What Is Fear: An Introduction to Feelings*. Englewood Cliffs, N.J.: Prentice-Hall, 1972. Explanation of a basic emotion that is often difficult to discuss.

Tester, Sylvia, *Moods and Emotions*. Elgin, Ill.: David C. Cook, 1970. A booklet discussing various ways to teach the subject of emotions in the classroom. Includes sixteen poster-size photos illustrating emotions.

Yashima, Taro, *Crow Boy*. New York: Viking, 1955. A young Japanese boy is rewarded for six years of perfect attendance in school. Yet, he is an outsider until a sensitive teacher finds a way to give him the recognition he deserves.

TEACHER RESOURCE MATERIALS

Amidon, Edmund, and Elizabeth Hunter, *Improving Teaching*. New York: Holt, Rinehart & Winston, 1966. One of the first texts for making teachers aware of their specific verbal behaviors and the consequences of them.

Carroll, Anne Welch, *Personalizing Education in the Classroom*. Denver: Love Publishing Co., 1975. Although this book addresses itself to the special education teacher, the material is applicable to a wide variety of situations. Contains special chapters on communication in the classroom and on groups.

Cooper, Pamela J. *Speech Communication for the Classroom Teacher*, 2nd ed. Dubuque: Gorsuch Scarisbrick Publishers, 1984. Extensive look at several areas of communication including interpersonal, non-verbal, teacher influence, and communication barriers.

Getting Started 3

Everyone at one time or another has "done some drama," whether as a participant or as a leader. That is because many of the simple games and activities familiar to all teachers and children can come under the umbrella of creative drama. A game like "Simon Says," an action song like "I Know an Old Lady," or a narrated skit like the ones often used in scout camps or recreational settings, are good introductory activities to creative drama. Many games, in fact, have been used exclusively in the work of some drama educators.[1]

What is useful about these activities?

a. They create relaxed, good feelings and promote security.

b. They give students a good physical workout and develop muscular coordination.

c. They promote group cohesiveness and focus on the importance of a unified effort in achieving a common goal.

d. They help the students achieve some of the many skills that will be useful for all drama work.

e. Many of the activities can be coordinated with other drama lessons or other curricular material.

f. They can be used as a warm-up or cool-down for longer sessions.

[1]Most noted is Viola Spolin and her classic book *Improvisation for the Theatre*. Evanston: Northwestern University Press, 1963.

Shy students may become reluctant if they feel pressured to participate.

Why are these activities also useful for the beginning teacher and beginning group?

a. They are easily organized.
b. The rules and discipline are built into the activity or game.

ACTION/MOVEMENT/PANTOMIME

Drama is action or doing. For young children, movement is also their natural means of exploring and discovering. Their constant activity integrates them physically with everything they observe. Even older children are still quite active in their behaviors. Movement in drama continues this mode of learning.

Although you want to help students express themselves freely and creatively through movement, you will want to work toward disciplined and thoughtful movement, too. We will be working toward both these goals.

Pantomime is the expression of ideas and feelings through bodily action. It includes facial expressions, posture, gesture, and all body language used to purposely convey a message. You will want to help students learn to interpret the actions of others and express themselves more effectively through pantomime. In this chapter, we will begin work on the basics of pantomime.

TEACHER DIRECTED DESK ACTIVITIES

As an introduction to drama for both you and the students, you may want to begin with the easiest kind of activity to organize. You will probably be more comfortable at first with the students playing fairly simple activities at the desk area.

Following is a listing of the various kinds of activities you may want to try. Notice also that these first games are quite teacher-directed and keep the students seated or standing in one place.

ACTION SONGS

Traditional action songs, including "This Old Man," and "I Know an Old Lady," are also useful for beginning drama work. You can make up your own, too. Students will like creating actions for parodies such as Tom Glazer's "On Top of Spaghetti" (to the tune of "On Top of Old Smoky") or George Mendoza's *A Wart Snake in a Fig Tree* (New York: Dial Press, 1968), a bizarre version of "The Twelve Days of Christmas."

ACTION STORIES

Many of these activities are well known in recreational circles, and many are taught by word of mouth. These stories are narrated by a

Playing at the desk area provides control as well as security.

An action song is a good warmup.

leader while small groups of students perform an action and/or sound whenever certain words are said.

You and your students can make up your own action stories by narrating a brief version of almost any story. The following is told in the style of a typical old–fashioned melodrama.

A WESTERN "MELLERDRAMA"

BELLE: Wipe eyes with corner of apron and say, "Sob, sob."

NELL: Put back of hand to forehead and sigh, "Ah, me."

SHERIFF SAM: Twirl two six guns, place in holster and say, "I'm your man."

SNEAKY SNIVELY: Twirl cape in front of face and laugh villainously, "Heh, heh, heh."

HORSE(S): Make sound of horses' hooves (on desks or on thighs).

HOUSE: (sing) "Be it ever so humble, there's no place like home."

RENT: (chant) "Money, money, money, money, money, money, money, money."

STORY: Our story takes place near Junction City. **Nell** and her widowed mother, **Belle,** have fallen on hard times. The landlord, **Sneaky Snively,** rides his **horse** up to the **house** to demand the **rent. Nell** and **Belle** plead for more time. Angrily, **Sneaky Snively** rides off on his **horse** into town to get **Sheriff Sam. Sneaky Snively** bursts through the saloon doors and orders **Sheriff Sam,** at the bar drinking sarsaparilla, to evict his tenants. **Sheriff Sam** and **Sneaky Snively** ride on their **horses** out to **Belle** and **Nell's house. Sneaky Snively** pounds on the door. **Belle** begs for mercy. **Sneaky Snively** sneers and demands that **Sheriff Sam** kick them out. **Nell** explains they would have paid, but **Sneaky Snively** tripled the **rent. Sheriff Sam** suddenly remembers that just last week old prospector Fred talked about a rich seam of silver being very near the **house.** Is it possible? **Sheriff Sam** accuses **Sneaky Snively** of wanting to tear down the **house** in order to mine the silver. **Sneaky Snively** tries to make a getaway on his **horse. Sheriff Sam** grabs **Sneaky Snively** just in time. "My hero," says **Nell.** "Curses, foiled again," says **Sneaky Snively.** As the sun sinks slowly in the west, **Sheriff Sam** rides off on his **horse,** taking **Sneaky Snively** to jail. **Nell** and **Belle** wave goodbye, clutching the **rent** money as they stand in the doorway of their **house.**

The End—Everyone takes a bow

SHORT ACTION STORIES AND POEMS
FROM LITERATURE[2]

Many short poems and stories have a lot of action that students can pantomime while you read them. The following are some suggestions to get you started.

"The Adventures of Isabel," Ogden Nash. (4) Isabel meets a bear, a witch, and a doctor and handles each with dispatch.

"Boa Constrictor," Shel Silverstein. (30) The complaint of someone being eaten by a boa. You may know this one as a song, too. Ask students, "How can you pretend to make yourself disappear?" and see how many ideas they come up with!

"The Cares of a Caretaker," Wallace Irwin. (30) An old woman has her work cut out for her trying to take care of life on the seashore.

"Cat," Mary Britton Miller. (4) A cat's movements are detailed. I read this one as it is written, but when students act it out, I change the last two lines to read, "And sits on her rug with her nose in the air," so they end in a seated position.

"Hungry Mungry," Shel Silverstein. (53) A nonsense poem about a boy who eats everything, including himself. For maximum effectiveness, encourage variety in pantomiming the one action of eating.

---

[2]Numbers in parentheses correspond to the numbered anthologies in the bibliography at the back of this book.

[⌣] ACTION GAMES

Traditional games like **"Follow the Leader"** and **"Simon Says"** are also useful in drama. In each case, you specify the actions the group is to do. In the game "Simon Says," players are to perform the action only when the leader precedes the command with "Simon Says." There is no need to eliminate players, and, in fact, that would really be counterproductive to our goals. You can simply note, "Ah, a few were caught that time," and continue the game.

You can vary the games and incorporate other curricular concepts. One teacher used "Simon Says" to review foreign language phrases with her class. Another used it for a review of the names of bones of the body. ("Shake your cranium; wiggle your ilium; rotate your clavicle.")

Other seat games utilizing action, coordinated movement, and practice in following directions are described below:

"Move to the Beat" While you beat a drum, students move in as many ways possible while sitting at their desks. Students move only when the drum beats and must listen closely. Try to vary the beats: slow and fast, loud and soft, different rhythms, make sudden halts, and so forth to make the game fun.

"Balance Movement Game" While standing at the side of the desk, students perform a variety of movements that you call out. Try having them stand on tiptoes, crouch and touch both knees, take one "baby" step forward, a quick hop back, and so forth. For added challenge, have students try balancing a book on their heads while performing the movements.

SIMPLE SENSORY AND EMOTION PANTOMIMES

Simple sensory and emotion pantomimes can also be acted out in limited space at the desks. Not only are these fun to do, they encourage the students to remember past experiences, recall information, and form mental pictures. These skills are helpful in most learning tasks and can be sharpened by pantomime activities.

[⌣] SENSORY PANTOMIMES

From our senses we learn about the world around us. We make observations, comparisons, discriminations, and form our concepts about the nature of things.

Sensory awareness is central to drama, as it is to all learning. Strengthening our sensory awareness and recall assists the imagination and is important to the actor as well as to the writer or any other artist. Since every story or other piece of literature has either direct or indirect reference to the senses, many sensory pantomimes can be developed from literature.

In sensory-awareness activities, you may need to do the following:

a. Describe details as well as encourage concentration. Often it is helpful to perform the real action and then perform the pantomimed action so that recall is clearer. For example, in pretending to read a book, you might actually do it first; then recall the experience through pantomime.

b. Pantomime along with the students in order to encourage their participation.

Taste: Pretend to eat a slice of pizza. ("Take your first bite. Careful, it's hot. It's your favorite kind with lots of sausage and chewy cheese," and so on.)
Suck on a lemon or eat a tart, juicy apple.
Bite into the hottest jalapeno pepper you have ever tasted.

Touch: Pretend to care for a bird with a broken wing. ("Gently examine it to see the extent of the wound. Try to comfort the frightened thing," and so forth.)
A velvet drape, a cactus, your sunburned arm, a hot iron, a sticky piece of candy, gritty sand on your desktop, or a sharp knife blade.

Pretend to eat a sour pickle.

Hear: Listen to the siren on a police car racing by.

Pretend to hear a little voice coming from inside your pocket.

React to fingernails scraping across the chalkboard.

See: Watch a tennis match or a ping pong game being played.

Read a mystery book under the bedcovers with a flashlight.

Observe the actions of a small insect crawling on your desk.

Smell: Open a carton of milk and find that it has gone sour.

Discover smoke coming from inside your desk.

Smell ammonia, cake baking, a skunk, or your favorite perfume.

Now try adding a little *conflict* to pantomimes. For example, in watching the tennis match, you could pretend that the player the students are rooting for is having a bad day. ("He misses the ball this time. The opponent makes the next serve, and it's off to the side. He runs to hit it but stumbles and falls," and so forth.) While reading the mystery book, perhaps footsteps are heard approaching.

Now try doing pantomimes with a little longer story line. For example, you could narrate a brief story of eating a picnic lunch, going on a hike, or any other experience that is strong in sensory stimulation. (See Chapter 6 for more ideas.)

ADDITIONAL SENSORY GAMES

You may decide that your class needs more exercise in sensory awareness. There are many traditional games that develop skills in sensory awareness. Many are useful for creative drama work as well as for other areas of the curriculum, such as science and language arts. Following are some examples you may wish to consider.

"I Spy"

This is an old favorite that is helpful for developing observation skills. Students take turns selecting an object in the room to be identified, saying "I spy something that is a cube." (You may use any identification like "a pulley," or "edible.") The rest of the students try to identify what the object is. Can be played in small groups.

"Scavenger Hunt"

Students are given a list of articles to collect within a given time limit: red pencil or pen, American flag, whale, reference to an astronaut, a mirror, a Haiku poem, story problem involving fractions, dictionary, ring binder, and so on.

"Guess the Sound"

Different sounds (flipping pages of a book, erasing the blackboard, turning a doorknob, or tapping a pencil, for example) are made while students have their eyes closed. The one who guesses the sound correctly could be allowed to make the next sound. This game can be played in small groups.

"Touch Box"

Put a number of items in a box for students to identify by touch. Items could include coins of varying denominations, cork, pine cone, metal screw, needle, decorative button, three-prong adapter plug, and so on.

EMOTION PANTOMIMES

In creative drama we will focus on emotions in numerous activities. Identifying, recalling, expressing, and being sensitive to feelings are also important in understanding characters in literature. Understanding emotions and how they are expressed is also important to our own well-being. You might want to begin the study of emotions with the following game:

"Pass the Face"

One student starts out making a face (perhaps sad), and shows it to the next person. That person imitates the face, pretends to remove it (like a mask) from the person, puts it on, and then changes the emotion (angry, happy, or surprised, for example). Continue until everyone has a turn. This game can be played in several small groups at the same time.

Other Possibilities

The following simple emotion pantomimes can be other beginning activities for your class. Notice that presenting a situation or an activity (rather than just saying, "Pretend to be happy" or sad or angry)

a. gives students something to respond to, making the response more believable
b. helps sustain the mood and the playing a little longer.

Examples:

Pretend you are alone at night, watching a very frightening movie on television.

With earphones on, you are listening to your favorite song being played.

You are a mad scientist mixing chemicals in test tubes in your laboratory.

These activities may also be lengthened by incorporating them into a story line or longer situation. For example, you can just add a conflict or another incident to the situation and change the emotion: "Pretend to be watching a very funny television show. Suddenly someone else switches channels and you're upset because you wanted to watch the other show. But as you start watching the new show, you see that it's your favorite sports show and they're right in the middle of an exciting moment . . ." and so forth.

BRIEF STORY PANTOMIMES

Once you have tried several of the activities covered thus far, you might want to try your own hand at creating some brief story pantomimes. All you need are a few sentences of storyline focusing on action. It is also helpful to include a variety of movement as well as levels and directions of movement—up and down, back and forth, left and right, bending over, turning around, going in reverse, and so forth. Changes of tempo, and perhaps even slow motion and triple time are fun, too.

If you also add sensory and emotion details, the activities will be more interesting to play as well as being more dramatic.

"PAINTING"

Students pretend to paint with a brush that slowly changes sizes as you indicate—from a very small artist brush to a broom or a paint roller on an extension pole. Paint the desk top, the air, the ceiling, and even the sky! Students can begin seated, then stand at the side of the desk, and then sit again. Encourage students to think of themselves as famous artists painting with great skill and confidence. Maybe they are painting a huge mural on the side of a building or painting a sunset. Perhaps they run out of paint at the end and have just enough left to sign their names in the corner of their painting. Leroy Anderson's "Waltzing Cat," Strauss waltzes or other free-flowing music should be played in the background for this activity.

"PLAY BALL!"

Students pretend to be bouncing different sized balls: a basketball, volleyball, tennis ball, and so forth. Change the weights (balloon, medicine ball) and textures (heavy, sticky, rubbery) of the ball. Maybe they are famous athletes in this one, trying out a variety of products for a sports manufacturer. Have them try some "fancy" moves. You could include fast dribbling or some intricate footwork. The Harlem Globetrotters' theme song, "Sweet Georgia Brown," is wonderful background music for this one.

IMAGINATION GAMES

All artists, including actors, use imagination. But even other fields of work, such as science, or other tasks, such as reading, require well-developed imaginations also. The following games can encourage the development of imagination.

"WHAT COULD IT BE?"

Use interesting, unusual objects which students are to imagine might be something else. A pair of scissors might become a dancing puppet, a spear for catching fish, or a lorgnette. A conch shell might become a large rosebud, a horn, or a water sprite's castle. Unusual kitchen tools or other gadgets are good to use. Students can bring in objects to share also.

"PASS THE OBJECT" –

Pretend to handle or use an object (example: a fuzzy caterpillar, a bowling ball, or a sharp knife), then give it to a student. He/she handles it appropriately, then passes a *different* one to the next student, and so on. Consider: a curious hamster, bubble gum, diamond

What do you suppose this is? What could it be used for?

necklace, a ringing telephone, melting ice cream cone, a lit candle, and so on. See if students can play the game without naming the object; you can check later for accuracy. The game may be played in small groups.

"SCARF GAME"

(You could also use any object that has flexibility, like a piece of rope, for this.) The first player uses the scarf in some way, perhaps as a veil, an apron, or a sling for the arm. It might become a bull-fighter's cape, a magician's turban, or a window-washer's rag. Have fun thinking of all sorts of other uses for whatever object you choose.

QUIETING ACTIVITIES

A final category of desk activities is quieting activities. These are particularly useful if you are playing several activities in one session or when your drama period lasts for a half hour or longer.

A creative drama period should come to a quieting end. Particularly if there has been a lot of movement activity, concentration, and hard work, it is often essential to calm everyone down and not let them go to other schoolwork at a high pitch.

One technique is to read a very quieting selection, such as a poem. There are many suited to this purpose. Often the characters in the poems are relaxed or tired and the actions are subdued. Following are some suggestions:

The snow sculpture melts slowly in a quieting activity to close the drama session.

"Fatigue," Peggy Bacon. (32) The subway ride at night features tired workers.

"Lullaby," Robert Hillyer (34) We are in a rowboat, drifting along peacefully.

"Slowly," James Reeves. (6) Everything moves very slowly in this poem.

"Stopping by Woods on a Snowy Evening," Robert Frost. (33) "The woods are lovely, dark, and deep . . ."

"Sunning," James S. Tippett. (4) (33) An old dog sleeps lazily on a porch.

Having students close their eyes for the quieting activity is helpful. Try to capture the quieting mood in your voice, or perhaps use a quiet record for accompaniment. (Schumann's "Traumerei," Debussy's "Claire de Lune," or "Berceuse" from Stravinsky's *Firebird Suite.*)

You can also create your own activity by narrating a few sentences about a candle burning and slowly melting, a sun setting, or floating on a tranquil lake. Quieting activities should relax the students and calm them down. More importantly, they should help students absorb the experiences that have been covered during the drama lesson.

4 Using More Space

Thus far, all the activities have not required much space. In this chapter we will introduce activities with more movement and more space demands. Hence, here are a few words on organizational procedures.

As was indicated earlier, use caution in choosing the space you work in. Many teachers have been led to believe that a lot of space is necessary for drama work. For me, nothing could be further from the truth.

Having a gymnasium to work in, for me, is usually a curse rather than a blessing. The space is so open that voices constantly echo and meaningful communication is extremely difficult. Furthermore, students associate a gym with active sports and the chance to blow off steam and energy. Their anticipation of doing that rather than experiencing a drama class is disconcerting and sometimes frustrating to them, which causes more problems for you. And, often large activity or all-purpose rooms create similar problems.

I believe very strongly in using the classroom and making use of the desk or table areas. If another kind of space is needed, the desks can be moved to the edges of the room. But, always make sure you really need more space and that changing the classroom arrangement is really desirable before you go ahead and do it.

ORDERLY, ORGANIZED PLAYING

Obeying rules and following directions are as important in drama work as in any other classroom work. In fact, they may even be more important, since drama work is so often a group activity.

Interestingly, adults working in groups actually behave very much like a classroom of children. Remember the last teachers' meeting you attended when the principal had trouble getting the group's attention? Or the last time you tried to get several guests seated for a dinner party? Frequently it is a phenomenon of group behavior and sheer numbers rather than age that causes difficulty in organization.

Although you are probably aware of them already, here are some hints to keep in mind:

1. Word directions explicitly and carefully. Students will usually do what is asked of them if it is clearly and firmly stated. Unfortunately, they usually do not tell you when they do not understand, so they simply go ahead and do something—even if it leads to chaos. That is your clue that your directions were unclear, and you had better intervene before it is too late to rectify the situation.

2. Give directions while students are seated and you have their attention. Once any group gets up and begins moving, you will have difficulty getting their attention again without reseating them—and that is not easy for you or them. (It is a little like the old song, "How ya gonna keep'em down on the farm, after they've seen Paree?")

3. If there is a problem, back up and start over. Do not try to muddle through something that just keeps getting more out of hand. You may need to repeat directions or even ask them what the problem is.

Problems can occur, in spite of your best planning.

4. Do not sugarcoat directions.
   "Remember now, you're statues and statues don't talk." (If you are a kid with an imagination, your statue can talk. At least one student will probably say, "*Mine* does!")
   "Let's pretend you're like sticky gum, so don't touch anyone else or you may all stick together." (What an invitation that is for the curious minded! Think of it as a "Wet Paint" sign. How many people go ahead and touch the paint to see if the sign is really telling the truth!) It is best just to be straight forward with directions.

5. Use attention-getting devices. You probably have several of these already in your repertoire. Sound other than your voice and visual cues are often helpful for drama work. (Examples: audible cues like ringing a bell or beating a drum; visual cues like flicking lights or raising hand.)

6. Cultivate your nonverbal controls to minimize the need for constant scolding or verbal reminders:

   a. Wait with folded hands or a finger to the lips for a group to settle down before trying to talk above their chattering.

   b. Stand next to a hyperactive or talkative student for proximity control. (Close presence of an adult figure can speak authority.)

7. Understand that problems will occur in spite of your best planning and intentions. Students often get excited as they get ready to participate in drama. Excitement leads to whispered talking. Sometimes you find yourself getting excited and rushing students before they are ready. Or you may do too much discussing of an idea, and they begin to get restless. For your own well-being, it is helpful to acknowledge the problem rather than blaming yourself or them. For example, "Whoa! I think I've been

Attention-getting devices are useful.

rushing too fast and you're getting too excited. Let's slow down a bit" or "I can see we have a problem, but I'm not sure I know what it is. Let's come back, sit down, and talk about it."

These hints, while they are not all inclusive, will help keep order and control so that everyone can focus on the drama activities rather than on discipline difficulties.

GAMES FOR SELF-CONTROL

The games and activities in this section will require more space, but they are also highly structured and encourage self-control and self-discipline. Students should learn that artistic discipline is necessary for an artist to perform at his or her best— just as a sound mind and body are important to the athlete. Indeed, athletic training and artistic training have many similarities.

While students will enjoy playing the games, you will be looking for skill development in concentration, disciplined coordination, and self control. The repeated playings of the exercises should result in increased skill. However, you should be aware that many similar exercises are practiced continuously by professionals, so the games can provide constant practice material at all ages and all levels of development.

SOLO WORK IN SELF-CONTROL

Caught in the Act

Students move any way they wish while both feet are "glued" to one spot. Give a signal to freeze: give signal again to move. Students move around the room *in the position they were frozen in*. Another signal stops them and the game repeats. Instruct them to freeze as animals, statues, monsters, machines, literary characters, showing emotions, and so forth.

Freeze Game

This game teaches that space must be used with responsibility. Students may move about the room as fast as they wish as long as they do not bump into each other. On signal (for example, a ringing bell) they must freeze. You may specify a certain scene or situation: shoppers hurrying to buy sales items; people dashing to jobs during rush hour; robots working at high speed to increase production quotas, and so forth. Start with a few students and gradually add on more. The goal is eventually to have the entire class playing the game at the same time.

"Freeze" game encourages physical control and self-discipline.

Slow Motion Activities

Slow motion is a technique used frequently in drama. Discuss slow motion so students understand it. Play slow music at an even slower speed as well as sidecoaching to assist them. *Suggestions:* playing a sport in a television replay; plants or animals growing and changing as in a nature film using time-lapse photography; an underwater adventure with Jacques Cousteau or exploring a sunken ship for treasure; experiencing a dream or nightmare; being in outer space; or other ideas the students suggest. Students may also want to try these ideas in small groups.

Falling

Falling is a popular activity and useful in many dramatizations. Students should approach this exercise with the realization that anyone can fall, but it takes real skill to do it with control and discipline. All falling should be done in slow motion and with a counting signal from you. It may also be helpful to have students close their eyes in order to concentrate on their own work. Be sure also that they do not fall on the "unprotected" parts of their bodies like elbows, knees, and heads. If they have already played this activity in the earlier grades, they should have gained skill to a degree, but most will benefit from continued practice. *Suggested topics:* a hot air balloon landing, a building being demolished, a theatre curtain lowering, a fireworks display, a marionette whose strings break one at a time, a waterfall or fountain, a ship sinking, the sun setting, a parachutist landing, and so forth. Let students create ideas in small groups as well.

In-service teachers practice moving in slow motion.

Conducting an Orchestra I

Students are orchestra leaders and must keep with the beat of a particular recording. Use a variety of rhythms, perhaps even switching songs. Students will probably respond best to popular recordings, but do not overlook the possibilities of the old standards and of classical music (marches, jazz, waltzes, Broadway show tunes, and so forth).

Take a Walk

Organize students in a circle. Pantomime walking through different substances—sticky tar, quicksand, spiderwebs, or on marbles, hot sand with bare feet, on steel girders high in the air, or on a swinging bridge.

I Won't Laugh

Players try to get "audience" to laugh by telling jokes or miming antics. (No touching allowed!) See who can be sober the longest. Create scenes: comedians before a bored audience; clowns entertaining sad people; show-off children with stern relatives, and so forth.

Noiseless Sounds

Students act out such things as coughing, sneezing, sighing, shouting, gulping or hiccuping, using their body but not their voices. Try

Student tries to break classmates' concentration in the game "I Won't Laugh."

this in slow motion. Challenge students by pointing out that anyone can do these actions the ordinary way. Only a skilled actor can do them silently and in slow motion!

PAIR AND GROUP WORK IN SELF–CONTROL

Often students need assistance in learning to work together. These activities require the students to work together in order to make the pantomimes believable. Since the games are fun to do, they usually make pair- and group-work appealing. Because the focus is on the activity rather than on the persons doing it, petty people-differences are usually forgotten.

Mirroring
Students face each other in pairs. One is the person using the mirror, and the other is the mirror. The mirror follows the leader in various actions. Consider a full-length mirror—exercising, dancing. Switch parts. Do the actions in slow motion to make it easier to stay together. After trying pair mirroring, students can also try pairs mirroring pairs. For example, a salesperson assisting someone buying new clothes are mirrored by two others. You might also add a friend or family member to make a trio. Eventually you might challenge the class to be an orchestra (See "Conducting an Orchestra II") playing in a mirrored ballroom.

Sound Pantomime

One student pantomimes while another creates the appropriate sound effects. At first the sound effects should fit the pantomime; then the pantomimer should fit movements to the sound-effects person. Try: pumping up a flat tire, dribbling a basketball, starting an old car, or eating soup and potato chips. For group scenes, as many as five actors might perform while five sound effects persons add the sounds. Try using nursery rhymes or folk tales, or let students create scenes. For advanced students, have sound effects persons try speaking dialogue for actors.

Two Person/Group Jobs

Students pantomime jobs which require two or more people. Actions must be coordinated to make the objects believable. Hang wallpaper; fold a flag or sheet; police carry a very tall murder victim down a circular stair. Groups: move a grand piano to a second floor or put up a tent.

Sculpturing

One person is the sculptor while the other is a piece of clay. The sculptor molds the clay into a statue. Groups of sculptors may also mold statue groupings. Use titles like ''Winged Angel,'' ''Victory,'' ''The Workers,'' ''The Fates,'' ''Children at Play,'' or others of your choosing. Stirring music played in the background encourages the sculptor's artistic movements.

Tug-of-War and Other Rope Activities

Players form teams to stage an imaginary tug-of-war. The rope must be believable and must ''stretch'' as it is pulled. The activity can end when you announce that the rope breaks. Players fall in slow motion to your slow count of 10. Other rope activities include: jumping rope (two turn and one or more jump); circus acts on a tightrope, including bicycle riding; scaling a mountain and rappelling down with rope; rescuing someone who has fallen through ice; rodeo roping; cowboy rope tricks; and so on.

Conducting an Orchestra II

In groups, one conducts while others play various instruments to recorded music. Then have students *become* the instruments that are played by musicians. Some instruments need two or more people to represent them.

"Tug of War" encourages concentration and focus.

One at a Time

Several players (five) pretend to be in a given setting, perhaps a living room. They are seated randomly. They move about the room as they like, but they do not interact. However, only one person may move at a time. The action of the next person moving freezes the first mover in place until that player decides to initiate movement again. For example, Person 1 might get out of a chair and turn on an imaginary TV. Person 2 might pretend to pick up a magazine from a table, which freezes Person 1 at the TV. Perhaps Person 3 crosses her legs and freezes Person 2. Then Person 1 might decide to return to his seat, and so forth. Students must become very sensitive to each other's movements or the game fails. They must also be assertive if they want to move. The activity is most difficult when players have their backs to each other. In these cases a slight sound cue (clearing the voice, taking a deep breath, and so forth) may be used. You monitor and coach when necessary, "Only one person can move at a time. . . . Wait, Ann, Frank just stopped you. . . . OK, Frank, go ahead. . . . " But the challenge will be for the student to learn to monitor themselves.

To help students learn the game, you can give players a number and call the numbers at random to indicate when they may move. Once students understand how the game is played, they initiate their own actions.

Variation: Students sit in a circle and do not move from their seats. All initiated action must be in a seated position. Work toward using smaller and smaller actions. Groups of five to ten work best. But try for even larger groups.

(*Note*: The spontaneity of this game makes it fun for the rest of the students to watch. But you can also have more than one game going at the same time so that more students can play.)

SEQUENCING ACTIVITIES INTO LONGER LESSONS

Now that you have been introduced to a number of activities in the last two chapters, you may wish to sequence several of them into one lesson plan. Specific choices will depend on your determination of the group's needs and interests.

I find it useful to have a theme to tie activities together. It is most important to make the activities progress according to levels of difficulty. (Refer to the chart on p. 11). With the activities and games covered thus far, you can select particularly from the following variables:

desk area activities	and move toward	those that use greater space
unison playing	and move toward	pairs and groups sharing their ideas
run-through playing	and move toward	concentrated playing, repeated playings, practice to improve

At this point, the other variables probably are not as distinct as they will be in later chapters.

Here is one example to demonstrate. Note the flexibility of choice and how an activity can be adapted to fit a theme.

Occupations or People at Work (theme)

1. "Guess the Sound" p. 41 (seat activity—use occupational sounds)
2. "Painting," p. 42 or "Play Ball" p. 42 (more movement but still at desk area)
3. (Choose one): "Conducting an Orchestra," p. 51 and p. 53; "Mirror an Occupation," p. 52; "Space Walk," p. 50; "Sculpturing," p. 53; or "Sound Pantomime with Occupation" p. 53: (All have greater movement with possibilities of group work and of sharing ideas.)
4. "Fatigue" poem, p. 44 (quieting activity)

SAMPLE LESSON PLAN
Staging Fights and Battles

Objectives

a. Learn that theatrical fighting is a disciplined art.

b. Learn how to "stage" fight scenes in stories in order to play them safely.

c. Be challenged by the fact that anyone can shove and push people around; only the skillful and trained can make fake fighting look real.

Preparation and Materials

1. **Space:** front of classroom for demonstrations; open to more space as lesson progresses
2. **Supplies:** (optional) fight scenes from literature to practice with at the end of the lesson
3. **Length of Session:** approximately 30 minutes

Opening Discussion

Students are usually intrigued and impressed with the fact that the "realistic" fights they see on television, in the movies, and on stage are organized and artful pretense. Talk about this from your own personal knowledge and get them to share their information. Do they know about stunt people? Do they know how some of their favorite scenes on television were staged?

Activity

"Today we're going to learn, the way actors and stunt people do, how to throw a hit without making actual physical contact with people. We'll learn to pretend how to receive and give hits in a convincing and believable way."

A. First, students work alone, imagining a partner. (You may wish to have a couple of students demonstrate this for the rest of the class first before letting everyone try.) They must practice and perfect their skill in stopping the blow at the precise moment before the contact. The point of contact they aim at may be imagined or may be a wall, their desk, or the palm of one hand.

Try three hits at first. You call (count) the blows slowly, checking to see how they are doing.

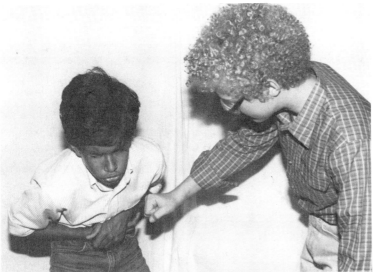

Students practice giving and receiving pretend hits in preparation for planning a fight scene.

You might pretend to be the one receiving the punches and give appropriate verbal response: "One, (pause), Ugghh! Two, (pause), "Ooh, you got me there," and so forth.

B. Next the students pretend to receive the blow. Again the partner is imagined. As well as calling the blows, you might tell them where the punches will be—1, stomach; 2, chin; 3, left shoulder.

Now you might pretend to be the one giving the blows and say: "One, take that!; two, and that!; three, that'll teach ya, ya ornery varmint!"

C. Now they can work in pairs. (Again, you may wish to demonstrate with two students before letting everyone try it.) Again you count. Allow perhaps five punches this time. Count slowly, perhaps even freezing after each count to make sure all rules are being followed.

D. Speed up *only* when they exhibit appropriate skill and sensitivity to each other. If you see any problems at all, stop immediately.

E. When everyone has had a chance to try it out, you might want to let them "stage" a fight from literature.

Suggestions: The King's Stilts, Dr. Seuss. New York: Random House, 1939. The Nizzards (large birds) and the Cats have a battle. The story says, "The fur flew fast but the feathers flew faster. It took only ten minutes." Let them all be the Nizzards fighting with imaginary partners and proceed as above.

As students gain skill in this kind of playing, they may be allowed to work out their own fight choreography. "Now that we've read the Robin Hood episode with the miller (93), let's divide into groups of five—the miller, Robin, and some of his men. We'll just do the part beginning with the miller opening his bag as he pretends to search for the money, continuing with the blows he gives the flour-covered men, and ending the scene when Robin gives three blasts on his horn. I'll give those blasts. Get into your groups now and plan who will play what part, and how Robin and his men react when the joke they have planned backfires. Also, you need to plan who will get hit first, second, and so on."

Quieting Activity (at desk)

Have them be a punching bag that slowly loses air and flattens out. You can count slowly to 10 at which time they must be seated.

Note: When students are capable of working out these ideas in cooperation with each other and rehearsing "staging" techniques, they are greatly pleased. It takes far more skill than a real playground brawl and is certainly more satisfying for all.

Narrative Pantomime With Children's Literature 5

A number of years ago, while looking for an easy way to get teachers and children started in a creative drama activity, we discovered that there were many stories and poems that we could narrate while the students pantomimed them. We called both these materials and the technique of playing them "narrative pantomime."[1]

Narrative pantomime is easy for both you and the students to do. It also provides a way for students to experience excellent literature, trying on favorite characters and joining them in their adventures. Narrative pantomimes encourage students to focus on the literature, to listen carefully in order to know what to pantomime and when to do it. Narrative pantomimes also give them security and self-confidence to try more challenging drama work later. Another advantage of these materials, particularly the stories, is that they give students an introduction to dramatic structure. There is a plot with a conflict and a beginning, middle, and ending—the basic ingredients for drama.

Because children must follow the literature's directions in narrative pantomime, there is built-in organization. You are in control. You will quickly learn what literature works best and will soon find yourself being able to edit material easily and even to write some of your own materials. These materials will also help you in narrative description, useful in the technique of "sidecoaching" in other activities.

At first, older students will probably prefer enacting the narrative pantomimes that have two or more characters because these materials resemble a skit or a play.

[1]See *Creative Drama for the Classroom Teacher* by Ruth Beall Heinig and Lyda Stillwell. (Englewood Cliffs, N.J.: Prentice-Hall, 1974 and 1981).

(An example might be George Mendoza's "The Crack in the Wall," the story of a hermit whose house falls apart, beginning with a crack that will not stop spreading.) Older students also prefer interacting with classmates and do not feel as isolated as they might with solo stories. But as the students begin to understand what narrative pantomime is and become more comfortable in their pantomiming abilities, they will also enjoy the materials that feature one character which the entire class can play simultaneously. An example of such material would be Phyllis Krasilovsky's *The Man Who Didn't Wash His Dishes*, the story of a lazy fellow's problem with housework.

Some material has several characters appearing one after another. For these materials the students can play all parts by themselves. For example, in the poem "Foul Shot" by Edwin A. Hoey, the students can first be the ball player, then the basketball, and finally the crowd watching the basketball game. Again, the entire class can play solo (by themselves) and simultaneously.

As you and the students become more familiar with narrative pantomime, you will want to try many varieties. We will talk about each in detail and give separate bibliographies for each. First, look at the general considerations you will need to make in playing narrative pantomimes.

LESSON PLANNING FOR NARRATIVE PANTOMIME

SELECTING THE MATERIAL

Material used for narrative pantomime must have enough continuous action to keep children actively involved from beginning to end. Since most authors and poets have not written their materials for narrative pantomime purposes, almost any selection can benefit from minor editing. Some material benefits from tightening the physical action, even to the extent of omitting sentences, as long as the plot is not destroyed.

The most dramatic materials build to a climax and have a quieting ending. Many stories and poems even have the character in a settled position at the end, a welcome aid in getting the students back in their seats or in a stationary position after playing. In some cases, you will want to add this feature with an added line or two or a simple rewording.

Sometimes you will find that additional action is helpful, particularly in picture books where much of the story is told through the art work. Adding descriptive detail to action can also enrich the drama experiences. The line may read, "The farmer worked in the field all day long." You might add the words "cutting and stacking the hay" in order to give students an idea of what they might pantomime.

"Look at the world upside down. . . . " (*Kalamazoo Gazette*)

EDITING DIALOGUE

Some stories have brief lines of dialogue. If they are short, the children will enjoy repeating them. Longer lines can be dropped. Some dialogue is easily pantomimed (for example, "No," "I don't know," or "Here"). Generally, the mouthing of words is distracting, so if you see the children doing this as you narrate, it probably means there is too much dialogue and it should be cut (or, that verbalizing should be added—see p. 69).

PRESENTING THE MATERIAL

There is no one way to present the material before enacting it. You might want to read the story first and discuss it to make sure the students understand it and know what they are to do. Other times you might want to read a story "cold" and have the students improvise on the spot. In any event, you will always want to be sure the students know what they are to do, have ideas for doing it, understand how to use space, and can handle any physical action safely. Sometimes it is helpful to have competent students demonstrate to the others how to play difficult or problem situations.

CREATIVE INTERPRETATION OF MOVEMENT

There is no one way to interpret the action in the narrative pantomimes. For example, in Carl Sandburg's "Lines Written for Gene Kelly to Dance To," the students are asked if they can dance a question mark. This could be interpreted in a variety of ways: the feet might draw a question mark on the floor; the hands might inscribe one in the air; or the whole body might form one, dissolving and reforming in a rhythmic dance. You will want to encourage the students to find their own ways of performing an action. The ideas can be discussed prior to the playing, and perhaps be tried out and demonstrated before the entire selection is played.

LIMITING SPACE

As discussed earlier, it is most useful to keep the students working at their desks or in a designated place on the floor. Often the desks can become part of the drama if you refer to them as beds, cars, tables, or whatever the material calls for.

For pair and group playing, be sure the children understand the limits of their space. In some cases it may also be necessary to let only half the class play while the other half observes. (Observers might help with the sound effects or other technical aspects.)

NARRATING THE MATERIAL

Much of the artistic burden of narrative pantomime relies on the narrator's reading abilities. Therefore, it is probably best not to let the students be the narrators, particularly at first. Later, when they become familiar with narrative pantomime, you may find superior readers volunteering to narrate and doing an excellent job. If you have several talented readers, you might want to let them all narrate one selection. Just divide the material at logical intervals.

You also need to know the story well enough so that you can keep an eye on the class's performance. If you have a soft voice, it may be necessary to allow only a few students at a time to play in order that your voice can be heard. Your timing and vocal intensity can also control the action and the noise level. If the students get a bit too noisy, just pause. As they quiet down in order to hear the next cue, you can speak in a softer voice. This should calm their playing down.

MUSIC

Some materials benefit from musical background, lending atmosphere, sustaining involvement, and encouraging ideas. Some suggestions for music are indicated in the bibliographies in this chapter. At first you may need to rehearse the narration with the music before trying it with the class.

EVALUATION

Both you and the students will be evaluating the playing throughout. Acknowledge the good work you see them doing, although it is best not to praise one idea over another. Your acknowledgement can pertain both to the students' playing and their management of themselves:

"You had so many interesting and different ways of being a cat. I saw some washing themselves; some were sitting on haunches; and I think I even heard some quiet purring."

"I liked the way you were able to stay in your own space and not interfere with others' work."

Self evaluation is also important and can be encouraged by asking:

"What's one thing you did that you liked the best?"

"What do you think you might do differently the next time we play it?"

Some may like to share their ideas for interpretation, both in telling about them as well as in demonstrating them.

REPLAYING

If students have enjoyed the material and their own expression of it, they may ask to repeat it. In repeated playings they can perfect their ideas with your encouragement and guidance. New goals may also be established.

"This time you may want to try some new ideas."

"I'll slow down this time in the part where you thought I read a little too fast for you to act out all the ideas you had."

NARRATIVE PANTOMIMES FOR SOLO PLAYING

The following stories and poems are arranged alphabetically according to titles. Numbers in parentheses refer to anthologies listed in the final bibliography. Suggested grade levels are listed in the left hand margin.

4–6 "Base Stealer," Robert Francis. (34) A baseball player's actions are described as he hesitates and then decides to steal a base in this poem. Experiment with slow motion on this one, as in televised sports replays. Let students run in place on the last line. You call "Safe!" to end the playing.

4 *Could Be Worse!* James Stevenson. New York: Morrow, 1977. Grandpa tells an incredibly tall tale about what happened to him one night.

4–6 *Fortunately*, Remy Charlip. New York: Parents', 1964. Good fortune and bad fortune go hand in hand in this adventure.

4–6 "Foul Shot," Edwin A. Hoey. (34) This careful, poetic description gives all the minute details of a basketball shot. In solo playing, students can be the player and then the ball. For a final touch, be a person in the crowd giving a *silent* "roarup," and then freeze.

4–6 *Great-Grandfather in the Honey Tree,* Sam and Zoa Swayne. New York: Viking, 1949. This is a very tall tale about a hunting adventure.

4–6 "The Hairy Toe," George Mendoza. (21) This delicious weird tale is similar to the tale of "Teeny Tiny." Everyone will want to say the line "Gwot, I ate it!" at the end.

4 *Hildilid's Night*, Cheli Duran Ryan. New York: Macmillan, 1971. A woman tries everything she can think of to get rid of the night until she becomes so exhausted she falls asleep.

4 *I Will Not Go to Market Today*, Harry Allard. New York: Dial, 1979. Day after day Fenimore B. Buttercrunch attempts to go to market for strawberry jam. But there is always a problem: a dam breaks, a dinosaur is in his front yard, and he even breaks his leg and is laid up for six months! But persistence wins out in the end.

4–6 "Lines Written for Gene Kelly To Dance To," Carl Sandburg. (56) This poem asks the famous dancer to dance such ideas as the alphabet, the wind, and so forth. The first section is the easiest to do, but the entire poem offers wonderful possibilities. Try it with a musical background such as Leroy Anderson's "Sandpaper Ballet." (Say a line, turn up the volume of the record for a few seconds, fade down and say next line, and so on.)

4 *The Man Who Didn't Wash His Dishes*. Phyllis Krasilovsky. Garden City, N.Y.: Doubleday, 1950. A lazy fellow's neglect poses problems in housekeeping. Students are amused at the solution of letting the rain wash the dishes! The desks can be the man's chair, kitchen table, and truck.

4 *The Man Who Entered a Contest*, Phyllis Krasilovsky. Garden City, N.Y.: Doubleday, 1980. A man decides to enter a baking contest. But when the cat knocks over the baking powder, unnoticed, the batter bakes all over the furniture. The man wins, of course. Students can play in pairs if you want to add the cat; other characters are easily omitted.

4–6 "The Passer," George Abbe. (38) This is a brief description of a football pass. Try it in slow motion. A college football fight song playing in the background, perhaps at slow speed, will lend atmosphere.

4–6 *The Pond*, Carol and Donald Carrick. New York: Macmillan, 1970. Sensitive, poetic descriptions of movements of water, insects, and all life near and in a pond are presented. Students can switch from one character to another. Try Debussy's "La Mer" or something similar as background music. Try as a shadow dance with scenery and lighting suggestions that are in Chapter 13.

4–6 "Rodeo," Edward Lueders. (34) This describes a cowboy readying to mount and ride a Brahma bull and is another possibility for slow motion.

4 *Sometimes I Dance Mountains*, Byrd Baylor. New York: Charles Scribner's, 1973. Ideas for dance pantomime are presented. Photographs

of a girl dancing illustrate movement ideas. Simple instruments (wooden xylophone, tambourine, drum, and so forth) can provide background effects. Try it as a shadow dance with scenery and lighting suggestions that are given in Chapter 13.

4–6 "The Sorcerer's Apprentice" (40) The young apprentice to a magician remembers only part of a magic spell and finds himself in much trouble. Begin action where the Sorcerer leaves. Try music of Paul Dukas for background. It can also be played in groups. (See other versions by Lesi Well, Boston: Little, Brown, 1962 and Wanda Gag, New York: Coward, McCann & Geoghegan, 1979).

4–6 "Trinity Place," Phyllis McGinley. (32) This description compares actions of pigeons in a city park with actions of humans. It is brief but has wonderful possibilities for sophisticated movement.

4 *We Were Tired of Living in a House*, Liesel Moak Skorpen. New York: Coward, McCann & Geoghegan, 1969. Some children decide to investigate other places to live and find that their house is not so bad after all. Fill in narrative detail from the pictures.

PAIR AND GROUP PLAYING WITH NARRATIVE PANTOMIME

As stated earlier, older elementary students will particularly enjoy playing stories that have two or more characters because these stories resemble a skit or a play. They feel a sense of accomplishment in creating their own dramas quickly and easily without having to memorize a script.

In paired playing the entire class (or as many as you can handle) is paired and the pairs play simultaneously. This procedure allows more students the opportunity to play.

You will also quickly note that when a story has two or more characters, the characters frequently interact socially and even physically. For example, "The Crack in the Wall" by George Mendoza is fun to play with one student as the hermit and one as the expanding crack. But since the hermit pounds and kicks the wall, you will want to make sure the students can perform such actions appropriately and safely before you let an entire class try this story. Such physical contact has to be pretended or faked as it is done in the movies and on television. (See Chapter 4 for a lesson plan on staging fights and battles.)

Other paired playing can be done with stories that have several characters. For example, in some stories, one character meets several other characters during an adventure. One student can play the major character while the second one plays each of the other characters. Often this procedure is preferred by the students as it gives them more opportunity to enact more roles.

NARRATIVE PANTOMIMES FOR PAIRED PLAYING

4 *Andy and the Lion*, James Daugherty. New York: Viking, 1966. A young boy reads about lions and imagines himself in an adventure similar to that of the fabled Androcles. You can begin with Part II.

4–6 "The Bear in the Pear Tree," Alice Geer Kelsey. (31) The Hodja meets a bear and hides from him in a pear tree. Subtle humor is important in this story.

4–6 *The Boy Who Would Be a Hero*, Marjorie Lewis. New York: Coward, McCann & Geoghegan, 1982. A lad who sets off on an adventure to become a hero almost becomes one when he meets a witch who is set on having a hero sandwich for her birthday. Try this with pairs— hero and witch plus minor characters. Since the witch's body appears in parts and later comes disassembled, you may also want to do this one in groups. Dialogue can be edited out for initial playings.

4 *Caps for Sale*, Esphyr Slobodkina. New York: Scholastic, 1968. Thieving monkeys take a peddler's caps. This version is easiest to use for narrative. It can be played in pairs, using one monkey to one peddler.

4–6 "The Crack in the Wall," George Mendoza. (11) A hermit loses his house to a crack in the wall that will not stop spreading. Pairs include the hermit and a crack that starts out "knife-thin, the length of the hermit's hand" and keeps reappearing on different walls until the whole place collapses. Plan carefully the hermit's examination of the crack. I let everyone fall at the end, but in slow motion to a count of 3.

4 "Gertrude McFuzz," Dr. Seuss. (58) Gertrude finds that growing a big, beautiful tail may not be what she really wants after all. The same child who plays Lolla-Lee-Lou can also play Uncle Dake.

4–6 *Gone Is Gone*, Wanda Gag. New York: Coward McCann, & Geoghegan, 1935. The old tale of the man who swaps chores with his wife only to discover her work is not as simple as he had thought. Another version is "The Husband Who Was to Mind the House." (4) (35) You can combine the best features of both stories.

4 *How the Grinch Stole Christmas!* Dr. Seuss. New York: Random House, 1957. This is the modern classic of a spiteful character who learns the true meaning of Christmas giving. While one child plays the Grinch, another child can be Max the dog and the Who child.

4–6 *How the Rhinoceros Got His Skin*, Rudyard Kipling. New York: Walker, 1974. A Parsee gets even with a rhinoceros who keeps stealing cakes. You will probably need to edit out the fact that the Parsee wears no clothes to avoid embarrassment in playing. This beautifully illustrated version by Leonard Weisgard is tastefully done. See also (24).

4 *Lizard Lying in the Sun*. Bernice Freschet. New York: Charles Scribner's, 1975. A lizard has a peaceful day in the sun until an eagle flies by. Play this in pairs with one child as the lizard and the second child as each of the other animals.

5–6 "The Mouse and the Flea," Charles E. Gillham. (5) Two friends get tired of each other and begin to play tricks on one another. This is an Alaskan Eskimo tale.

4 *Mrs. Gaddy and the Ghost*, Wilson Gage. New York: Greenwillow, 1979. Mrs Gaddy lives in an old farmhouse with a ghost. When all efforts to get rid of him fail, she decides to move. But when she sees how dejected the ghost is, she decides to return. Mrs. Gaddy talks to herself, but these little monologues can simply be mimed. This one is fun for Halloween.

5–6 "Wait Till Martin Comes," Maria Leach. (46) A man has a scary adventure in a haunted house with four cats. A second actor can play all the cats. The man can be "rocking" in a rocking chair while he observes all the goings on. This is appropriate for Halloween.

4 "What Was I Scared Of?" Dr. Seuss. (37) A typical Seuss character is frightened of a pair of pants with nobody in them until it finds the pants are afraid of it! Fun for Halloween.

GROUP STORIES INTO PLAYS

Often narrative pantomime stories will have several or even numerous characters. Students will want to make these stories into skits or informal plays with perhaps everyone in the class having a part.

The size of the cast and the number of characters in the story will vary. Often the number of characters can be easily increased by double casting the parts or by adding crowd scenes. If you prefer to divide the class into small groups with each group working on a different play, you may need to decrease the cast size. This can be done by having students doubling up on the number of parts they play.

Some of the characters in group stories have small parts; but if they are interesting characters, the children will want to include them all. For example, in *Ittki Pittki* there is, in addition to the title role, the prince, the wife, four sons, the prince's messenger, the doctor, the funeral director, and all the customers and mourners. Some appear only briefly, but they are all important to the plot.

By adding characters or by double casting, an entire class can often play in one of these group stories. For example, in *The Beast of Monsieur Racine* by Tomi Ungerer, there are crowds in both the railway scene and in the auditorium at the Paris Academy of Science. The picture book shows numerous interesting characters which the students can develop in greater detail. The same is true of Tomie de Paola's *Strega Nona*, which features an entire town inundated with spaghetti from a magic pasta pot.

If you prefer to have a small cast of characters, then several minor parts in a story can be played by the same person. You might even want to let two small groups enact a story simultaneously. At first, it may seem a little like a two-ring circus, but it does give more students a chance to play. And the remainder of the class who are watching can see different interpretations of characters and lines.

You may even want to encourage groups to work out their portrayals on their own, giving each group a different story to enact. In order to keep the decision-making tasks easier, the working groups probably should not be larger than five to seven students, including the narrator. Students may draw lots to see who plays which part. An informal drama "festival," with each group sharing its performance with the rest of the class, can be the end result of this more elaborate procedure.

ADDING DIALOGUE

If a class enjoys a story and likes replaying it, they may begin to perfect it much as they might in rehearsing a play. This happens because these stories develop so easily into a play format.

Consider for a moment that when you put on a play, the first step you take is to select a script. And, what is a script but the dialogue or speeches of the characters? Actors must memorize the speeches (or script) and then add the action or stage directions so that the plot unfolds.

However, in the process being recommended here, we begin with the pantomimed action first, organizing and rehearsing it. Now, if desired, dialogue may be added to the pantomime. As the students work with the story, they may see opportunities for dialogue. All you may need to do is pause in the narration and allow them to improvise their dialogue. In some cases, and with some stories, the students may carry the story along so completely that narrating will be needed only sporadially. It may even be eliminated in time.

SHARING

As the students gain more confidence in themselves and in their work, they may ask to share it with an audience. However, sharing should be the collective desire of the group rather than being imposed by you.

Students often have more success in sharing these narrated materials than they would with a scripted play. Fear of forgetting lines, usually the biggest worry in performing a play, can be eliminated since the dialogue is not essential to these stories. There is less pressure than with a scripted play since these plays go on as long as the narrating and pantomiming continue. If some students are hesitant with dialogue, they can still participate in the playing, while those who are ready for improvising can add it.

Older elementary students may find it a rewarding experience to share their stories with students in the lower grades. Of course, they will want to share the stories that are most appealing and understandable to that age group. You may wish to check additional story possibilities in the companion text to this one, written for lower elementary grades. Many stories can be appreciated on two levels of understanding and are as interesting for the older students to perform as they are for the younger children to see.

AUDIENCE

When sharing the play with classmates you have an excellent opportunity to emphasize what an audience is and how it shows its appreciation of theatrical events. An audience watches to learn and enjoy. It is polite and shows respect for the actors. Those students who form the audience from time to time should be as courteous to their classmates as they will want them to be when the roles are reversed.

ADDING TECHNICAL ASPECTS

Students will enjoy adding technical aspects to their plays, particularly if they are planning to share them with an audience. It is best to keep these additions simple and not clutter or overpower the most important part of a drama—the actors and the story.

Costumes can be simple pieces of material that are draped or tied around any child of any size. Cast-off curtains, blankets, tablecloths, and fabric remnants do nicely. Hats and scarves are also useful.

Props should be made of simple materials. Many can still be pantomimed. And, indeed, sometimes this procedure is more aesthetically pleasing than using real objects.

You and the students can find ways to use objects creatively. For example, students once played a version of "Jack and the Beanstalk" and for the beanstalk used a broom and a chair. Jack stood on the chair and held the broom high. Then, as he "climbed the beanstalk," he went hand over hand along the broomstick. As the

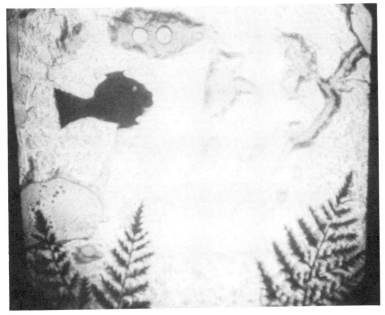

A plastic bag, filled with a small amount of water and cooking oil, with added food coloring and aquatic ornaments, will give interesting visual effects when projected on a screen or sheet. Background scenery for *The Pond* by Carol and Donald Carrick.

broom lowered to the floor, the illusion of climbing was cleverly, yet simply, executed.

Scenery is usually never required. Students can get very literal about what is needed and should, instead, be encouraged to use their imaginations. Again, simplicity is the key.

Music and sound effects, if they aid the interpretation of the story, can also be added.

Finally, some students will enjoy working on the technical aspects of the production more than performing in the story itself. Some may even show abilities in managing, designing, and executing these simple technical aspects. Encourage this and give as much attention to these technical artists as to the actors. You may even find some students exhibiting directing and overall management skills. The theatre requires many artists to achieve the total picture. Who knows how many of these artists are waiting to be born in your own classroom?

NARRATIVE PANTOMIME FOR GROUP PLAYING

4 *The Bears Who Stayed Indoors*, Susanna Gretz. Chicago: Follett, 1970. Five bears and a dog named Fred spend a rainy day playing spaceship. The bears' actions are so cleverly written and fun to play that even older students should enjoy this one.

4–6 *The Beast of Monsieur Racine*, Tomi Ungerer. New York: Farrar, Straus & Giroux, 1971. A retired French tax collector discovers a rare beast, befriends it, and takes it to the Academy of Sciences. The surprise ending will delight all. May be played in threes (two are the beast) or with the added crowd scenes. Try a series of frozen pictures (see Chapter 7) for the line, "Unspeakable acts were performed."

4–6 *The Big Yellow Balloon*, Edward Fenton. Garden City, N.Y.: Doubleday, 1967. With his yellow balloon, Roger manages to lure an unlikely parade of a cat, dog, dog catcher, lady, thief, and police officer. Organize this one carefully. Precise timing is required for maximum effect.

4 *Caps for Sale*, Esphyr Slobodkina. New York: Scholastic, 1947. Thieving monkeys take a peddler's caps. Although this story is popular with younger children, older students often like playing the monkey's antics. This version of an oft-told tale is the easiest to use for narrative pantomime. Try groups of five, or two peddlers and the rest monkeys.

4–6 *Casey at the Bat*, Ernest Lawrence Thayer. Englewood Cliffs, N.J.: Prentice-Hall, 1964. This is the well-known poem of the ball player who strikes out and causes Mudville to lose the baseball game. This edition has wonderful gay 90's pictures. The poem should not be edited, so action needs to be created in several sections. Another effective way to do it is through a series of frozen pictures. (See Chapter 7). The frozen pictures might also be done as shadows. (See Chapter 13). Two other picture book versions of this poem are by Wallace Tripp, New York: Coward, McCann & Geoghegan, 1978 (animal characters) and Ken Bachaus, Milwaukee: Raintree, 1985.

4 *Curious George*, H. A. Rey. Boston: Houghton Mifflin, 1941. This is the original story of the curious little monkey who cannot stay out of trouble. Edit for solo playing at least once to give everyone a chance to be George. Again this is a story for the young, but many older children find monkey behaviors fascinating to play. Check other sequels for more adventures of this famous character in children's literature. Most of the stories have a number of additional characters for George to interact with.

4–6 *Drummer Hoff*, Barbara Emberley. Englewood-Cliffs, N.J.: Prentice-Hall, 1967. This is a simple cumulative story of a cannon being loaded and fired off. Older students will like the challenge of mechanical movement in this one. You might like to watch the Weston Woods film company's animated version of this award-winning picture book for movement ideas. Be sure to add flowers growing at the end, as shown in the final scene. Many background musical or sound-effects possibilities exist, but do not overpower the simplicity of the text. You might also try this as a shadow play with live actors (See Chapter 13).

4 *The Duchess Bakes a Cake*, Virginia Kahl. New York: Charles Scribner's, 1955. A bored Duchess tries her hand at baking and winds up on top of a huge cake. This is told in rhyme; dialogue can be pantomimed. There are numerous characters. Some students can play more than one part, if desired.

4–6 *The Funny Little Woman*, Arlene Mosel. New York: E. P. Dutton, 1972. A giggling little woman in Japan chases a rolling rice dumpling underground. When the statues of the gods are unable to protect her, she is captured by the wicked Oni who force her to make rice dumplings for them. She escapes with a magic wooden paddle that brings her great wealth. There is some dialogue, but it can be easily mimed. It is a good story for masks. (See Chapter 13).

4 *The Goblin Under the Stairs*, Mary Calhoun. New York: William Morrow, 1967. A boy and his parents each have a special way of viewing the goblin who lives in their house. And the goblin lives up to each one's expectations. The narrator can also play the part of the neighbor.

4–6 *Harriet and the Promised Land*, Jacob Lawrence. New York: Windmill, 1968. This story of Harriet Tubman can be done in frozen pictures (Chapter 7) or as a shadow play (Chapter 13). The text is illustrated in beautiful, stark woodcuts.

4–6 *Horton Hatches the Egg*, Dr. Seuss. New York: Random House, 1940, 1968. Horton the Elephant, who is "faithful 100 percent," hatches an egg for the lazy Maizie bird. It can also be done as a shadow play. See Chapter 13.

5–6 *It Could Always Be Worse*, Margot Zemach. New York: Farrar, Straus & Giroux, 1976. Rabbi advises a crowded, irritable family to keep taking animals into their house. Then, when he advises taking the animals out, the house seems spacious. Freeze the mayhem in the house each time the father visits the Rabbi.

4–6 *Ittki Pittki*, Miriam Chaikin. New York: Parents', 1971. Ittki Pittki, a mid-Eastern cloth merchant, fears he has been accidentally poisoned at the prince's palace and returns home to wait for death. This funny tale has a moral as well.

5–6 *Lentil*, Robert McCloskey. New York: Viking, 1940, 1968. A boy saves the day for a small town in Ohio with his harmonica playing of "She'll Be Comin' 'Round the Mountain." The villain, old man Sneep, sucks a lemon to keep the band from playing welcoming music for the town's benefactor who is being greeted at the train. There are plenty of characters. Although it features minimum dialogue, plenty of opportunity to improvise exists.

4–6 *Mrs. Beggs and the Wizard*, Mercer Mayer. New York: Parents', 1973. Mrs. Beggs owns a boarding house. A strange renter seems to be the source of many unusual happenings, and Mrs. Beggs is forced to use her witchery kit to get rid of him. Several interesting boarding

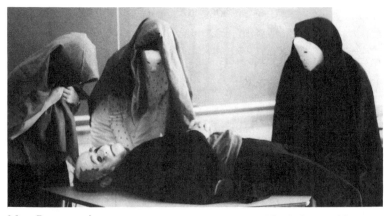

Mrs. Beggs conjures up strange creatures to get rid of the troublesome Wizard.

house characters are presented. The ending can use a quick blackout.

4–6 *My Grandpa is a Pirate*, Jan Lööf (English translation by Else Holmelund Minarik). New York: Harper Row, 1968. A young boy and his grandfather go off on a pirate adventure one summer afternoon while Grandma takes a nap. There are lots of characters and exciting action in this one.

4–6 *Oté,* Pura Belpré. New York: Pantheon, 1969. A Puerto Rican folk tale about a man and his family who are plagued by an unwanted, nearsighted little devil.

4–6 *The Pond*, Carol and Donald Carrick. New York: Macmillan, 1970. Sensitive, poetic descriptions of movements of water, insects, and all life near and in a pond are presented. For group playing, you might want to try some simple choreography. Dancers in leotards are a possibility as well as shadow dancing behind a well lighted sheet or a shadow play (See Chapter 13). As with solo playing, try Debussy's "La Mer" or something similar as background music.

4–6 *Seven Skinny Goats*, Victor G. Ambrus. New York: Harcourt, Brace Jovanovich, 1969. Jano, a young goat herder, does not realize his flute playing, which causes the goats and everyone else to dance, is not appreciated. Control the frenzied dancing with music. Whenever it stops, the dancers must immediately cease. You might also have them dance with one foot "glued" to the floor as in the game "Caught in the Act" in Chapter 4. Playing a recording of Sid Lawrence's "Swinging Shepherd Blues" at fast speed can also add to the fun.

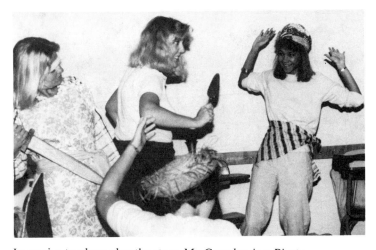

In-service teachers play the story *My Grandpa is a Pirate*.

4–6 *The Sneetches*, Dr. Seuss. New York: Random House, 1961. Sneetches with stars on their bellies feel superior to those without. An enterprising salesperson, Sylvester McMonkey McBean, takes advantage of the situation. It is fun for some students to become the machine. Design it carefully. What parts are there in the machine and what does each one do? Because the story is Seuss and in rhyme, you will want to keep it just as it is, including the dialogue. Encourage the students to fill in appropriately mimed action during the speeches rather than mouthing the words. Seuss is easy to memorize for those who might want to add dialogue to the playing. The students may already be familiar with the story and the television production.

4–6 *The Sorcerer's Apprentice*, Richard Rostron. New York: William Morrow, 1941. The young apprentice to a magician remembers only part of a magic spell and finds himself in much trouble with brooms that fetch water but will not stop. When the apprentice tries to stop the brooms with an ax, his troubles keep doubling. It is fun to add people enacting bottles, books, and other sorcery items that float about as the water rises in the Sorcerer's workshop. Try adding the famous music by composer Paul Dukas. (See other versions by Lesi Well, Boston: Little, Brown, 1962 and Wanda Gag, New York: Coward, McCann & Geoghegan, 1979.)

4–6 *The Stonecutter*, Gerald McDermott. New York: Viking, 1975. This is a well-known Japanese folk tale simply told with numerous charac-

College students enact "The Sneetches" in garbage bag costumes.

ters and no dialogue. McDermott's illustrations give many ideas for a shadow play also. (See Chapter 13).

4 *The Story of Ferdinand*, Munro Leaf. New York: Viking, 1936. This classic story of Ferdinand, the bull who would rather smell flowers than fight in the bull ring, gives students an opportunity to learn about bull fighting customs. A parade of bulls, matadors, picadors, and others is always fun to add before the bullfighting scene. Use classical bullfighting music or Herb Alpert's "The Lonely Bull."

4–6 *Strega Nona,* Tomie dePaola. Englewood Cliffs, N.J.: Prentice-Hall, 1975. Strega Nona, or "Grandma Witch," has a magic pasta pot which Big Anthony misuses, and the town is flooded with pasta. Numerous characters are presented. Students often like to pretend to be the pasta pot, joining hands in a circle and jiggling to show the boiling. They might also like to become the spaghetti that boils up and over the pot and covers the town.

4–6 *The Three Poor Tailors*, Victor G. Ambrus. New York: Harcourt Brace Jovanovich, 1965. Three tailors go off on the back of a goat to see the city and find fun, adventure, and trouble. It requires groups of four: three tailors, with a fourth player to enact the soldier, innkeeper, and guards. It is more fun just to imagine the goat.

4–6 "Urashima Taro and the Princess of the Sea," Yoshiko Uchida. (12) Urashima is enticed to live in the sea and spends much more time

In-service teachers play dePaola's *Strega Nona.*

Three Poor Tailors (story by Victor Ambrus) ride off on a goat to seek adventure in the city.

there than he imagines. On returning home, he finds out just how much time has lapsed. The dialogue can easily be edited out. It is effective as a shadow play with live actors or with shadow puppets.

4–6 *The Way the Tiger Walked*, Doris J. Chaconas. New York: Simon & Schuster, 1970. Porcupine, zebra, and elephant try unsuccessfully to imitate the tiger's regal walk while monkeys watch the show. When the tiger imitates *their* walks, they return to their natural movements. It requires subtle humor and can be done simply or perfected into a finely tuned precision piece, perhaps with rhythm instruments for sound effects.

4–6 *Who's in Rabbit's House?* Verna Aardema. New York: Dial, 1977. In this African Masai tale, Caterpillar is in Rabbit's house and is scaring all the animals away by pretending to be a huge monster. The pictures show the folk tale presented as a play performed by villagers

Frog, Rabbit, and Elephant are surprised to find that it is only Caterpillar in Rabbit's house. (*Who's in Rabbit's House?* by Verna Aardema)

wearing masks. Although there is dialogue, the narrator can still read this while actors mime in masks.

4–6 *Yeh-Shen*, Ai-Ling Louie. New York: Philomel, 1982. This is a Chinese retelling of the Cinderella story with a fish taking the place of the fairy godmother. The tale is told mainly in action and dialogue can be mimed easily. The illustrations are free-flowing and suggest stylized pantomime, aided by flowing scarves and masks. A shadow play is also possible. (See Chapter 13).

6

Further Uses
of Narrative Pantomime

Once you have become familiar with narrative pantomime, you will quickly see that there are many other uses for it. You have probably already found a number of your own stories and poems suitable for narrative pantomime.

NARRATIVE PANTOMIMES FROM LONGER BOOKS

Sometimes whole chapters from a single book can be easily adapted for narrative pantomime. For example, there are numerous episodes in Armstrong Sperry's *Call It Courage* or Scott O'Dell's *Island of the Blue Dolphins* that you can easily excerpt or splice together for excellent narrative pantomime experiences.

NARRATIVE PANTOMIME AND PUPPETS

Many of the narrative pantomimes in the previous chapter as well as in this one can be done very successfully with puppets. (See Chapter 13 for more information on puppetry.)

The narrative pantomimes can be used as a way of exploring the various movements the puppets are capable of. Because the puppet's body has certain limitations of movement, much inventiveness will be required. But children will enjoy the discovery process and will get a basic anatomy lesson as well.

You will need to decide what kind of puppets you want to experiment with. A stick puppet will not be able to move as much as a hand puppet, for example. Yet the basic puppets may be very effective with some stories. Very simple shadow puppets, for example, have been used successfully in telling *The Story of Babar the Little Elephant* and *Casey at the Bat*.

NARRATIVE PANTOMIME WITH ADDITIONAL CURRICULAR SUBJECTS

Again, as you become familiar with narrative pantomime, you will quickly see that there are a great many excellent materials focusing on other areas of the curriculum such as social studies and science. Following is a list of excellent stories for older elementary children covering animal life cycles, career education, biography, and so forth. You can use these materials as they are, with editing in some cases, or as a stimulus for your own writing. Because they provide such rich learning experiences for students, you will not want to overlook any of the following possibilities or other similar materials you may find on your own.

Note: The materials focusing on animal and insect life will be of interest to many fourth graders. Students in fifth and sixth grades will probably be more interested in the materials focusing on people. You will, however, be the best judge for your own particular class.

4 *All on a Mountain Day*, Aileen Fisher. New York: Thom. Nelson, 1956. This book has a chapter about each of the wild animals on a mountainside, from rabbit to bobcat.

4 *Amelia Bedelia*, Peggy Parish. New York: Harper and Row, 1963. Amelia, a housekeeper, takes all her instructions literally. This popular character has been the subject of many adventures. You and your students will not want to overlook any of them. All are good lessons in word usage. Usually it is easiest to let everyone play Amelia.

4 *And Then What Happened, Paul Revere?* Jean Fritz. New York: Coward, McCann & Geoghegan, 1973. An accurate and amusing story of a national hero by one of the most popular history writers for children.

4–6 *Balloon Trip*, Huck Scarry. Englewood Cliffs, N.J.: Prentice-Hall, 1982. In this book we travel on an extended balloon trip, learning of the many intricacies of this exciting sport.

4 *Beaver Moon*, Miska Miles. Boston: Little, Brown, 1978. An old beaver is forced out of his lodge and searches for a new home.

6 *The Black Pearl*, Scott O'Dell. Boston: Houghton Mifflin, 1967. Ramon tells of his adventures with Manta Diablo, a fearsome fish, and of the search for a black pearl in Mexican waters. Many excerpts from this longer novel are useful.

4 *The Blind Colt*, Glen Rounds. New York: Holiday House, 1941. A blind colt must learn of the world, its joys, and its dangers. It is excellent for animal study as well as the topic of blindness.

4–6 *BMX*, Dave Spurdens. Sterling Publishing Co., 1984. This presents excellent data and photos (color and black and white) on Bicycle Motocross. There are story possibilities in the sections on riding, stunts, proper clothing, and maintenance.

4 *Brighty of the Grand Canyon*, Marguerite Henry. Chicago: Rand McNally, 1953. The story of a burro who spends his winters at the bottom of the Canyon where it is warm and his summers on the North Rim, where it is cool.

5–6 *Call It Courage*, Armstrong Sperry. New York: Macmillan, 1940. A South Sea island boy, son of a tribal chief, has many fears of the sea and sets out to conquer them.

4–6 *Chimney Sweeps*, James Cross Giblin. New York: Crowell, 1982. A nine-hundred-year history of chimney sweeps is presented with illustrations and photographs. Chapter 5 takes us through a day in the life of a chimney boy's day in London in the 1800's.

6 *Coyote in Manhattan*, Jean Craighead George. New York: Thomas Y. Crowell, 1968. A story about a teenaged black girl who wants to join a high-school group who has voted her out. She finds a caged coyote and sets him free so that the group will change their opinion of her. The story focuses as much on the coyote and his encounter with the city as it does on the girl.

4–6 *C. W. Anderson's Complete Book of Horses and Horsemanship*. New York: Macmillan, 1963. This has many descriptive passages including a chapter on riding techniques.

4–6 *A Day in the Life of an Emergency Room Nurse*, Margot Witty. Mahwah, N.J.: Troll Associates, 1980. A nurse, through text and photographs, shows what her experiences in an emergency room are like.

4–6 *A Day in the Life of a Forest Ranger*, David Paige. Mahwah, N.J.: Troll Associates, 1980. A forest ranger goes through a typical day which involves everything from paperwork to relocation of animals. Photographs are included.

4–6 *A Day in the Life of a Television News Reporter,* William Jaspersohn. Boston: Little, Brown, 1981. This book, complete with photographs, shows a typical day of a television news reporter in Boston, from an early morning call about a robbery to the evening news broadcast.

4 *Doctor in the Zoo*, Bruce Buchenholz. New York: Viking, 1974. A fascinating account of the many duties of a zoo doctor is presented with black and white photos.

4 *Felipé the Bullfighter*, Robert Vara. New York: Harcourt, Brace, & World, 1967. A young boy in Spain tries his hand at fighting a small bull. The beautiful color photographs add to the understanding of the story. Very little editing is needed, although it will be more dramatic if the action is condensed into one day's time.

4–6 *Flying to the Moon and Other Strange Places*, Michael Collins. New York: Farrar, Straus, and Giroux, 1976. This is a first-hand account of space from one of the early astronauts.

4 *Fox and the Fire*, Miska Miles. Boston: Little, Brown, 1966. A young red fox searches for food and is interrupted by a barn fire.

4–6 *Gorilla, Gorilla*, Carol Fenner. New York: Random House, 1973. This is a poignant description of a gorilla's life in the zoo with flashbacks to his life in the jungle.

4–6 *How a House Happens*, Jan Adkins. New York: Walker, 1972. This presents the steps in the process of building a house, complete with diagrams.

A narrative pantomime of "The House that Jack Built," with simple cardboard scenery and paper masks, is shared with an audience outdoors.

4 *How to Dig a Hole to the Other Side of the World*, Faith McNulty. New York: Harper and Row, 1979. Instructions are detailed for taking an imaginary 8,000 mile journey, beginning with a shovel and a soft place to dig to a no-spaceship with super-cooling system, fireproof skin, and a drill on its nose.

4–6 *i am the running girl*, Arnold Adoff. New York: Harper & Row, 1979. Rhonda trains for a running meet. It is told in poetic form.

4–6 *Indian Hunting*, Robert (Gray-Wolf) Hofsinde. New York: William Morrow, 1962. This describes Indian weapons, hunting methods, and the ceremonial rites of the hunt. Other books by this author may also be of interest.

6 *Island of the Blue Dolphins*, Scott O'Dell. Boston: Houghton Mifflin, 1960. An Indian girl is left alone on an island in the Pacific and manages to survive. There are many episodes to use from this exciting book based on a true story.

6 *Julie of the Wolves*, Jean Craighead George. New York: Harper & Row, 1972. An Eskimo girl must choose between the world of her ancestors and the world of modern white people. Her sensitivity to the wolves and time spent with them comprises much of the story.

5–6 *Kon-Tiki and I*, Erik Hesselberg. Englewood Cliffs, N.J.: Prentice-Hall,

The Indian mother shelters her children from the storm.

1970. This is the account by one of the six explorers in Thor Hyerdahl's expedition that sailed a small raft from Peru to the Polynesian Islands.

4–6 *The Long Ago Lake*, Marne Wilkins. New York: Charles Scribner's, 1978. This gives fascinating data on outdoor life in the Wisconsin north country in the 1930's.

4–6 *Lucky Chuck*, Beverly Cleary. New York: William Morrow, 1984. A picture book illustrates the story of teenaged Chuck who pumps gas and has a motorcycle. Chuck goes for a ride and frequent references are made to the motor vehicle code which he follows. When he forgets himself and has an accident, he gets a traffic ticket. The last picture shows Chuck wondering how much gas he will have to pump to pay for the fine. It is good for teaching road safety with humor along with the fun of riding the motorcycle.

4–6 *Lumberjack*, William Kurelek. Boston: Houghton Mifflin, 1974. The author describes his personal experiences as a young lumberjack in Canada.

4 *The Moon of the Winter Bird*, Jean George. New York: Thomas Y. Crowell, 1970. The dramatic experiences of a sparrow trying to survive in northern winter weather are presented.

5–6 *My Side of the Mountain*, Jean George. New York: Dutton, 1959. The various adventures of a young boy who tries his hand at living by himself in the Catskill Mountains are presented. It is an excellent nature study.

4–6 *Night Dive*, Ann McGovern. New York: Macmillan, 1984. A twelve-year-old girl accompanies her mother, a marine biologist, and other divers on night scuba-diving adventures. Several stories show undersea life, exploring an old shipwreck, as well as the rigors of scuba diving. It has color photographs.

4 *Nobody's Cat*, Miska Miles. Boston: Atlantic-Little, Brown, 1969. This presents the adventures of an alley cat in the city and his struggles.

4–6 *The Philharmonic Gets Dressed*, Karla Kuskin. New York: Harper and Row, 1982. Over a hundred members of an orchestra, including the conductor, are shown getting dressed and ready for a performance. You can read each section and let students choose the clothes they want to put on (by pass the underwear if it seems inappropriate) and the instruments they want to play. A few might be chosen to be the conductor whose part can be rewritten to be female. At the end, play a short symphonic piece and let the orchestra be conducted. (See "Conducting an Orchestra" in Chapter 4).

4 *The Pine Tree*, George Maxim Ross. New York: Dutton, 1966. A pine tree struggles for survival. It is a simple story but is dramatically written.

4–6 *The Plymouth Thanksgiving*, Leonard Weisgard. Garden City, N.Y.: Doubleday, 1967. Simply presented are the details of the events leading up to the first Thanksgiving. Numerous characters for groups or the entire class to play are included.

5–6 *The Printers*, Leonard Everett Fisher. New York: Franklin Watts, 1965. This is one of a series of over a dozen handsomely illustrated books on colonial craftspersons, including glassmakers, wigmakers, cabinetmakers, and homemakers.

4–6 *Roadrunner*, Naomi John. New York: E. P. Dutton, 1980. The hurrying desert roadrunner, a comic figure, spends his day chasing, running, and racing with twists, circles, and sudden stops. Here is the real story of the popular film cartoon character.

5–6 *Robinson Crusoe*, Daniel DeFoe. New York: Charles Scribner's Sons, 1983. A man is shipwrecked and lives for years on a lonely island. There are many episodes to choose from in this novel.

4–6 *Rodeo School*, Ed Radlauer. New York: Franklin Watts, 1976. A detailed narrative account of the training and techniques rodeo riders need to know.

6 *Saint George and the Dragon*, Margaret Hodges. Boston: Little, Brown, 1984. This is the retelling, in picturebook format, of a portion of Edmund Spenser's *The Faerie Queen*. George, accompanied by the fair maiden Una, slays the dragon in a three-day fight. The fight scene itself is good for narrative pantomime and can be played in groups of five: Una, George, and three for the dragon (one each for head, wings, and tail). This is a good story to accompany a study of the Middle Ages in England.

5–6 *Shaw's Fortune: The Story of a Colonial Plantation*, Edward Tunis. New York: Collins Publishers, 1966. Data on all facets of plantation life are beautifully and carefully illustrated.

4 *Tarantula, the Giant Spider,* Gladys Conklin. New York: Holiday House, 1972. This explains that tarantulas are useful insects that need not be feared.

5–6 *Tiktaliktak*, James Houston. New York: Harcourt Brace Jovanovich, 1965. An Eskimo boy is trapped on a rocky island and must make it back to food and safety.

4–6 *The Teepee: A Center of Native American Life,* David and Charlotte Yue. New York: Alfred A. Knopf, 1984. This presents excellent data with illustrations on teepees, the sophisticated dwelling of the Great Plains Indians. Story material is possible in the teepee construction and the role of women in the task.

5–6 "To Build a Fire," Jack London. Many editions. A man in the Yukon, after a brave struggle, loses his battle against the 75 degree below zero temperature. This is a long story that can easily be shortened.

"Reel in that big fish. . . ."

4 *Vulpes, the Red Fox*. John and Jean George. New York: Dutton, 1948. The descriptive and sensitive story of the life cycle of a fox is presented.

4 *Wharf Rat*, Miska Miles. Boston: Little, Brown, 1972. This is a realistic portrayal of a rat's survival when threatened by an oil slick near the docks.

4 *The White Palace*, Mary O'Neill. New York: Thomas Y. Crowell, 1966. This is a beautifully illustrated story of a salmon's life.

5–6 *Wolf Run: A Caribou Eskimo Tale*, James Houston. New York: Harcourt Brace Jovanovich, 1971. Rather than face certain starvation, a young Eskimo boy sets off to find caribou against almost hopeless odds.

6 *Wrapped for Eternity: The Story of the Egyptian Mummy*, Mildred Pace. McGraw Hill, 1974. It presents fascinating information about a fascinating subject, particularly for older children. For a simpler version, see *Mummies Made in Egypt* by Aliki Brandenberg. New York: Thomas Y. Crowell, 1979.

WRITING YOUR OWN MATERIAL

As you work with narrative pantomime, it will become rather obvious what works well and what does not. Soon you will feel comfortable trying your own ideas, focusing on the experiences you want your students to enact. Eventually you will be able to narrate short passages "off the top of your head," which is similar to the technique of sidecoaching (encouraging or talking students through drama experiences). Remember the following tips:

1. Keep the action continuous and moving along from one event to another.
2. Keep the action as immediate as possible. Time lapses and repeated shifts from place to place can lessen the dramatic impact.
3. In sidecoaching particularly, the sense of immediacy can be aided with the use of present tense and "you," either stated or implied in the wording. "Now, (you implied) zip up your jacket and put on your backpack . . ."
4. Be aware of the beginning, middle, and end of any selection. Build to a climax and follow it with a satisfying and quieted resolution.
5. As you narrate or sidecoach your material, add or delete details of action according to the students' needs. Sensory and emotional description is often helpful to add. Some students will be very imaginative while others will need ideas given to them. Watching the students as they play will be the best way to know how much assistance they need. You will have to find a happy medium between the most and the least imaginative student.

The following examples are presented to stimulate your own thinking and get you and your students started.

SAMPLE LESSON PLAN
Cookin' For Paul Bunyan

Original Narrative Pantomime

Objectives

a. Give students an experience in paired pantomime in a dramatic storyline.

b. Present some details about a fictional American hero in the exaggerated style of the tall tale.

Preparation and Materials

a. **Space:** Desk area.

b. **Materials:** Copies of one or more editions of Paul Bunyan tales. Suggestions:

   Kellogg, Steven. *Paul Bunyan.* New York: William Morrow, 1984.

   McCormick, Dell J. *Paul Bunyan Swings His Axe.* Caldwell, ID: 1955.

   Rounds, Glen. *Ol' Paul the Mighty Logger.* New York: Holiday, 1941.

c. **Visual aids:** Pictures of logging, perhaps showing both the old and the newer methods.

d. **Session length:** Approximately 30 to 40 minutes.

Motivation

Show some of the pictures from the books about Paul Bunyan, the giant woodsman whose mighty deeds are told from Maine to California. If you have pictures of logging and logging camps, you might show those also. Review some of the details about Paul Bunyan and his Blue Ox, Babe. Everything about Paul is the biggest— his footprints made small lakes, his axe was as wide as a barn, and he chopped down whole forests in a single day. Even if students do not know much about him, you can still play this pantomime. It may motivate them to do further reading about Paul and the many tales about him. They may even want to write a tall tale episode, perhaps even one that can be played as a narrative pantomime.

Preparation for Playing

For the story they should know that Paul was a logger and that his camp was supposedly the biggest in the world. Hundreds of people worked there. It took two hundred cooks to feed all the workers; the tables were six miles long. In this story, the students will pretend that they have been hired on as cooks for Paul and the head cook, Hot Biscuit Slim. Allow them time to find a space that two can work in comfortably, but not interfering with others' space. Designate (or let them decide) who will be Cook 1 and Cook 2.

Playing

(*Begin narration*) "It's early in the morning and you're still asleep on cots. But you're startled out of a deep sleep by the clanging of the bell. You jump out of bed and quickly pull on your clothes. Suddenly you remember that it's—the day to make pancakes for breakfast. You run to the ten-acre griddle pan to grease it for the hot cakes. You help each other strap the flat sides of bacon on your feet. Make sure they're on tight. Good. Now skate back and forth over the hot griddle. Hot Biscuit Slim told you to stay together and go back and forth carefully so you don't miss a spot. But you soon notice that some of the other cooks are playing tag. It looks like fun so you play tag with each other. Ah, but you are just learning, and you don't know how hot the griddle can get. You both fall and burn your trousers. Ouch! Better take it easy and do it the way Slim told you to.

"The steam from the hot grease makes a thick cloud over the griddle. It's hard to see. Get out of the way! Here comes a flood of pancake batter pouring out of a chute onto the griddle. Quick! Skate off the griddle and get your skates off. Grab a large, flat shovel. These cakes are so big it takes five men to eat one, so it will take both of you to turn it. You watch to see when the pancake has baked. (You'll know when you see bubbles on the top.) Now, it's ready. Lift the sides carefully with the shovel and turn it over. Ah, nicely done to a crispy brown. And smells delicious. But there's no time to waste. The lumberjacks are sitting at the six-mile long table and are very hungry.

"Load the pancakes onto a large platter. Lift and toss. Lift and toss. Good. Now, strap on your roller skates. Pick up the platter together and skate down the length of the huge table to serve the men. By the time you get to the end of the table, all the pancakes are gone. They sure do eat a lot, but they work hard, too. The men can rest now, but your work goes on because now you must get lunch ready. Take off the roller skates and get over to the soup kettle.

"The huge kettle holds eleven hundred gallons of soup and the water is already boiling in it. You'll be using a rowboat to get to the center of the soup, but first you have to load the rest of the ingredients in the boat. Cook 1, get in the boat so Cook 2 can hand you the ingredients: three bushels of carrots, two bushels of peas, a bushel of onions, two bushels of turnips, and fifty heads of cabbage. Cook 1, sit down in the boat. Cook 2, tie on the raft full of potatoes and four roasted pigs behind the rowboat and sit on top of them. Now, Cook 1, row toward the middle of the kettle. When you're rowing, you're going backwards, so Cook 2 will have to help guide toward the middle of the kettle. Careful, the water is hotter than the griddle. When you get to the middle, throw in the carrots, a bushel at a time. Careful, don't let the hot water splash on you. And be sure you don't take everything from one side of the boat or it's going to get unbalanced. That's it. Steady. Now the cabbage. Cook 2, take a taste from your dipper. Um . . . not bad. Time to add the potatoes. Stand up slowly and shove the potatoes in carefully. Good. Now drop in the four pigs, one by one. Uh! Whew! What a jobs this is!

"Now, both of you taste the soup again. Ummm, delicious. After it simmers for a few hours it will taste even better. The men will love it. Now you row the boat back to the edge of the kettle. It's getting really hot and steamy now. Whew! It's a good thing you're not on the supper shift so you get a chance to relax. Get the raft and the rowboat out of the soup. Someone else will clean them up for the next time. You're off duty now. So you drag yourself back to the bunkhouse where you collapse on your cot. Feeding those hungry lumbermen is a hard, but important job! You'll probably be included in those stories about Paul Bunyan, but for now all you can think about is sleep."

SAMPLE LESSON PLAN
Going Camping
Original Narrative Pantomime

Objectives

a. Experience pantomime movement in a storyline.
b. Recreate an out-of-doors adventure.
c. Learn some details of backpacking and hiking—clothing, gear, and safety rules.

Preparation for Playing

"You've always wanted to go backpacking in the woods by yourself, but your folks have said you had to wait until you were older. Now you've just received a backpack for your 12th birthday and they've said you're ready to go backpacking on your own just for the day. And today's the day!"

Playing

"Let's get dressed in the right clothes. Today you'll wear jeans and a sweatshirt. Now, importantly, get on your heavy socks and the boots. Make sure the socks are on smoothly and the boots are laced just right so your feet will be comfortable.

"Now, open your pack to check your supplies and pack up the things you'll need. Check the mess kit with its knife, fork, and spoon. Now seal up a hotdog and a bun with plastic wrap so they are air-tight. This will keep them fresh. Now, carefully roll up your sleeping bag, being sure to get it small and compact. Check your knife. Be sure to take a piece of old newspaper to start the fire ·and some matches. Don't forget your compass! Put some water in your canteen and fasten it to your belt. Now, fasten a shovel on the pack and pull the straps tight.

"Now lift the backpack over your arms—first one, then the other—opps! kerplunk! You sit down with a bump. The backpack is heavier than you thought! Well, stagger to your feet. You'll get used to it. And off you go—out the door and down the path to the creek in back of your house. And now you're in the woods. You walk through the woods for quite a while, checking your compass to make sure you go in one direction. You stop once to take a drink of water from the canteen. Umm, never knew how good plain old water could taste!

"Finally, you come to a clearing and decide to set up camp.

"Whew, it feels good to get that backpack off your shoulders."

Take off the backpack. Whew, feels good to get that load off your shoulders. Stretch a bit to get the kinks out of your shoulders, back and arms. Now get the shovel and dig a hole in the ground one foot deep and three feet around. Now gather some large rocks to border the hole. Next you need an armful of twigs and drop them into the pit. Now carefully stack the sticks in a criss-cross fashion to form a kind of teepee shape. Crumple the piece of old newspaper you brought and put it underneath the branches. Now get out the matches and light one. Ah, the fire crackles and hisses nicely.

"Use that old log there by the fire as a stool and sit down on it. Get the hotdog and bun out of your backpack. Get out your knife and whittle the end of a branch so you'll have something to cook the hotdog on. Put the hotdog on the branch and hold it over the fire. After a while it's plump and looks ready to burst. Put it in the bun and enjoy.

"You unroll the sleeping bag and lie down on it. You won't be staying overnight so you don't get inside it. But this is just getting it broken in.

"You lie back looking at the sky for a while. It's so peaceful here. But you notice the sun starting to move quickly toward the west and know you'd better get back home soon.

"You start to put out the fire when suddenly some gusts of wind fan the flames and they start to fly up. A few dried leaves near the fire catch some sparks. Gosh, that's a little scary. But you know what to do. You quickly throw water from your canteen on the fire. Now, grab the shovel and dig three shovels full of dirt onto the fire, stirring it around to make sure all the fire is completely out. Hurry! Wow, that was close. Now you know why Mom and Dad made you wait until you were old enough to go backpacking.

"You repack the backpack and look around to make sure you don't forget anything. Tie the shovel on last. Hoist the pack up again on your back. Now you head back in the opposite direction. You trudge through the woods, noticing some of the same things you spotted before. The way doesn't seem as long this time. That's good, because the sun's almost out of sight now. Ah, there's the stream just ahead. Jump across! Six more leaps to the front door, and slam! Home again. The first trip was a success!"

SAMPLE LESSON PLAN
Scene From "The Legend of the Moor's Legacy"
Original Narrative Pantomime

Objectives

a. Experience a group narrative pantomime based on a scene from a story students have read.

b. Try on the characters and a dramatic situation presented in a famous story by an American writer.

c. Become more familiar with the details in the exotic setting of a story.

Preparation and Materials

a. Space: several areas large enough for four students in each group

b. Equipment: (optional) record player and record of Spanish guitar music and sandalwood incense to burn

c. Session Length: 30 to 40 minutes, assuming two playings needed for entire class to participate

Preparation for Playing

The narrative is based on a scene from Washington Irving's "The Legend of the Moor's Legacy," (40) one of the stories in *Tales of the Alhambra*. In the story, Peregil, a poor water-carrier, befriends a Moor who is ill and cares for him in his home, even though it is against the law to shelter a Moor. The Moor dies and gives Peregil a sandalwood box for his kindness. When it is learned that he may possess wealth, Peregil is arrested by the greedy mayor, or *alcalde*. But the sandalwood box reveals only a scroll and a piece of candle, so Peregil is released, though the mayor keeps his donkey in payment for the investigation. Peregil finds a Moor shopkeeper who translates the writing and discovers that it is the key to treasure. They agree to meet at midnight, the specified time, and test the charm.

In this one scene, there are parts for four students in each group: Peregil, the Moor, and the two "enchanted" persons who also play the stone entrance to the cave and provide the sound effects. A darkened room, and some Spanish guitar music playing softly in the background will lend to the mood. You can also burn some sandlewood incense at the moment of the candlelighting.

(Two players in each group have their backs to Peregil, forming the cave's entrance. Peregil stands at the entrance of the cave, waiting for the Moor to arrive.)

Playing

(Narration begins.) "It is chilly tonight, and Peregil shivers and wraps his cloak a little more tightly around him. As he waits, he thinks about his unhappy lot—being so poor and with so many mouths to feed.

"And now he examines for the hundredth time the sandalwood box left by the Moor. Are the Moor's words true? Does the box really hold secrets? He opens it up and carefully takes out the small candle and the fragile piece of paper with the strange Arabic writing on it. He looks at the words, trying to make them out, but they mean nothing to him.

"Peregil begins to become impatient for the Moor to arrive. Now a form can be seen through the trees in the distance. Ah, it is the Moor. You greet each other silently, and now you both hurry quickly to test the power of the box. As you hear the watchtower clock strike midnight, Peregil lights the candle and holds it while the Moor reads the incantation on the scroll. The perfume from the candle sends a sweet odor through the damp air.

"Then suddenly there is a distant rumbling like thunder. ("Cave entrance" gives sound effects.) Suddenly the cave entrance opens and reveals a long winding stairway. (After cave entrance "opens," the two players become the enchanted guards.) You huddle together as you descend below. Shield the candle light, for if it goes out, you will be entombed forever in the cave. As you reach the bottom step you see a large trunk with huge bands of steel encasing it. At each end of the trunk you see two motionless guards, enchanted, and their eyes stare straight ahead.

"Around the trunk there are many treasures, and you realize that you have indeed found wealth. You slowly and cautiously examine it—pick up a coin, try on a bracelet, examine a precious stone. Yes, it is real! And it is yours! You each take as much as your pockets can hold. There is more than enough and you are not the greedy sort.

"You hurry to finish because the candle is small and may burn out. You climb back up the long, steep stairs. You take one more look at the enchanted guards, wondering if they saw what you did. They have such a knowing look about them. But you must hurry, there is no time to waste.

"You blow the candle out, and the cave entrance closes with thunderous sound. ("Guards" become "cave entrance" and create sound effects again.) You grope your way through the trees to an open space. You agree to meet again on another night. To show good faith with each other, Peregil is to keep the paper while the Moor takes the candle. You part, each happier and wealthier—for the moment, at least—than you have ever been in your whole life. You both disappear into the shadows of the night."

7 Pantomimes for Guessing

When students play the narrative pantomimes in the preceding pages, they focus on self-expression and the playing of ideas and stories for their own satisfaction. In this section, the emphasis will be on developing pantomime skills further, conveying and translating specific nonverbal ideas and messages.

Acting out pantomimes for someone to guess is an age-old game as well as an art form. The childhood game of "Statues" can be played endlessly as players enjoy being "swung" into frozen positions for "It" to guess. You can make use of such games, capitalizing on their entertaining features, as well as encouraging the development of pantomime skills. You can also use numerous other curriculum topics for the pantomime games.

GUIDING PANTOMIME PLAYING

Because pantomime for guessing requires an audience/performer situation, try to avoid having one student at a time pantomiming in front of the rest of the class. This procedure places too much pressure on the performer, who may become shy and inhibited or develop show-off behaviors. Also, if the other students have to wait their turn too long, they can become bored. Therefore, all of the following games are designed to have as many children involved as possible, while still focusing on skill development.

You will be encouraging the pantomimers to communicate ideas nonverbally as clearly as possible and motivating the guessers to develop skills of observation, analysis, and synthesis in translating the messages. Challenges and learning experiences are thus equally shared by both pantomimers and audience guessers.

Pantomime, like all nonverbal communication, is ambiguous. This is its fascination. We speculate on it, guess, and test our accuracy constantly. You will need to aid the students to understand that it may take a little time to figure out what a pantomimer is doing. And, a pantomime may look like several things at the same time.

As the students pantomime, you should identify, through verbal feedback, the various clues the students are giving:

"I can tell you all have been really studying that book on armor. All five of you were pantomiming so believably I could practically feel the weight of each article of clothing you put on."

Sidecoach, speculating out loud on the thinking process in making a guess, perhaps even giving a possible idea or two. Note how this can help the players as well as the guessers.

"Notice how the 'soldiers' are positioned in this frozen picture. Remember when we discussed the different kinds of weapons that were used in different periods of history? That should help you guess which war scene this is."

Discuss how pantomime is not always clear and how one action or object might be mistaken for another.

TEACHER: Aletta, how did you know that Luis was looking into a mirror on the wall and not a picture hanging there?

ALETTA: Because he was smoothing down his hair when he was looking at it. If it was a picture, he'd have just looked.

Limit the guessing whenever possible. This challenges the performers and the guessers to do their best work. If a pantomime cannot be guessed, the players simply state what they were doing. This also discourages pantomimers from trying to fool the audience.

Shy students may seem disappointed or think they have been unsuccessful if their pantomimes are not guessed immediately. Sometimes they will even say you have guessed the right answer—even if you have not. With them you might say, "That's a hard one! You have us stumped. You will have to tell us what it was," to point out the ambiguity of pantomimes.

Outgoing students often seem disappointed, angry, or think they have been unsuccessful if their pantomimes *are* guessed immediately. Often they like to confuse an audience so they can continue performing. They may even say the guess is not correct or not accurate enough. For these students you might say, "You did that very well. We guessed right away," to encourage giving good clues.

PANTOMIME GAMES

⊡ HALF AND HALF

One half the class acts out a pantomime for the other half to guess.

1. Divide class into two groups. Groups make two lists of related topics to pantomime.
2. If the topic is "verbs and adverbs," one group tells its adverb and the other group must act out one of its ideas as the adverb suggests. (Example: "riding a bicycle *happily*," "washing an elephant *thoroughly*," or "painting a room *sloppily*.")
3. The guessing group guesses the action after a specified time; then takes its turn.

Tips: You may prefer to have the verbs suggested and the adverbs guessed. Other paired ideas might be: tools/trades, countries/customs, and so on.

⊡ COUNT FREEZE

Several players pantomime simultaneously in front of the rest of the class, each performing his or her own ideas on a given topic. Pantomimers may work individually, in pairs, or even in small groups.

1. Select topic. Special topics for pairs and groups might be to demonstrate an activity that takes two people (playing checkers, riding a tandem bicycle) or a group (holding net for person to jump out of burning building, hanging a longer banner across a street).
2. Choose several volunteers to pantomime.
3. Count to five or ten while audience watches (counting may be as slow or as fast as seems necessary) and then say "Freeze."
4. Audience guesses aloud only after the players are frozen.

Tip: This game is popular enough to play at any grade level. As students become more experienced, encourage more detail in the pantomiming and in the guessing. (Example: "baking a lemon meringue pie" rather than "baking" or even "baking a pie.")

⊡ PANTOMIME SPELLING

Words are spelled out by each student acting out other words beginning with the appropriate letters. For example, the topic might be animals or mammals. Students choose to spell out "cat" using other animal words such as c—camel, a—alligator, and t—tiger. Or the topic might be state capitals while the pantomime category is occupations. "Austin" could be spelled by acting out a—aviator; u—undertaker; s—secretary; t—teacher; i—ice skater; n—newscaster.

1. Play as "Count Freeze" above.
2. Number of players determined by number of letters in word spelled.
3. All letters acted out at same time. Audience can try guessing the word even if they are not sure of each letter. (Like working a crossword puzzle.)

Option: You may wish to let students guess in small groups, pooling their guesses and making a group decision.

ACTING OUT NAMES/TITLES

Similar to charades, this pantomime has several students at a time acting out the titles of songs, stories, or books. For example, four students together might act out the book title *A Swiftly Tilting Planet* (Madeleine L'Engle). "Swiftly" could be indicated by student running quickly in place; "tilting," by third student leaning, and "planet" by fourth student rotating and circling while in a "rounded" shape.

In-service teachers spell out T-A-M-P-A using occupations: T-truck driver, A-artist, M-magician, P-pianist, and A-acrobat.

1. Play as "Count Freeze" above.
2. Number of players determined by number of words in title.
3. Again, all words acted out at same time.

Tip: As in charades, the small words can be indicated with thumb and forefinger close together. (Or, student could hold blank card.)
Variation: Syllables of longer names or titles might be acted out as well. For example, acting out the names of states (Washing-ton); state capitals (Indian-apple-us) or book titles (Robin-son Crew-sew).

☺ FROZEN PICTURES

Small groups plan a scene appropriate to a given topic and freeze themselves into position. Scenes might be from favorite stories such as *Tales of a Fourth Grade Nothing* (Judy Blume); from history, "Napoleon's Defeat at Waterloo;" from famous paintings, *Sunday Afternoon on the Island of La Grande Jatte* (Seurat); or from current events, "President Inaugurated."

☺ SEQUENCE GAMES

Pantomime actions on cards are acted out sequentially by players.

1. Prepare cards, using pictures or written instructions, in a particular sequence with cues for each previous pantomime.
2. Cards are distributed at random to individuals, pairs, or even three players per card.

Frozen picture of Washington crossing the Delaware.

Cue: Someone will motion to you and point to the ship.
You: Pretend to be a patriot sneaking on board the ship to dump the tea.
(Sequence Game)

3. Cards are played in sequence with player(s) correctly interpreting the cue to the next pantomime. There is much suspense in the waiting for one's cue and the chance to play as well as to see the chain of events or story unfold.

Example: The first card reads:

*You begin.

YOU: Smooth out the floor of your tent. Pound in the stakes. Set up the frame. Pull out the ropes until the tent is up. Pound in the stakes. Sit.''

The second player's card reads:

Cue: After someone sets up a tent,

You: Gather some wood and begin to stack it near the tent.

Other cards could include instructions on making a fire, cooking food wrapped in foil, washing utensils in stream, and so forth to complete a story on camping.

Tips: Cues may be written in red ("Stop and look") and the directions written in green ("Go ahead"). You should have a master list of all the actions in sequence in order to monitor the playing. Students might also like to try their hand at creating and making the cards for their own sequence games.

Topics which are particularly fun and work well are activities which follow a step-by-step procedure (how to make something) or have a storyline. You can convert favorite stories to sequence games also.

Actions can also be alphabetized, perhaps even omitting the cues. For example, the topic might be "Sports." First might be the miming of A—archery, B—basketball, C—canoeing, and so forth. The alphabet itself can serve as the cue. See *The Marcel Marceau Alphabet Book* by George Mendoza (Garden City, N.Y.: Doubleday, 1970) for an excellent example of this.

ADD-ON PANTOMIMES

These are similar to the sequence games except that the students act out their own ideas to fit with the previous player's.

1. You select a topic or let students select their own.
2. First player pantomimes an activity such as painting a room.
3. The rest of the players assist the first by adding on the actions of perhaps wallpapering, laying carpet, installing new light fixtures or plumbing, and so on to create the scene of *redecorating a house.*

Tips: It is more fun—and more dramatic—not to guess out loud, but just quietly add on. An entire scene of activity unfolds before the audience's eyes, almost magically.

You may wish to have students whisper their answers to you before they add on their ideas in case there are incorrect guesses. "Painting a room" could be mistaken for "washing a picture window."

Advanced students may want to create *pantomime scenes* rather than just a series of related activities. Example: child brings stray dog into room; mother enters and indicates dog must go; another child enters and the two play with the dog; a student may decide to enter as the dog itself, pouncing on furniture; father enters and all plead with him; and so on. See if the students can bring the scene to some kind of ending.

VARIATION ADD-ON

An object is created by several people, each adding on his or her part. The first student might become the drill pipe of a rotary drilling rig while others add on the rest of the parts (rotary table, pulleys, kelly, and so forth) one by one.

Tips: Small groups may decide ahead of time what they wish to create.

Audience can guess at any time during the adding on or they may be asked to wait until the group has finished.

For the adventuresome, one student becomes the first part of an object while others add on as they wish and as they *guess* the object. Of course, there is more room for error with this method, but it is fun to see the varieties of interpretation.

BUILD A PLACE

Students create a room or location by pantomiming the various furnishings or objects needed.

1. Mark off a space on the floor to indicate the walls of a room or location with doors or entryways. Use chalkboard erasers, books, or chairs for the four corners. Indicate the doors by pantomiming opening and closing, and so forth. For building a room area, use two doorways so that several students at a time can play.

2. Players pantomime bringing in one item at a time into the space, placing it appropriately and using the doors and entryways to enter and exit. If the space is a room, they must go through the doors and not the walls. They must also remember where each previous item is and not walk over or through it.

3. Guess each object after it is brought into the room.

In-service teachers bring imaginary objects into an imaginary room in the pantomime game "Build a Place."

4. After a couple of objects are in the room, students should use one of the previous objects in some way after bringing in their chosen item. For example, after bringing in test tubes to the scientist's laboratory, the player lights the Bunsen burner brought in previously.

Tips: You may need to help students remember the details of the room and where each item is placed. Side-coach: "I wonder what Monica and Ali might be carrying. Sure looks big and heavy. You'll have to remember where everything else is in the room so you don't bump into anything."

Even spaces that are not enclosed (as a room) can be created in this game. Students have enjoyed building stores, factories, parks, city layout, ships, states (can use masking tape to lay outline of state; students mime appropriate activity or product important to certain city or area, standing in the appropriate place), and countries.

INTRA-GROUP PANTOMIMES

Pantomimers enact ideas just for the audience members in their small group. The advantage of this method is that the audience is small and the pantomimes go quickly, reducing the focus on the person. Even the most reluctant student or the shy student will find it difficult not to get caught up in this game.

1. Divide class into several groups of five or six persons.
2. In each group, two will guess what the others pantomime in a limited time period of perhaps 2 minutes.
3. Instructions might be: "Pantomime all the words you can think of that rhyme with "oat." (Example: boat, coat, wrote, note, dote, float, goat, quote, vote, and so on.)
4. The pantomimers do not confer with each other; each thinks of his or her own ideas and enacts as many of them as time permits.
5. The two guessers work as quickly as possible and write down the ideas. If an idea cannot be guessed quickly, either the pantomimers or the guessers may say, "Pass."

Tips: Avoid counting up the number of words on each list afterward and introducing competition into the game. A better learning experience is to discuss the words that were "most unusual," "hardest to guess," or "most frequently used words." Combine the lists for other purposes and projects: a class display of brainstorming for ideas, for example.

Caution the students to work quietly *so they do not give away their ideas to the other groups*. (This game can get a little noisy, and this reasoning works better than just telling them to keep quiet!)

Use topics that have numerous possibilities or answers. For example: jobs of pioneer families; things we save or collect; leisure time activities; things our feet can do; words with three syllables, and so on.

ADDITIONAL IDEAS FOR PANTOMIME

The following additional topics for pantomime may be used with one or more of the methods discussed in the chapter. Students can choose their own topic to pantomime; or you may wish to assign certain topics, perhaps having ideas written on cards.

Who Am I (Are We)? Act out historical or literary characters, famous scientists, people in current events, and so on.

What Am I (Are We)? Students can pantomime animals, inanimate objects, machinery, or other nonhuman entities.

What Am I (Are We) Doing? This may be as simple as acting out verbs or more complete ideas like making a cake, driving a car, or milking a cow. Pantomimes may be more challenging and add conflict, such as testing a waterbed before purchasing, washing an unwilling dog, or setting up a tent in a windstorm.

What Am I (Are We) Seeing, Hearing, Tasting, Smelling, Touching? Pantomimers react to various sensory stimuli which may cover such topics as seeing a ghost, listening to loud music, tasting unsweetened lemonade, smelling ammonia fumes, or touching a hot iron.

What's the Weather? Players enact clues for audience to guess the seasons or the climatic conditions. They may act out seasonal sports or daily chores related to certain times of the year, putting on appropriate clothing for the weather (hot, cold, rainy, windy), or demonstrating various natural disasters.

What Am I (Are We) Feeling? Students act out various emotions. As an additional challenge, limit students to using only certain parts of the body to show emotion (face, hands, feet, or back). (You can hold up a sheet to make just the certain body parts visible.) Emotions can also be combined with the "doing" pantomime by showing an action as well as how you feel about doing it (e.g., a household chore you do not like to do). The pantomime may be extended to acting out a brief scene showing more than one emotion or a scene in which something happens to change the feeling. For example, "You are happily packing a picnic basket when you suddenly notice that it's raining. So now you can't go on the picnic and are disappointed."

Where Am I (Are We)? Pantomime being in various locations such as a zoo, a hospital, desert island, haunted house, carnival midway, elevator, and so forth. Students may also focus on particular cities or countries studied.

Let's Get Ready To Go. Pretend to pack supplies for various adventures such as going on a fishing trip, preparing for a hike, loading a covered wagon, or equipping an explorer's ship, preparing for a space launch, and so forth.

Transportation. Players pretend to travel in various ways, which may be categorized such as modern (electric car, space ship), historical (horse and buggy, high-wheeler bicycle), foreign (rickshaw, camel) or fantastical (flying carpet, seven-league boots).

Family or Group Portrait. Members of a family or a group prepare as well as pose for their portrait. It may be an historical family (Abraham Lincoln's family) or group (First Continental Congress), a royal family or group, a literary, an animal, or a cartoon or television family or group.

Dress Up. Pretend to be certain characters dressing in their appropriate garb, such as Pippi Longstocking, a knight, an astronaut, a desert nomad, or an Egyptian priest.

Foods. Pretend to grow, harvest, or prepare and eat familiar and foreign foods: lobster, spaghetti, wild rice, coffee beans, peanuts, cocoanut, and so forth. Students can also do four basic food groups (fruits and vegetables; bread and cereal; dairy products; meat, fish, and poultry or other protein).

Health and Hygiene. Players can demonstrate various good (or bad) habits such as brushing and flossing teeth, getting fresh air and exercise, cleaning house, and so forth.

Energy and Water Conservation. Students demonstrate various ways to conserve electricity and water consumption at home, school, and in business and industry. (Turning off unneeded lights, repairing leaky faucets, turning heat or air conditioning down, and so forth.)

Occupations. Students can act out various jobs, perhaps pretending what they would like to be when they grow up. They may also focus on groupings such as community helpers, occupations in colonial times, occupations in other locations or countries.

Tools. Demonstrate various tools people used in the past or present to perform certain occupations or tasks: doctor's stethescope, blacksmith's bellows, carpenter's level, and so on.

Machines. Demonstrate simple tools such as levers, wedges, and pulleys, as well as more sophisticated machines such as electrical appliances or construction equipment. Students may demonstrate operating the machinery or becoming the machines.

Sports. Enact favorite sports or favorite athletes. These may be categorized into team sports, Olympic events, winter sports, and so forth.

Animals. Different groups of animals might be enacted: pets, zoo animals, circus animals, mammals, amphibians, or mythical animals.

Biography. Enact a famous or historical person performing a typical activity or acting in a famous event. Students may focus on various categories such as Famous Women (Rachel Carson, Barbara Jordan, Maria Tallchief), Black (or other minority) Heroes or Heroines (Martin Luther King, Frederick Douglas, Mary McLeod Bethune), or Famous Scientists (Albert Einstein, George Washington Carver, Marie Curie).

Inventions. Pantomime using or being the invention. Class guesses the inventor as well as the invention (Eli Whitney, cotton gin; Robert Fulton, steam engine; Samuel Morse, telegraph, and so forth).

Musical Instruments. Pantomime the instrument of choice or one from a category such as orchestral instruments, marching-band instruments, percussion, woodwinds, and brass. Oriental or instruments associated with a particular country or culture (Scottish bagpipes) might also be included.

Safety. Pantomime the *do's* and *don'ts* of various activities: bicycle riding, water sports, camping activities, household or school activities.

First Aid. Demonstrate techniques for removing a foreign body in the eye, aiding a choking victim, treating frostbite, giving first aid for burns, and the like.

Festivals and Holidays. Act out various activities associated with holidays in the United States (Fourth of July, Thanksgiving, Memorial Day); celebrations (Christmas, Hanukkah, Halloween, Valentine's Day), other cultures and countries (Chinese New Year, Mexican birthday, French Bastille Day). Audience guesses the custom and the country.

Word Pantomimes. Several games can be played using categories of words or parts of speech. For example, in an "Opposite Game" the audience guesses the opposite word of the one pantomimed (hot-cold). This game may also be played with homonyms (weigh-way; guesser spells both). Other words might be those with long vowel sound, spelling words, and vocabulary words.

Countries and Customs. Students enact a custom and audience guesses both custom and country: British afternoon tea; Spanish or Mexican bullfight; Japanese kite-flying contest.

Sign Language. Learn some Indian sign language (Aline Amon, *Talking Hands—Indian Sign Language*. New York: Doubleday, 1968), finger spelling, American Sign Language (Mary Beth Sullivan and Linda Bourke, *A Show of Hands*. New York: Harper Trophy edition, 1985) or other nonverbal language systems. Use these in place of the pantomime cues for guessing games.

PANTOMIME SKITS AND STORIES

As students become skilled in pantomime, they may want to do more elaborate pantomimes, individually or in pairs and groups. Some of these may even develop into complete stories.

Encourage plot structure by discussing the concept of beginning, middle, and end of stories. This procedure will focus on story building as well as helping groups in their planning and organization. For example, if groups do not specifically plan an ending for their skit or story, they may ramble on ad infinitum.

Your focus here is still pantomime for guessing. Some students may ask to talk, but you will want to encourage them to see how much they can communicate without words. As children's language increases each year, they tend to forget how much communication they can still accomplish nonverbally.

In these pantomimes, they also must watch carefully in order to identify clues and guess. And, although we usually think of listening as related to hearing, good listening also involves watching for nonverbal cues. These skits will give them opportunities to observe closely for extended periods of time.

With longer stories, it will not be necessary to guess each detail, although evaluation of the effectiveness of communication is still important. Discussion questions for evaluation may include:

What was the most understandable moment?

When did you have difficulty following the story?

Was it clear who the characters were? List them.

When were the characters and their feelings most believable?

Was there a satisfying ending?

SKIT ACTIVITIES

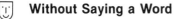 **Without Saying a Word**

In groups the students must both plan and play a fairy tale or other short story without talking to each other *the entire time*. Writing notes or mouthing words is not allowed. This game is challenging, but rewarding. To make it somewhat simpler, verbally brainstorm titles or topics and list them on the board. Groups then select from the list (without going to the board and pointing). After the groups have rehearsed (still without talking), share the stories. In managing the sharing, it is best for you, too, to use pantomime. Do not be surprised if one or two people in a group are acting out a different story from everyone else. Only after all the sharing is anyone allowed to talk—and then be prepared for about two minutes of nonstop chattering while everyone checks to see how accurate their interpretations were.

Proverbs and Sayings

Students develop a pantomime skit to illustrate a proverb or saying. Examples: "Make hay while the sun shines," "A stitch in time saves nine," "A friend in need is a friend indeed."

News Story of the Week

In groups, students illustrate a current news story. Having a newspaper at hand can provide ideas for the skits as well as stimulating interest in reading about them.

Television Shows and Commercials

Students can act out favorite television shows. Story commercials (those that can be pantomimed and do not require dialogue) may also be enacted. You may wish to relate this to a study of television and the various types of shows: situation comedies, soap operas, variety shows, and so forth. The commercials may relate to a study of advertising techniques such as using famous personalities.

Favorite Stories

Students may act out some of their favorite stories from basal readers, independent reading, or one seen on television for the class to guess. This activity can "advertise" books to the class or serve as book reports.

You Are There

Skits may be based on scenes of scientific or historical significance. Facts about the events may be listed on cards, or the students may be encouraged to do research in preparation.

Test drive of the first automobile;
first airplane flight of the Wright Brothers;
driving the golden spike for the Transcontinental Railroad;
Alexander Graham Bell making the first telephone call;
discovery of King Tut's tomb.

The Invention

Students act out their version of the discovery of the following inventions: laughing gas, suspenders, rubber band, fire, mirror, pop-

The Scarecrow meets Dorothy and Toto. A pantomime drama accompanied by the score from MGM's *The Wizard of Oz*.

corn machine, fireworks, the wheel, potato chips, snowshoes, or bubble gum. For comparative purposes, refer to *The Invention of Ordinary Things* by Don L. Wulffson (New York: Lothrop, Lee & Shepard, 1981) which tells the story behind the invention of such things as the zipper, breakfast cereal, and the toothbrush.

Charades

This age-old game can be played by older elementary students. Once the game is learned, it is probably best played in small groups so that more students have a chance.

Two teams are formed. One team gives its topic to one of the players from the opposite team to enact for his or her team to guess. A time limit is imposed, though you may wish to deemphasize this feature.

Traditionally, players are given song, play, book, film, or tele-

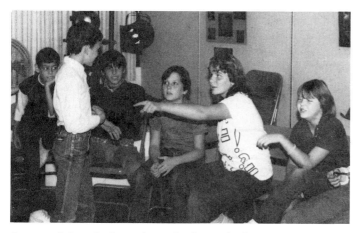

A game of charades is good practice for perfecting pantomime skills.

vision titles as well as common sayings to act out. Usually the words are acted out one at a time, although they need not be acted out in the order in which they appear in the title. Sometimes only one syllable at a time is acted out.

The pantomimers have several aids they can use:

a. They may tell the guessers, "This is a _____ (title or saying.) There are _____ words in it. I'm going to act out the _____ word."

b. The player may say, "This is a short word." The guessers then simply call out as many short words they can think of until the correct one is called. Words such as "a," "an," "the," or various pronouns and prepositions can be handled quickly in this manner.

c. The pantomimer may act out a word that *sounds* like the original word if that would be easier to guess. The word "car," for example, might be easier to act out and guess then the word "far."

For additional curricular emphasis, story titles might be from basal readers or popular library books. Sayings might be historical quotes such as "Walk softly and carry a big stick" (T. Roosevelt).

8 Verbal Activities and Improvisation

You will always be looking for ways to encourage students to express themselves through verbalizing, improvising dialogue, and interacting with others in drama activities. As you have probably already noticed, the students in your classroom vary in their readiness to verbalize. Some comfortably improvise dialogue at the drop of a hat, while others are more reticent in self-expression.

You will want to have available to you a range of verbal activities to choose from which will correspond to the different skills your students exhibit. This chapter will give you many selections, ranging from the easier to the more difficult. Remember, however, that while the simple activities can be particularly useful for encouraging shy students to participate, they can also be creatively challenging to all.

BEGINNING VERBAL ACTIVITIES

SOUND EFFECTS

Creating sound effects can be an excellent learning experience as well as great fun for all. The voice is a marvelous instrument of sound and can have an extremely wide range of possibilities when we take the time to explore it. Without saying a word at all, there can be great flexibility of communication.

Students will enjoy doing this kind of experimenting. And you will soon discover that there are many places in the curriculum for this activity. While students have fun, they will also be learning facts, experimenting with the physics of sound, and creating settings and environments of the mind. Sound effects can be highly dramatic by themselves or when coupled with other material.

Sound Effects from Literature

There are many excellent stories and poems in literature that students can experiment with that provide a variety of topics for sound. Students will also be drawn into a study of literature interpretation.

The easiest way to begin these activities is simply to narrate the material (as you did before in narrative pantomime) and to pause for the students to make the sounds in the appropriate places. The list of literature suggested at the end of this section covers a broad range of subjects for you to choose from. For example, ''The Devil's Pocket'' has continuing echo sounds, while ''Paul Revere's Ride'' provides opportunities for an entire drama of sound effects.

Tips:

1. Some sounds are best made by one student or by just a few students, while other sounds will require the entire class. Experiment to see what procedure will give the best results.

2. Control the sounds by using an indicator for volume control. Some leaders use an arrow made of wood or cardboard or an oversized pencil. One teacher used a cutout picture of an ear on a stick and simply raised and lowered it to indicate on and off and intensity of volume.

3. It is probably best not to let students operate the volume control— at least not at first.

4. Do not try to do too much at a time. Students may get tired of a long selection in one sitting.

5. Try tape recording the selections after they have been rehearsed a few times so students can hear themselves. It will be easier for them to evaluate their work this way. Consider these as radio dramas, where one's imagination can soar, visualizing entire scenes based on narration and sound effects. See *The Magic of Sound* by Larry Kettelkamp (New York: Morrow, 1982). Chapter 4, ''Fun with Sound Effects,'' tells how to make, amplify, and record a variety of sounds.

6. Try adding some musical sounds or other nonvocal sounds for variety. Rhythm band or Orff instruments have endless possibilities. Experiment also with objects in the classroom that make noise.

Follow the arrow to know when to make the sound and how loud it should be.

SUGGESTED LITERATURE

(*Note*: Numbers at the beginning of each entry indicate suggested grade levels. Numbers in parentheses refer to numbered anthologies listed in the bibliography at the end of this book.)

> 4–6 *Clams Can't Sing.* James Stevenson. New York: Greenwillow, 1980. A simply told, but challenging and delightful sound-effect story of two clams who prove to the other animals on the beach that they can contribute to the orchestra concert. This presents an opportunity to pull out all your (and your students') creative stops when it "gets fancy."

> 4–6 "The Devil's Pocket," George Mendoza. (11) Two boys have a mysterious adventure throwing a penny into an old, abandoned quarry. Echo effects and exciting tension make this a real "Twilight Zone" kind of story that is good for Halloween.

> 6 *Paul Revere's Ride*, Henry Wadsworth Longfellow. New York: Greenwillow, 1985. There are opportunities in this famous poem for such sounds as climbing wooden stairs, startled pigeons, horse's hoofs on sand, and so forth. With extended planning, a shadow drama (with people or puppets or even a combination) could evolve from this.

Original Sound Effects Materials

Once you have selections above, you will be ready to compose some of your own. You might even create a group story with the students or encourage them to write their own.

1. The stories can be based on a number of other materials being studied. For example, a story about a natural disaster and the preparations and safety precautions surrounding it might be explored. Or a location, such as a foreign city and the different sounds heard there might be created. You might consider an event, such as a space launch, and develop a story around those sounds.

2. Another variation of sound effects is to select favorite stories and assign certain sounds to each of the characters. Each time the character is mentioned in the story, the sound is made. Consider the characters' looks and personality in order to determine the most appropriate sounds. (Finger cymbals, for example, might be the sound for a Princess; a drum might signal the villain, and so forth.) This is a valuable characterization lesson for both drama and literature study.

SEQUENCE GAMES

As in the pantomimes for guessing, you can create sequence games for verbal activities, too. In this case, the sequence game is really like performing a short play script. Or, it might be compared to "Reader's Theatre."

Script Reading

Playing with sequence games can be one way to approach script reading and play writing, particularly for stories told in dialogue format. (See, for example, the story of "Peter Perfect" on p. 121.) With these materials you will see opportunities to encourage appropriate

Interpretive reading skills are encouraged in verbal sequence games.

interpretive reading of the lines, pointing out how timing and vocal dynamics help establish character.

Usually students ask to repeat the sequence games so they can switch cards and perfect their delivery. After several playings, there is usually an automatic improvement in reading. Students will need time to work on script reading, beginning with run-throughs and the chance to get into the spirit of the material.

In the theatre this is known as "studying the script." Students will appreciate knowing that a considerable amount of rehearsing time in the theatre is spent on discussing character and experimenting with different interpretive reading of lines.

Reader's Theatre

Reader's Theatre is the name given to the art of interpreting literature by means of several individuals reading the dialogue of various characters. There are usually no props or costumes, which puts the emphasis on the literature and the oral reading. Although in Reader's Theatre a few players generally face an audience, for classroom reading students can remain at their desks. Generally, it is more fun to place seats in a circle so all can see everyone else.

As with the pantomime sequence games, for verbal sequence games the cards are made up with a cue and a line to read. The cards are distributed at random.

The first card might say:

*You begin the game.

YOU: Stand and pretend to hold a mike in your hand, close to your mouth and say: "Good afternoon, ladies and gentleman, and welcome to the small, small world of sports." Bow and sit.

Another player will have the card that reads:

CUE: ". . . welcome to the small, small world of sports." Bow and sit.

YOU: Stand and pretend to hold a mike in your hand, close to your mouth and say: "Brought to you by Flexy Hula Hoops." Sit.

and so forth until a sequence of events or a story is told.

Sequence cards based on a poem or story make a game of reading aloud.

Sequence Games from Literature

There are a number of stories and poems which have interesting dialogue or statements in a series that provide excellent material for sequence games.

Riddle and joke books and trivia information are also fun and often informative. Also, students are so fascinated by these books that they are highly motivated to create their own scripts for sequence games. Following are some suggestions:

(*Note*: Numbers at beginning indicate suggested grade levels. Numbers in parentheses refer to numbered anthologies in the bibliography at the end of this book.)

4–6 *Arm in Arm*, Remy Charlip. New York: Parents' Magazine Press, 1969. A small treasury of various materials from jokes to short sayings presents many possibilities.

6 *Ashanti to Zulu*, Margaret Musgrove. New York: Dial Press, 1976. This is an alphabet book of various African tribes. You will probably want to shorten the descriptions. Only a few words, if any, are needed as cues, since the information is alphabetized.

4–6 *Bringing the Rain to Kapiti Plain*, Verna Aardema. New York: Dial Press, 1981. A Nandi tale from Africa about how the herdsman Kipat helped end the drought is told in the style of "The House that Jack Built." It can also be done as a shadow play with many ideas from the beautiful illustrations.

4 *Don't Forget the Bacon*, Pat Hutchins. New York: Greenwillow, 1976. A grocery list—six farm eggs, a cake for tea, a pound of pears, and don't forget the bacon—turns into nonsense as a young girl struggles to remember each item. In the end she forgets the bacon!

4 *Drummer Hoff,* Barbara Emberley. Englewood Cliffs, N.J.: Prentice-Hall, 1967. This simple but classic cumulative story is also included in the Narrative Pantomime bibliography because of the mechanical-type movement suggested. (See Weston Woods animated film version for more ideas.) As a sequence game, students can add the narrated lines to the pantomime.

5–6 *Encyclopedia Brown's Record Book of Weird and Wonderful Facts*, Donald J. Sobol. New York: Delacorte Press, 1979. The facts and information are frequently tied together so that many parts read very much like a script. There is ample opportunity for several games from this collection. Students can even create their own skits from this material. (See also *Encyclopedia Brown's Book of Wacky Animals*, 1985 as well as other sequels.)

4–6 "The Gardner's Song," Lewis Carroll (4). This is a nonsense poem by a master writer.

4–5 *Git Along, Old Scudder*, Stephen Gammell. New York: Lothrop, Lee, and Shepard, 1983. A humorous invented character, in the manner of the old explorers of the 1800's, tells his own story of making a map one day—though he winds up lost. It can relate to the need for map making.

4–6 "Grey Goose" Traditional. (34) The story of a gray goose that was too tough to be killed and eaten. Twenty-five lines can be done one to a card with the chorus of "Lawd, lawd, lawd" said by everyone after each line. You can also add pantomime.

4–6 *Hello, Mr. Chips!* Ann Bishop. New York: Dutton, 1982. This is a fun and informative look into the world of computers by way of jokes and riddles.

4–5 *Hush Up!* Jim Aylesworth. New York: Holt, Rinehart and Winston, 1980. Everyone in Talula County is taking a nap on a hot day until a nasty horsefly lands on mule's nose and creates a domino effect of trouble. It is fun to do the mime with this one also.

5–6 *Jokes to Tell Your Worst Enemy*, Scott Corbett. New York: E. P. Dutton, 1984. There is much here to choose from—a mixture of jokes, short stories, poems, and so forth. You can mix and match or focus on one subject—such as the sections entitled "History Rewritten Mother's Way" (for example, Paul Revere's mother will not let him out at night for his famous midnight ride).

4–6 *The Judge*, Harve Zemach. New York: Farrar, Straus and Giroux, 1969. This is a comical story of various prisoners warning a judge of a horrible monster coming their way. *Suggestion*: Add "Hear ye! Hear ye! The court is now in session" and "Here comes the Judge," (the latter repeated three times) at the beginning. At the end, pantomime the monster (three students linked together) eating someone with the line, "There goes the Judge," repeated three times.

5–6 *The Last Cow on the White House Lawn and Other Little-Known Facts about the Presidency*. Barbara Seuling. New York: Doubleday, 1978. This is a fascinating book of trivial (and not so trivial) information. Let students try their hand at creating their own script for this one.

4–5 *"Let's Marry," Said the Cherry*. N. M. Bodecker. New York: Atheneum, 1974. A poem tells in short, rhymed couplets the wedding plans for the cherry and the pea.

5–6 "The Meehoo with an Exactlywatt," Shel Silverstein (26). This is a combination of a knock-knock joke and the old Abbott and Costello "Who's On First?" routine—with repetitive possibilities as well.

4 "One Two," Shel Silverstein (26). This is a short parody on an old nursery rhyme.

4–6 "Peter Perfect, The Story of a Perfect Boy," Bernard Waber (29). This is a story comprised of various persons' statements about a boy who does not exist.

5–6 *The Star-Spangled Banana and Other Revolutionary Riddles*, compiled by Charles Keller and Richard Baker. Englewood Cliffs, N.J.: Prentice-Hall, 1974. Puns, word play, and riddles based on historical data are presented.

4 *Tyrannosaurus Wrecks*, Noelle Sterne. New York: Thomas Y. Crowell, 1979. This is a collection of dinosaur riddles. It is good for word study.

4–6 *A Wart Snake in a Fig Tree*, George Mendoza. New York: Dial Press, 1968. This is a bizarre version of "The Twelve Days of Christmas."

4–5 "Whatif," Shel Silverstein (26). A child speculates on all the horrible things that can happen to a kid. It is amusing, but with undercurrents of seriousness.

5–6 *What's a Frank Frank?: Tasty Homograph Riddles*, Giulio Maestro. New York: Clarion Books, 1984. This contains illustrations of homographs—two words spelled the same way but with different meanings. It is excellent for a fun language arts lesson.

4–5 *What If . . . ?* Joseph Low. Hartford, CT: Connecticut Printers, Inc., 1976. Unusual questions are posed with amusing answers to solve the problems.

4–5 *Yuck!* James Stevenson. New York: Greenwillow, 1984. Two witches are cooking up potions but say Emma is too young. With the help of her animal friends, she succeeds. Cartoon drawings have dialogue "balloons." You can add pantomime to this one.

Original Sequence Games

After trying some of the above materials, you will soon find many of your own sources for sequence games. You may even be inspired to make up your own. Students, too, will want to give it a try. Perhaps small groups of students can prepare games for the rest of the class to play. And the possibilities for incorporating other areas of the curriculum are numerous.

Joke and riddle books work nicely. If you use the answers in place of cues, students will be encouraged to think through the answer to the riddles they hear in order to see if their cue will fit.

You can review famous statements from literature, history, or other sources in a sequence game.

> CARD 1: (You begin.) "I cannot tell a lie."
>
> CARD 2: (Answer) George Washington. "Give me liberty or give me death."
>
> CARD 3: (Answer) Patrick Henry. "We have not yet begun to fight!" (and so forth).

or, after a study of mythology:

> CARD 1: You begin. "If Athena can weave better than I, let her come and try."
>
> CARD 2: (Answer) Arachne. "I knew I should have used a super glue instead of wax!"
>
> CARD 3: (Answer) Icarus. "The only man I'll marry is the one who can outrun me." (and so forth)

BEGINNING IMPROVISATION

In creative drama, dialogue is usually played *improvisationally*. This means that it is created spontaneously, on the spot, as the students respond to the dramatic situations they are involved in. It is more natural than the memorization of "canned" speeches and is an excellent exercise in learning to "think on one's feet." The spontaneity of improvisation captures everyone's attention—even the players themselves. No one knows exactly what will be said, but what you do know is that it will evolve from a "real" person rather than from a printed script.

As you work toward the goal of encouraging improvisation of dialogue, you will need increasingly more challenging activities. We will begin first with the activities that do not require extensive response and build progressively to more extensive improvisation.

The verbal activities in this section will help build the students' confidence in verbalizing as well as helping lay the groundwork for more challenging activities in the following section.

ONE – LINERS

Often it is easiest to begin with one-liners since students need to say or create only one line of speech.

One-Liners with Pictures

1. Keep a file of pictures of people or animals in interesting poses or situations or exhibiting unusual feelings. Pictures should be large enough for everyone to see easily. Large ads from magazines, calendar pictures, and posters work well for this activity.
2. Show pictures to the students and ask them what they think the person might be saying.
3. They pretend to be the person in the picture, saying the statement the way they think the person or animal might say it.

One-Liners with Props

1. Interesting props can also stimulate one-liners. The comedian, Jonathan Winters, became famous for his ability to create imaginative comments when browsing through an old attic or a trunk of cast-off clothing.
2. Borrowing this technique, students can select a prop, then demonstrate a use for it while saying an appropriate one-liner.

Example: Somewhere we acquired a large hoop attached to a long stick. (You do not always remember where these things come from!) It has become an oversized magnifying glass which has stimulated the following line: "Elementary, my dear Watson;" a large butterfly net (without the net), "Boy, that was a hungry butterfly!" and a monstrous banjo, "Thank God, I'm a Country Boy."
Other props might be a hula hoop, caulking gun, perfume atomizer, and so forth.

Ad Talks

Many famous one-liners already exist from advertisements and commercials. By now everyone knows the famous "Where's the beef?" line, for example. Other intriguing lines can be found by flipping through magazines. In my collection I have such statements as:

"How good is the bologna in that sandwich?" "It's better in the Bahamas," "Is your house being watched?"

These are placed on cards and then used in a variety of ways such as the following:

a. Distribute the cards randomly. Students may read them in any order, pretending that they make sense or have some logic. Try using different voices with them also: computer/robot, witch, politician, and so forth.

b. Distribute a number of cards to each player. One person begins and others choose from their "dialogue packet" and respond. (Whoever stands first gets to say his/her line.) Mixing an equal number of questions and answers can produce interesting results. (*Example*: "Looking for a new place to go to?" "You never know who you'll meet at an army reserve meeting.")

c. Distribute alphabetized cards randomly. Then follow the alphabet to find the next statement. It is more fun if students are given several cards to choose from.

d. Other kinds of one-liners might be historical slogans like "54-40 or Fight!" or "Tippecanoe and Tyler, too!" Clever book titles are also great fun. Students can make their own lists and mix and match in whatever creative ways they wish.

STORYTELLING

Storytelling is an excellent verbal activity to help students imagine and create plots. It also encourages the building of details and making of inferences.

Statements clipped from a variety of sources and placed on cards provide good material for the "Ad Talks" games.

Students may build group short stories using the round-robin technique, with each volunteer adding another line to the story.

When ideas flow freely and students are comfortable with storytelling, you may need to set limits on each one's contribution. Using an egg timer or a bell, make it into a game. A ball of knotted yarn is another intriguing way to conduct storytelling. As the "yarn is spun," the ball is unraveled. When the knot is reached, the ball is passed to another student.

Storytelling with Wordless Picture Books

One of the easiest ways to begin storytelling is to use wordless picture books which have no text but tell a story in pictures.

Students interpret what they see happening in the pictures, using their own words and sometimes even adding dialogue.

Not all wordless picture books tell a story, and not all pictures are big enough to show to an entire class. Careful choice will, therefore, be important. Smaller books may be used for group work. Some of my favorite examples for older students are the following:

4–6 *The Damp and Daffy Doings of a Daring Pirate Ship,* Guillermo Mordillo. New York: Harlan Quist, 1971. Pirates encounter one obstacle after another in seeking a treasure. But they are undaunted, and as the book ends, they are building a new ship after their old one sinks.

4–6 *The Gray Lady and the Strawberry Snatcher*, Molly Bang. New York: Four Winds Press, 1980. The gray lady runs from a strawberry thief until, in the heart of the forest, he discovers blackberries.

4–6 *How Santa Claus Had a Long and Difficult Journey Delivering His Presents*, Fernando Krahn. New York: Delacorte Press, 1970. Droll-looking "angels" come to Santa's rescue in this tale.

5–6 *The Inspector*, George Mendoza. Garden City, N.Y.: Doubleday & Co. 1970. An inspector does not notice the dangers surrounding him. His dog attacks each and slowly turns into a monster himself. This is a bit gory if you are squeamish, but most students will love it.

4–6 *Journey to the Moon*, Erich Fuchs. New York: Delacorte Press, 1969. This documents the original eight-day mission to the moon in 1969, indicating what occurred each day. Text is separate from the pictures so students can check their accuracy.

5–6 *The Package*, Laurie Anderson. Indianapolis: Bobbs-Merrill, 1971. A package goes from one intriguing person to another. The focus is on characterization and motivation in this one.

4–6 *The Silver Pony*, Lynd Ward. Boston: Houghton-Mifflin, 1973. A young farm boy is taken on an adventure to various parts of the world and even a journey to the stars before returning to reality and receiving the gift of a real pony. This features extensive drawings.

Storytelling with Pictures

Single pictures (or even a series) of interesting people or animals involved in unusual situations can also stimulate storytelling.

At first you may need to start out the story with a rousing or imaginative beginning to get creative juices flowing. (Picture of a man all bandaged up. "This is Melvin Q. Batts. Nothing ever goes right for poor Melvin. One day. . . .") You may also need to introduce the conflict and help students focus on the story's conclusion. *Variation*: Use several pictures with a related theme or setting. After beginning the story with one picture, add other pictures to stimulate the continued storytelling.

Storytelling in Character

Students will also enjoy telling stories, pretending to be another character. They may also want to try out character voices, gestures, and attitudes in their storytelling.

There are many literary sources that show storytellers in action. For example, Pa Ingalls entertains his children with short adventures from his past in Laura Ingalls Wilder's series of "Little House" books. Students can also imitate the tall tales of heroes like Pecos Bill and his bride, Sluefoot Sue, giving their own account of the legends surrounding them.

There are also possibilities for storytelling in other areas of the curriculum: Indians of long ago telling myths or stories around a campfire, soldiers relating harrowing escapes in war campaigns; or pioneers telling of hardships as well as happy times in moving west.

For yet another variation, select pictures, newspaper articles, or facts from the *Guinness Book of Records* and have students tell the story as if they were the person involved. ("See me standin' here with the biggest fish that was ever caught in Lake Manitou? The bait was the real secret. . . .")

More Storytelling Variations

1. "What's the Word?" When students show skill in storytelling, they may wish further challenges. Try telling stories using new vocabulary words, spelling words, foreign words, and so forth.

2. "Alphabet Story." Tell a story with each sentence beginning with a letter of the alphabet in sequence. ("**A** story is told about three

robbers. **B**ad ones they were, if you know what I mean. **C**ouldn't shoot straight, though, so they never worried the sheriff much.")

3. "What's that Sound?" Tell a story suggested by a series of sounds. (Open a desk drawer, shut a door, and scream.) What story does that suggest? Or, start with one sound to begin the story and continue the story with each added sound.

4. "Skeleton Stories." Make up stories using the skeletal framework of props, characters, or settings to stimulate ideas. Motivation will be enhanced if you have the props on hand along with pictures of the characters and settings. Examples:

Props: a key, a piece of jewelry, and a telephone

Characters: a pirate, a baseball player, and Snoopy

Settings: deserted island, an elevator, a courtroom

Experiment with combining the categories, too. Endless possibilities exist for this one. (These can also be played out as skits.)

VERBAL GAMES

Games in which students pretend to be other characters set in verbal situations are useful for stimulating dialogue. These games are easy to organize and can involve the entire class. The goal of these games is to explore dialogue situations and to search for information and ideas.

1. Groups of five to eight students take turns being panel members. The rest of the students are audience/questioners.

2. You serve as the moderator/host. In initial attempts, you may need to help with the questioning until students become more adept. It may also be helpful to have some questions written out on cards for students to ask.

3. To encourage roleplaying and help students relax and get into the spirit, props and/or simple costume pieces may be employed, such as hats, decorative sunglasses, scarves, or masks.

Experts

Panel members are declared to be experts on a subject. Some examples might be: owners of a "car" wash for elephants, people who have ridden in an alien spaceship, or real estate agents who rent condominiums for pets. The purpose of having students be experts is to allow them the security to give their opinions freely. After all, *they* are the experts. Bizarre topics also aid self-confidence, since there is no precedent to follow.

Trinkets such as these can stimulate ideas for the Experts game:
    a. knitters of miniature leg warmers for birds
    b. inventors of homes for insects
    c. designers of hats for fairies
    d. barbers who specialize in the troll trade

Try to give roles to everyone in the class. While the experts talk about their "car" wash for elephants, for example, the audience might be people interested in opening their own franchise. Newspaper reporters could question the spaceship riders, and pet owners might be those most interested in pet condominiums.

Tell the Truth

1. A panel poses as a particular famous person who may be living (current events), historical (social studies), or fictional (literature).

2. The audience poses questions to determine who the person is. Questions may be limited to twenty. Panelists can answer only "yes" or "no."

What's My Line?

1. This game, based on a classic television show, features a panel who have an unusual occupation that the audience tries to guess within twenty questions. Panel members all have the same occupation and take turns answering the questions.

2. A questioner may continue to question the panel until receiving a "no" answer.

This game can be useful for a unit in career education. Occupations can be of the future (flight attendant on a space ship). Occupations of the past (town crier, court jester, stage coach driver) could fit into social studies.

Liars' Club

1. Another variation of a television game show operates on the premise that the speakers know the true use of a particular object. Some students may know the objects in question, but most will need to create believable explanations.

2. Objects may be antiques, unusual objects, or new products on the market. Some suggestions are an eyelash curler, rug beater, Chinese yoyo, Braille stencil, knitting stitch holder, candle snuffer, vegetable steamer, staple remover, and so forth.

3. For other curricular emphasis, children might pretend to be archaeologists trying to identify how the object was used by a particular culture they have been studying.

Variation: "Language Liar's Club" can be played by guessing definitions of new words. A panel offers their definitions, with only one person knowing the correct one. Suggested words are *epee, turgid, neologist, brouhaha, sacrosanct, lugubrious,* and *oleaginous.*

Props for "Liar's Club", (clock-wise) stereoscope, darning egg, button hook, wooden potato masher, and (center) antique vaporizer.

I've Got a Secret

Again, borrowing from television's past, this game can easily be adapted for classroom use. Several on a panel could share a secret for the audience to guess. Panel may answer only "yes" or "no." Limit to twenty questions.

Examples:

Category: Fictional character from Mother Goose. "This secret involves something this person did while dressed in a certain way." (Wee Willie Winkie—ran through town in his nightgown).

Category: Historical character. "This secret involves a message this person delivered. What was the message?" ("One if by land and two if by sea." Paul Revere) Or, "This secret involves something this person had that was made of wood." (George Washington's false teeth)

Character Panel Discussions I

This activity has many variations. Panel members are given roles to play or they may establish their own, usually with varying viewpoints.

The audience, who play either themselves or a character role, question the panelists. (If audience members play a role, they should identify themselves before asking their questions.)

The goal of the game is to seek information and ideas. Final decisions are not necessary.

The following suggestions are only some of the many possibilities:

1. A panel of characters in a given story may be questioned by the audience as to their actions and motivations for behaviors not detailed in the stories. This gives all students the chance to probe characters' lives and personalities further. Instead of you asking questions in a class discussion, students can question the characters themselves.

2. For example, several of the main characters in *A Wrinkle in Time* could be questioned. You might wish to focus on the children or on the characters they meet in outer space.

3. Several panel members may play a single role, such as the Witch from *Hansel and Gretel*. Audience members might be various citizens of the town Hansel and Gretel live in. Questions asked might be "What was your house made of?" "Who else did you catch and what did you do with them?" "How did you get to be a witch?"

4. Panel members may be characters who have a common trait or behavior. Perhaps they are characters who constantly get into trouble, like Tom Sawyer or Harriet the Spy. Consider also mythological

characters, presidents, inventors, or explorers and the questions that might be asked of them. (*Example*: Presidents who held office during wartime: "What was your biggest concern about the war during your administration?" "If you had it to do over, what would you do differently?")

5. Discussions could also take the form of a guessing game. Assign characters to the panelists. They answer questions anonymously. The audience must guess who they are.

IMPROVISING DIALOGUE IN SCENES AND SKITS

Improvised dialogue is most dramatic and often most easily generated when tension or conflict is present. Have you ever noticed how talkative people become when there are two (or more) sides to an issue to debate or simply discuss? People seem to talk the most when there are problems to face. So, you will get more participation from the students if you choose topics where dramatic conflict and tension are present. They will also get caught up in the fun of the playing and be drawn into excellent problem-solving exercises as a result.

It is not always necessary to bring any discussion or debate to a final close. The airing of views is initially the most important goal. If you or the students do want to conclude—to settle upon some decision—you should probably set this goal at the beginning: "Try to find an answer to your problem." While not all students will be able to do it, problem-solving will be a challenge to those who can. Often a unique and unexpected compromise comes out of these discussions, and that can be a great source of satisfaction for everyone.

SOURCES FOR DIALOGUE MATERIALS

Literature is full of such dialogue situations. Some stories have crucial scenes focusing totally on verbal interaction. Remember the verbal guessing game between the Queen and Rumplestiltskin as she tries to find out his name? *Wind in the Willows* has numerous situations in which Toad has to talk his way out of difficulties; or a poem like "Univac to Univac" (38) suggests that computers gossip about humans' limitations when they are alone with each other.

There are dialogue situations from history. For example, Governor John Winthrop had to convince the people of Massachusetts that the water in the New World was pure enough to drink. Consider also the discussions and arguments that preceded many policy decisions of governments and other legislative bodies. Or, in science there are the many inventors and discoverers who have had to explain to and sometimes persuade others of their viewpoints in order to get financial assistance or acceptance of their ideas. Virtually every area of the curriculum has topics that can be explored through dialogue activities.

ACTIVITIES FOR VERBAL INTERACTION

Simple Debate (Method I)

1. Divide the class in half and present each with an opposite viewpoint to uphold. You can simply play this at the desks.
2. With this technique, everyone has a part to play and identify with even though they may not feel confident enough to voice their opinions. Let students switch roles after a while so they have the opportunity to see both sides of an issue.
3. You play the role of discussion moderator/mediator.

Literature Example: In Roald Dahl's *Charlie and the Chocolate Factory*, Willy Wonka has difficulties with several children. One little girl, Violet, swells up like a blueberry and turns purple after disobeying orders not to chew the experimental gum. The Oompa-Loompas, or factory workers, have to take her away to the juicing room. Willy, the owner of the factory, is upset with Violet for disobeying his rules, but he would like to have her problem solved, too.

Although Violet really has no choices given to her in the book, you can use the situation for a simple debate with half the class being Oompa-Loompas trying to convince the other half of the class, who play Violet, that being juiced is her only option. Violet argues for other solutions.

You, playing Willy, can call on those who have ideas to express. You may also pose questions to each side, if this assistance seems helpful. ("What will happen to Violet in the juicing room? What sorts of machines and equipment do you have in there? Violet, why did you disobey the orders? Has this ever happened to you before?") *Mathematics and Language Arts Example:* A similar arbitration scene might be played between the two kingdoms of words and numbers in Norman Juster's book *The Phantom Tollbooth* (89). King Azaz and his subjects consider that words are far more significant than numbers and therefore his kingdom is more important than his brother's. The Mathemagician, on the other hand, is sure that numbers are more important.

One half the class plays the people of King Azaz's kingdom; the other half plays the people of the Mathemagician's kingdom.

You can play Milo, the curious visitor, and moderate the two sides of the argument. Encourage the students to give various reasons for their belief in the supremacy of words or numbers. For variety, you might have two students join you in arbitrating. They can play Tock the Watchdog and Hamburg, who accompany Milo on his journey.

Simple Debate (Method II)

1. Present an idea to the class for the scene. You can use the above examples, but here is a new one. You are selling candy (or other item) to raise money for a school event (or other cause). Your neighbor, whom you always ask to buy from you, has decided not to support any more of your projects.

2. Brainstorm with the students some of the different reasons they might have for selling their item and why someone should buy it. Then brainstorm some of the reasons the neighbor would give for not wanting to support the project.

3. Now pair the students and let them rehearse/try out the scene briefly—at their desks—all talking at the same time. (It will be a little noisy, but you will survive.) Switch roles and repeat.

4. Let the students share their ideas as follows:

   a. Select several volunteers for sharing. You might have five pairs in front of the class. (Do not forget that you can double cast and have more than one student in a role.)

   b. Give each pair a number. The pair may talk when you call out their number.

   c. Call numbers randomly and give each pair a few moments to share.

There are several advantages to this procedure for sharing. First of all, a number of students are allowed the opportunity to share, so they do not have to wait long to get a turn. Second, you are in control of the sharing. If some students have little to say, you simply call another number to relieve the pressure on them. Some students, if they cannot think of something to say, may begin to giggle with embarrassment or possibly start to fight. By being able to simply call another number, you can bail them out, too. (You can call their numbers again after they have had a little break to collect their thoughts.) This procedure also makes it easy to cut off those who would go on forever if you let them.

Extra Challenge: Highly verbal students will enjoy this additional challenge: they must pick up the thread of the previous pairs' (or group's) conversation and continue it. This forces them to listen carefully to the rationale of other players and develop it further.

Character Panel Discussions II

This format, suggested in simpler form in the last chapter, can be used as a structure for presenting different viewpoints. Again, these are easy to set up since the students can remain in their seats. The following are some possibilities for you to consider:

A.
1. You (or a competent student) pretend to host a television talk show or a public forum.

2. All the panelists (4–6 students) are the various stepmothers from folk and fairy tales who feel they have been given a "bum rap." They tell their side of the story and try to convince the audience they are not so bad.

3. The "audience" questions the details of their stories.
   (You can also use this technique with other characters and personages in literature or in history: villains, witches, traitors, and so forth.)

B.
1. Again, you host or moderate a talk show or forum. Choose a character usually assumed to be a villain and see how he or she might be looked at in a new light. For example, in *Little Red Riding Hood*, is it possible that the Wolf might be a sympathetic character?

2. Panelists could be his supportive mother, employer, or Boy Scout leader who speak in his behalf and answer questions the audience poses. To keep the tension, an equal number of panelists should speak on behalf of Red Riding Hood and her Grandmother.

3. Audience asks questions of either "side." *Note:* It is usually easier and more fun to do this one without having the original characters present.

C. Historical events may also be played in this format.

1. A panel of members of the Virginia Company might try to convince the audience to settle in the New World.

2. The audience knows about the hardships and failures of the earlier colonies, however, and is reluctant.

D.
1. You may also assign characters and viewpoints to the panel and the audience.

2. Write instructions and pertinent data for each character on note cards and distribute them. If the class does not know who is receiving what instructions, the scene can be even more realistic.

Example:

a. A town meeting is called; you might play the mayor.

b. Two panelists present the side of those who want a new factory built. One might be the president of the company and the other, a local contractor who will do the building. Both emphasize the number of jobs that will open up in the community, which has an unemployment problem.

c. The other two panelists might represent environmentalists. One has data about the company's past record of waste disposal abuse, and another believes the plant location will pose unsolvable problems.

d. Members of the audience are the citizens of the community. Some are unemployed; some work for the construction company which will do the building. Some live next to the plant site. The remainder are not sure how they feel about the issue.

CREATING AND PLAYING SKITS

Students will eventually be ready to create their own skits. This section will give you further suggestions for this type of work.

PLANNING AN ENDING

Usually the biggest problem when students create their own skits is planning an ending. You may need to press for this, as the students often do not realize the importance of it until they are actually playing their scene. If the scene has strong conflict and an ending has not been planned, then arguments, shouting, or a physical fight may be all they can think of. And, sometimes they cannot even bring *that* to a close!

Once I instructed some fourth graders to be sure to plan an ending for their scene. Then I asked if they knew why I had requested it. One answer was, "So we'll all know when to quit." I think that says it pretty well, and it is a story I often share with students to stress the importance of planning an ending.

In spite of your precautions, there still may be times when students reach a dead end. You then have several options.

a. You may walk up to them privately and quietly ask, as a reminder, "Do you have an ending?"

b. If an ending is not forthcoming, you may be able to narrate them out of the difficulty.

c. It may even be possible to step into the scene as a mediator character and negotiate.

In the following example, the students had developed skits based on returning an item to the complaint department. One group could not settle its argument, so the leader intervened.

"And so the complaint manager and the irate customer never got a chance to find out who would win the argument, for a bell sounded the closing of the department store. And to the strains of the Muzak playing 'God Rest Ye Merry, Gentlemen,' they all went home."

AUDIENCE FOR SKITS

As before, you may have to guide sensitive audience behavior. Some students are not unduly critical of each other and may, in fact, identify with and be sympathetic to students who falter.

But there are those who will become impatient with their classmates. They think *they* would know what to say or do in the same situation, so they may call out instructions. "Maybelle, tell him you don't want to go!" "Psst, George, give him a shove!" Sometimes, just a quiet reminder will do. At other times they may need to have it explained that prompting from the audience interrupts the players' thinking and does more harm than good.

EVALUATION

Students sometimes say they need more rehearsal time or that they do not like what they have planned. Obviously, they are aware that elements are lacking, and the best remedy may be to allow them to keep improvising together and working out their ideas rather than evaluating them.

When students have confidence in skit making, you may decide to ask them or classmates to give their evaluation. Positive evaluation is paramount, so you will need to word the discussion questions carefully. Your own positive feedback will be important, especially if some students insist on being overly critical of classmates.

What did you like about the/your scene?

What moments were the most enjoyable for you? Why?

If you could do it over again, what would you want to change? Why?

How successful do you think the ending was to the/your scene? Why?

SKIT IDEAS

Familiar Stories

Students often find it easier to create skits from familiar material such as fables, short stories, or favorite television situation comedies, television shows based on children's literature (*Little House on the Prairie, Wonderworks, Afternoon Specials*). You may want to have students in small groups read a specific story or watch a certain television show in preparation for reenactments.

Silent Movies

Show a silent movie or a film with the sound turned off. Students create dialogue and speak it as the film is shown, coordinating the speeches with the actors' movements. It may be easiest to use one film (or one scene) and let groups rehearse their ideas quietly at the same time. Then each group can present its version.

Skits from Ad Talks

Skits may be created from Ad Talk statements described on pages 123–24. Groups of students draw three or more cards at random. They must create a skit around the statements, improvising as much dialogue as they like, as long as they include the three statements. Often, the more unusual or unrelated the cards seem to be, the more creative the students become. (Consider lines like: "Who was that masked man?" "It's not what you know, it's who you know," "Help, I can't take it any more," "Hey, who took my secret decoder ring?" "What went wrong?" and so on.)

Proverbs

Students develop skits to illustrate proverbs. What stories do the following suggest? "Two heads are better than one." "All that glitters is not gold." "A fool and his money are soon parted."

News Story of the Week

Students recreate their version of a news event. Having newspapers at hand can provide ideas for the skits as well as stimulating interest in reading further about them.

Stories from Advertisements

Newspaper ads can stimulate the imagination to speculate on the story surrounding them. Items that are for sale or messages in the "Personals" section might pose possibilities. For example: "House for sale. Furnishings included. Vacating immediately. Best offer.'' might make one think of a story like ''The Amityville Horror.'' Or, ''Learn to speed-read in one week. Success guaranteed or your money cheerfully refunded.''

Opening Lines

Skits can be based on opening lines, such as the following:

1. It seemed a perfect day for the event. Crowds were gathered for the momentous, historic occasion. One person in the crowd, however, seemed out of place.

2. Silently and without warning it came on them like a thief in the night. Not until the following morning were they aware of what had happened.

Famous Last Words

Create skits that begin or end with intriguing lines like the following:

''You never listen to anything I say.''

''I told you we should have called the police.''

''I know exactly what I'm doing.''

Commercials

Create commercials not usually seen on television:

1. Recycle products. Create a commercial for things that might otherwise be thrown away (old shoes, cracked mirror, boxes of assorted sizes, bald tire, and so forth).

2. Sell products from the past (guillotine, suit of armor, covered wagon, spinning wheel) or the future (life-like robots, personal space ships, wrist watch television sets).

(Note: Can relate to a study of persuasive advertising techniques like bandwagon approach, testimony, appeal to status, and so on.)

Random Skits

a. Prepare sets of cards with places, props, and characters.

b. Groups select one (or more) card from each set.

c. Plan a skit using cards selected. May add more of each category.

d. Shuffle cards for infinite variety of combinations.

Settings: elevator, lost and found department, information desk, haunted house, cave, desert island, hijacked airplane,

Characters: spy, detective, genie in a bottle, Frankenstein monster, Superman/woman, ghost, police officer, Snoopy,

Props: treasure chest, magic wand, flying carpet, poison apple, cape to make you invisible, sneezing powder, seven-league boots, old jalopy, air balloon with a slow leak, and so forth.

Role-Playing Situations

Once students have had some experience with dialogue scenes and other creative drama activities, it will be easier to do role-playing suggested in many social studies texts. Students dramatize various ways of handling personal and social problems. Even if the dramatizations show unacceptable behaviors, the consequences of those behaviors are usually indicated either in the skit or in the discussion following.

Prop Stories

a.   Keep a selection of props and some costume pieces.

b.   Select three or four for each group to base a skit on.

c.   After the stories are planned, students may add other props and costumes to the skits.

Dialogue Guessing Games

Very verbal students will like the challenge of this game.

Props can stimulate story ideas.

"Just keep saying 'There's no place like home.' "

"This case calls for some super detective work!"

a. Students work out a scene on their own, without identifying the characters in it.

b. You stop the scene periodically so the audience can guess from the clues who the speakers might be. Here are two examples:

Examples:

I don't want you coming around here again!

But what harm did I do?

Harm? What about the food you ate and the furniture you broke?

Well, the food wasn't my idea of terrific—and the furniture wasn't very well made anyway!

(Goldilocks and Papa Bear)

I know you can do it; I have a lot of faith in you.

Well, I've sewn a lot of things, but this is a real challenge.

Here's the design we have in mind.

Ah, but five points are just as easy to make as six . . .

(George Washington and Betsy Ross)

9 Encouraging Creative Work

Many students create easily and freely. Others will need encouragement and guidance from you in developing into creative thinkers. This chapter will help you find ways to encourage creative work. First we will look at some fairly simple creative activities and ways to guide their playing. In the second half of this chapter, we will show you a way to help children create their own stories for dramatizing.

WHAT IS A CREATIVE ACTIVITY?

In creative drama, whenever we ask students for their own thoughts and ideas about what to play or how to play it, we are encouraging creativity. The activity may range from acting out one's own idea in a brief pantomime to creating an original story.

☺ EXAMPLES OF SIMPLE CREATIVE ACTIVITIES
   FOR SOLO UNISON PLAYING

   1. Favorite Story: ''Suppose you're Henry Huggins (75) in school listening to his teacher tell about the class play. He doesn't want to be in it, so he's trying to keep from being called on. The book says only that he slides down in his seat, but there are other things one could do. What would you do as Henry, staying at your desk, trying to avoid being called on?''

(Students might pretend to drop a pencil and spend a long time picking it up, look busily for a book in the desk, or retie a shoe.)

2. Study of Space Flight: "The astronauts have a number of duties to perform while they are on their space mission. We've talked about a number of these; you may know of others you can add. As I count to five, you try acting out five astronaut jobs."

3. Study of Shapes: "This time, pretend you're using something that is in the shape of a cone—maybe you'll be a cheerleader using a megaphone, or a clown putting on a cone-shaped hat, or maybe you'll be eating an ice cream cone."

4. Interpretation of Musical Selection: "As I play Stravinsky's *Firebird Suite*, you can be the magnificent, golden Firebird who flies into the forest from the other side of the earth and eats the maize. What else does this majestic Firebird do before the young archer arrives and captures him for the Tzar?"

5. Exploratory Movement Based on an Intriguing Picture: "This picture shows a man in a suitcase, almost as if he is folded up inside it. I thought you might like to try being this person. You probably need to think of a reason why he would be in the suitcase. Is he coming out or going back in? What does he do when he unfolds himself and gets out—or what happens to him when he goes inside? What sort of work does he do or what kinds of mission might he be on? How will you end your story about him?"

EXAMPLES OF SIMPLE CREATIVE ACTIVITIES FOR PAIR AND GROUP PLAYING

Similar activities may be created and played in pairs and groups.

1. Based on Patricia Hubbel's poem, "Shadows," (8) (35): "Decide between the *two of you* who will be the shadow and who will be the person the shadow is following and imitating. You'll have to decide who the person is and what he or she does all day long." (Music might be "Me and My Shadow.")

2. Being Clowns: "Clown routines are carefully worked out although they often look very spontaneous. After you divide into *groups,* you will need to decide what kind of clowns you are—sad-faced, silly, or some other possibility. What will your routines be? What specialty will you each have? What is the high point of your routine together? I'll play Kabalevsky's *The Comedians* for your background music."

3. Health and Safety Lesson: "This picture shows five people in a crucial moment. There seems to have been an accident of some sort. In your groups, decide how the situation might have begun and create a still picture of that moment. Then you'll act out the moments leading up to this picture and freeze again."

GUIDING CREATIVE WORK

Before one can feel free to create, one must be in an accepting, nonjudgmental environment. Consider the following techniques you can use to help students feel as comfortable as possible in their work.

1. Brainstorm some ideas verbally before playing. ("What kinds of appliances are there that use electricity?") Or, brainstorm by simply playing. ("While I play the music, you act out using as many different electrical appliances you can think of before the music stops.")

2. Keep the playing brief at first and have as many students as possible play in unison (with little or no audience watching). This technique lets children work privately without the pressure of being judged by others.

3. If you need to check on what the students are doing, keep the ideas private. As the students play their ideas, you can ask them to freeze while you come around and talk to them individually. (Your responses need only accept the idea. "Ah, that's interesting." "Ohh." "Um, hum." "Really?" and so forth. No judgments of good or bad need be made.)

4. Side-coaching.

   a. As the students play, remind them of the different ideas they mentioned in discussion, note some of the ideas you see being played, or suggest other possibilities for them to consider.

   b. Use recorded music to stimulate students' thinking as well as to provide a background to fill in any awkward silences.

5. When the playing is ended, you can comment on what some of the ideas were without identifying the players. ("I saw some people putting insulation in the attic, chop-

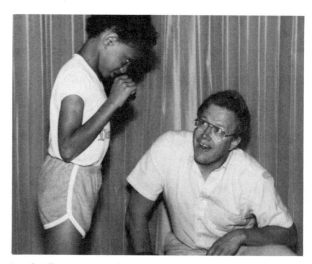

Leader listens appreciatively to student's pantomime idea.

ping wood for a wood-burning stove, some turning off lights—all kinds of ways to save energy.'') This technique shows acceptance of the students' ideas and lets the rest of the class know what the various ideas were.

6. As students become confident in creating, they will want to share their ideas with each other. Those who wish may do so, either by telling what they did or by demonstrating their ideas, sometimes even for audience guessing. But be cautious of pushing anyone who is not yet ready. Remember the flower bud that cannot be forced to open before its time.

CONTROL TECHNIQUES IN CREATIVE WORK

Sometimes we are afraid to let students be creative in their playing because we feel they will get out of control. Providing a definite structure or framework for students' creativity can lessen our anxiety.

1. Always be definite about when the students should start and stop their pantomiming.
   a. You may simply say, "Begin—Freeze."
   b. You may count, saying, for example, "Think of three things you can do as I count to three—1, 2, 3."
   c. "When the record begins, you may move; when it stops, you freeze."
   d. For more extended playing, you may be more inventive and say: (mysteriously) "When the lights go off, that will be the signal that Halloween night is here. And all you witches, goblins, ghosts, and other assorted characters will come out from your hiding places (desks) to create your own Halloween mischief (solo at the side of the desk) in the moonlight. But when the clock strikes five o'clock (hammer on a small gong), you must return to your hiding places again where no human eye can see you."
   e. Students' inventiveness and the length of playing time needed will vary with each individual or group. Therefore, just tell them to sit down when they have finished their work and wait quietly for others to finish. While this technique may seem strange at first, you and the students will soon become accustomed to it and will find it helpful for many activities.

MECHANICAL MOVEMENT

Mechanical movement is another technique you can use for controlled, creative work. You can be the operator who manages the "on" and "off" switch.

Suggested Characters: robots, windup or mechanical toys, marionettes, clocks with characters that move as the hour strikes, and so forth.

A Possible Story Outline: Robots go on a picnic. It rains and the robots all "rust" and are "frozen." You might oil them up again, one by one, so they can go home.

Students work out their ideas for creating the various parts of a machine.

Group Work: Create machines, both real and imaginary. Try household appliances, indoor and outdoor machinery of all sizes. For imaginary machinery, students might invent "a homework machine," "a machine to wake you up *and* get you out of bed in the morning," or "a dream machine." Machines from literature might include the doughnut machine from *Homer Price* (78).

"SETTING PICTURES IN MOTION" OR "COMING TO LIFE"

For still another technique, students create a picture that is frozen but comes to life on cue. For even more structure, each student is assigned a number. When you call out all the "1's," they move, "2's," add on to the "1's," and so on. You can even reverse this counting so the picture returns to its frozen position once again.

Examples:
a.   "In this short poem, "The Shopgirls" (32), we are told that when the shopgirls leave the stores and the working day is over, certain things in the store come to life. What might some of these things be and how would they move? What position might they freeze into at daybreak?"

b. "In Jay Williams' story "Tyl on a Tightrope" (55), Tyl tosses the soldiers' boots to them, forcing them to scramble to find their own. Before acting out the story, we'll try this scene. In groups of eight, you will be frozen in your various positions just before Tyl throws the boots. Each of you will have a number, and you can move only when I call your number."

c. "Now that we've studied early railroad-building in the United States, we can create our own railroad crew. Divide into groups of five. In each group you'll decide who will be those who lay the ties or "sleepers," "shakers" who hold the spikes, those who hammer, those who carry the water, and one supervisor. When you've worked that out, I'll give numbers to each. (Appropriate music might be "I've Been Workin' on the Railroad" or "John Henry.")

CREATING STORIES

Many students are capable of creating stories on their own that they can enact with little assistance from you. Others, however, may be dependent on you to give them ideas to work with and guidance through plot outline. In this section we will look at some of the ways you can help your students create and play out plots of their own.

In the process of plot building, you will be giving students a framework for developing a story that is meaningful and satisfying to them. The stories are action based and played out in pantomime. But you will also learn how to extend the story by adding verbal experiences after the pantomiming.

Steps in the Process of Creative Plot Building

1. Present an intriguing idea that can be played in pantomime to the students. The playing may be solo, in pairs, or in groups.
2. Guide the students through a series of approximately five discussion questions to assist them in planning their own stories. The questions help them create a beginning, middle, and end to their stories as well as a conflict and a resolution.
3. Sidecoach the unison playing of the stories. (Sometimes half the class plays for the other half and then we switch.)
4. Followup discussion may be with you in character role or other verbal activities.
5. Replaying (optional).

Now let us look at each step a little closer.

CHOOSING AN IDEA

The topics for a creative story, whether fact or fiction, can come from a number of sources as you tap your own imagination.

Literature:

"Harriet the Spy (74) is the kind of person who finds it exciting and important work to check on people, taking notes of all they do. She wants to be a writer someday and thinks that's what writers should do. Her spying missions take her to a number of different and unusual places. Suppose you are someone like Harriet and you, too, spend your days looking for and observing all sorts of people. . . .''

Social Studies:

"Let's suppose that you are a member of an archaelogical team working at a new excavation site. It's your job to carefully uncover all the artifacts, photographing their exact placement, and put identifying tags on them so you can learn more about them. . . . '' (group playing)

Science:

"As the world-famous team of Dr. Pinna and Dr. Lobe, the ear experts, you will need to use your secret invention to make yourself small enough to travel in your patient's ear in order to find the source of the problem. . . .'' (pair playing)

Music:

"Listen to this music called 'Neptune' from *The Planet Suite* by Holst. Imagine you are a space explorer and this music is what seems to be coming from a new planet you're about to land on. What kind of place do you think the planet will be?''

DISCUSSION

Discussion questions follow general plot outline. Five well-worded, intriguing questions are usually sufficient to develop the story. (You can combine several short or related questions into one.)

Generally the *first* question introduces the idea, the *second* and *third* questions build the adventure, by the *fourth* question the conflict is introduced, and the *fifth* question brings the story to a close.

Through the questions you ask, students plan the details of who they are, what they are going to do, what problems they might have, how they will solve them, and how their story will end.

Hints in Wording the Questions

1. The questions must continually focus on *action* since the stories are going to be pantomimed.

2. Keep the questions following the chronological order of the story, moving it forward. Do not back up and change the direction of a story or ask questions that are not directly related to it.

3. Ask questions that are open-ended and that encourage embellishment of ideas. If a question can be answered with just a "yes" or "no," it will build minimal plot.

4. Ask intriguing questions that will draw the students into the idea. The characters should be significant and important. Sometimes you can make them experts in their adventure—"the world's smartest detective," for example. Use words like "special," "clever," and "unusual."

5. Adding tension to the story as it evolves will intensify the drama. Perhaps there is the pressure of time—a job must be finished by midnight or a magic spell will wear off.

6. It is helpful to word the questions tentatively so the students can change their story as they hear more ideas discussed. "What *do you suppose* you'll do next?" for example leaves the way open for flexibility.

7. Do not try to get answers from everyone on every question. Discussion continues only as long as it is motivating the students and the ideas are flowing. Most students will want to get to the playing as soon as possible.

As students gain skill in this kind of story building, they may not always need a lot of discussion time. You may be able to give the entire outline of your discussion questions and let them plan it all in one gulp. It is not unusual for some students to give you their entire story after you have asked only one question. They may already be several steps ahead of you!

The importance of the class-wide discussion is for the evolving of numerous ideas, the cross-fertilizing of thinking, and the expanding and elaborating of creativity. Students may hear ideas that will mesh with theirs; or they may hear an idea they like better than their own. You, too, may even be inspired with new ideas. Discussions are most valuable when this kind of creative process is taking place.

Discussions are also helpful to you since they will let you know what ideas you can expect to see in the playing. You will then be able to interpret the pantomime much better. And you will have a better idea of what questions and feedback to expect in the verbalizing later.

PLAYING / SIDE-COACHING

At first, your students may only create very brief stories of perhaps only thirty seconds to a minute in length; gradually, with a topic that interests them, they should increase their playing time to three minutes and possibly even longer.

Not all students will play for the same length of time. Therefore, it is best to have them sit down when they have finished their story and quietly watch others.

Even though students are making up their own beginnings and endings for their stories, you should give signals for both. Your signals will add more to the playing if you make them as imaginative as possible.

> "When you hear the clanging of pots, you'll know the cook's signaling you cowboys for the new day of driving cattle on the open range. You'll know the day is ending when you hear the soft strums of the guitar by the campfire."

When most of the students have ended their playing, you can narrate/sidecoach an ending for those still playing if it look as if they need help. (Some can go on forever if you let them!) It is also wise to narrate/sidecoach an ending if you see the playing deteriorating at any time.

Side-coaching Hints

1. As before, music will play an important part in encouraging the students' ideas and providing a background for their dramas.

2. Since students have created their own stories to play, they may not need more than just a few reminders of the various stages of their plot—the beginning, the action, the problems they may be encountering, and the solutions they may have. Many will be too engrossed in their playing to pay much attention to sidecoaching.

3. Sidecoaching is usually needed more for individual playing than for pair and group playing. When students work with each other in these stories, they rely more on their classmates than on you for assistance.

4. In your sidecoaching you can also lend to the drama by playing a character role. In the following example students are creating stories about race-car driving. They are in groups that include the drivers and their pit crews. You can lend authenticity and drama in the role of the official announcer of the race:

> "It's a great day for the races, all you fans out there! The cars are lined up for the beginning of this day-long race. The excitement here is high—the atmosphere is tense. The engines are roaring, and the race is about to begin. At the wave of the flag, each team is on its own. Good luck! And they're off! What will be the outcome of this race is anybody's guess. . . . ."

5. Usually it is best to word the sidecoaching tentatively since the students' ideas are all different and you really do not know all the details of each story. Also, the students are not moving through the various stages of their stories at the same speed.

"It *seems as if some* people have already left on their mission. . . . "

"I *wonder if anyone* has run into a problem yet. . . ."

"You're all such clever detectives, I'm sure you'll all be able to *find the clues you need* to solve the case. . . ."

6. Do not interject any new idea in the side-coaching. If you call out ideas such as, "Look out for that shark!" or "Suddenly you discover gold!" you will only confuse the playing. These ideas are appropriate to narrative pantomime but would be interruptions in these original stories.

DISCUSSION / DIALOGUE FOLLOWUP WITH LEADER IN CHARACTER ROLE

When the playing has ended, many students will want to tell you what happened in their stories, elaborating on the ideas they mentioned earlier. There may be times when you will ask them to write their experiences in story format, diary, newspaper article; or you might have them draw a picture, or just discuss what happened.

However, you will not want to miss the opportunity to extend the story/plot idea through character dialogue. If you play a character role, you have the chance to explore so many more ideas and concepts with the students.

Ideally you want to extend the story and build on the students' creativeness. Often it is helpful to use props, pictures, costume, or anything else that will stimulate ideas. Opinions, evaluations, descriptions, or other categories of verbalization can also be explored. You may even introduce new problems to be solved.

Dialogue with Verbal Children

Generally it is best to ask questions of the group as a whole and then call on volunteers. If students are highly verbal, you need to move quickly from one student to another.

Sometimes highly verbal students will be interested in joining you as questioner. You might then give them a general role as "my assistants," "my colleagues," and so forth.

If students have played their dramas in small groups, they may see even more opportunities to create dialogue. And, if the majority of the class is highly verbal, you will want to utilize other verbal activities such as Panel of Experts (p. 127) or even Verbal Skits discussed in Chapter 8.

Dialogue with Reticent Students

If the creative story has been intriguing and the questions are captivating, often even the shyest person will want to become involved. However, it is a good idea to be prepared with simple questions that can be answered "yes" or "no" for students who find it difficult to speak up in a classroom. ("Did you have an exciting adventure?" "Did you find what you were looking for?" "Were you scared?" and so on.) Even nodding or shaking the head in answer to a question can be a big undertaking for some students.

As another precaution, it is helpful for you to have an "out"— a reason you can give in case a student appears ready to speak and then freezes up at the last moment. For example, as a "newspaper reporter" you might say to an inventor, "I can understand your not wanting to talk to me; this invention of yours is probably top secret stuff."

REPLAYING (Optional)

Once the students have tried an idea they like, they may ask to play it again. They may have new ideas. Some may want to include ideas they have heard from others. Or, they may want to work with a partner after playing solo.

You can take the opportunity to have them evaluate their work by asking what they might like to change or what they particularly liked about their previous playing.

SAMPLE LESSON PLAN
Robots

Objectives

a. Experience creative mechanical movement and creative verbal experience based on topic of robots.

b. Practice in creating a story with a beginning, middle, and end.

c. Deal with the concept of mechanical robot's possibilities for work.

d. Imagine problems that could be encountered in mechanical devices and create appropriate solutions.

e. Have opportunities to respond to character questioning related to the experience.

f. Have opportunity to become more familiar with computer concepts such as programming, GIGO (garbage in/garbage out), user friendly.

Preparation and Materials

a. Space: area in center of room with desks around edge of room

b. Supplies: ad statement cards; small nondescript piece of machinery

c. Equipment: record player

d. Books: catalogue advertising a personal robot or use one of the robots discussed in *Robots in Fact and Fiction* by Melvin Beyer (New York: Franklin Watts, 1980)

e. Music: use any "mechanical" musical recording, "Aquarium" from Saëns' *Carnival of the Animals* or other quieting music

f. Visual Aids: pictures of robots

g. Length of session: 60 minutes

Warmup

Introduce the advertisement for a personal robot that rolls on rubber wheels, has a stationary tray-type arm, a manual grasping hand to carry objects, flashing eyes, and a tape recorded voice.

a. Do a warmup activity of robots doing calesthenics or aerobic dancing to music. (Give students the opportunity to move as the robot would move, translating calesthenics designed for the human body to a robot's body.) Divide students into two groups, taking turns with brief exercise activity. Try interpreting how a robot would do toe touches, jumping jacks, knee bends, and so forth.

b. Do magazine ad statements (See p. 123) using a robot/mechanical voice.

Creative Plot Building Activity

Discussion Questions

a. "Suppose you were a robot? What type of job might you do? Where do you work?" (in an office doing odd jobs; in a house doing simple housework tasks; belong to a kid like me who has him as a servant)

b. "What are all the things you have to do in a day's time? What's your typical day like?" (deliver mail, run copy machine, get coffee; dust, empty wastebaskets, run a vacuum cleaner; follow a kid like me around to carry books and stuff, bring a kid like me breakfast in bed, and do a kid's paper route)

c. "Suppose today, as you're in the middle of all your work, something goes wrong. What might that be? And what happens to you and all your work?" (Well, I could start doing things all wrong and pour coffee in the mail box and run lots of blank paper; I'm cleaning because a lot of company's coming, and I'm trying to mop and spill the bucket of water and short all my circuits and go haywire; I throw the papers on the porches, but I got programmed too strong and the papers start breaking windows and knocking stuff around.)

d. "Oh, dear, well we'd better get things back to normal again. What could happen to stop all this damage and make things right again?" (I have to be sent out for repairs and get straightened out and finish the day; someone comes and blows me dry with a hair dryer and I still have to be fixed but at least I stop messing things up; some people tackle me and punch in the right code so I can do it right.)

e. "Now I'd like to know what robots do when they've finished a hard day's work. What do you do to relax?" (I watch tv in the lounge; I have my own room so I go there and listen to records; I like to play chess with myself and see if I can trick me.)

Directions for Playing   "I think we can give this a try. Since there isn't enough space for everyone this first time, we'll take half of you for the first playing and half for the second. I'll play some mechanical-sounding music for you to pantomime to. Get in your places. And be sure you stay in your own space, especially since you said so many things would go wrong. I'll let you know when you're switched on. When you finish your story, just freeze where you are." (Record starts.)

Side-coaching   "Robots, get ready for a new day. You're switched on–Now. Oh, boy, a robot's day never seems to end. It's work, work, work all the time. You've sure been thoroughly pro- grammed—so many jobs are being done. I hope the people who own you are aware of the complete job you're doing for them. Ah, and today is that special day when you're to do your special job. It's so very important that everything goes right. Everybody's counting on you. Oh, dear, I think I see some things looking not quite right. Is it possible? Oh, I hope someone can save you from making such a mess of things. Whew, good, I think some robots must have been helped. They seem to be getting back to normal— or at least they've been stopped from doing any more damage. Some are completely done in I see. And now almost all robots are finished. We'll shut off the last few as the music ends." (Fade mu- sic out.) *Note:* The above is said only when needed during the play- ing.

Second group of players enact their stories.

Leader in Character Role   "Now that you robots are back to nor- mal again, I'd like to check with you on some things. Allow me to introduce myself. My name is McGillicutty and I'm a marketing analyst. I've heard about you robots, and I want to talk directly to

Playing a story about a robot.

you about your capabilities so I'll know how to market you in this country."

Questions: (students encouraged to use the "computer sounding" voice used earlier in the Magazine Ad Statement activity.)

a. "Just how user friendly are you? Is it possible to make you even more user friendly then you are? And, if so, how might we do that?"

b. "Which of your parts need replacing most frequently? What is the cost for that?"

c. "I've heard it said that some of your early customers had complaints. For example, some said you didn't work fast enough; you were too noisy; and one even claimed you talked too much. Would you care to respond to any one or all of those complaints?"

d. "Oh, by the way, here's a small piece of machinery I found on the floor. I think it might be a part of one of you. Who claims it? What is it and what does it do?"

e. "I understand you are the first model of personal robot and that there are others in designing and manufacturing right now. How are the new models different from you and are the differences significant?"

f. "One final question—and this is strictly personal and off the record. You can level with me. As a robot, do you ever have a desire to become even more human than you are now? Why or why not?"

"Thanks for talking with me. I have to go write my report now. I know you've had a very busy day, so I'll let you relax now."

Option: Instead of questioning in leader role, you could set up a panel of robots who are questioned by the class playing prospective buyers. If they all like talking as robots, you might want to set up paired conversations with robots interviewing other robots for jobs.

Quieting Activity   "Robots, please return to your packing cases. We need to have you sent out for servicing and overhauling after your experience today. You're all inside? Good. I'm shutting off all your power now." (Play restful music for a few moments like "Aquarium" from Saint-Saëns' *Carnival of the Animals.*)

SAMPLE LESSON PLAN
Boston Tea Party
Objectives

a. Experience a creative movement and creative verbal experience based on an event in American history.

b. Create a story with a beginning, middle, and end, including conflict and resolution.

c. Experience working in a small group to create and play a story. (*Note*: Although this same story can be played solo or in pairs, the lesson plan is designed for small group playing.)

Preparation and Materials

a. **Space:** Each group will need enough space to play their stories without overlapping into another group's space. You may need to allow only half the class to play at one time.

b. **Supplies:**

  1. Record player and recording. Music (such as Richard Rodgers' *Victory at Sea*) to set the mood of intrigue would probably work best.

  2. (Optional) Artists' drawings of the event

c. **Length of Session:** Approximately 40 minutes

Warmup and Motivation

Recall the event, perhaps showing artists' drawings. Discuss feelings of colonists about the tea tax and the group known as the "Sons of Liberty."

Discussion Questions

"Let's suppose that it's 1773 in Boston and you are the group of people called "The Sons of Liberty," who object to the high tax on tea. You disguise yourselves as Indians, board a tea freighter at night, and throw the tea overboard."

a. "Now, what are your plans for disguising and arming yourselves for tonight? Your disguise should be good enough to fool the British." (Students' answers might include arm ourselves with tomahawks, hatchets, and bows and arrows; put red ochre on our faces; wear buckskin jackets and moccasins.) (*Note*: Because students are working in groups, they will need to talk their ideas over with each other before answering. You may prefer to give students all the questions at once and let them work out their entire story in groups. In that case, you may wish to just listen in on their group planning to make sure they are covering all the questions.)

b. "Next you need to plan your strategy for getting down to the harbor and out onto the ship without being spotted. How will you do that?" (Our job will be to divert the sailors on watch so everyone else can get aboard; we're going to shout like Indians making war cries to scare them; we wait until night when there are fewer people at the harbor and the officers are asleep on shore and we can sneak on board.)

c. "Once you get to the harbor and get on board the ship, how will you take it over and get to the tea? How will you take care of the crew?" (We'll lock the crew in the fo'c'sle; we have to rip off the hatch covers so we can get to the tea; we may have to use winches to get the tea chests out of the hatch.)

d. "It's always good to be prepared for problems. You know, it's possible there are some British spies on the lookout. What sort of problems do you anticipate, and how will you solve them?" (We'll send someone out to spot the British sailors so they can warn us if they come; we might not get all the crew members locked up and some come to fight with us and we'll have to tie them up; someone could be hurt with the tea chests and it hits someone and knocks them overboard and we have to save them.)

e. "After the mission is completed, you'd better lay low—maybe even go into hiding. How will you do that?" (We have to hide or bury our makeup and costumes and hatchets so we don't get arrested; we have horses and are going to ride out into the countryside to hide—away from Boston; we're going to change into our regular clothes and pretend we don't know anything about it.)

Directions for Playing

If half the class is to play first, get them placed. When they have finished their stories, they should sit and wait for others. They are to play only as long as the music plays. When they are ready, you say, (whispering) "My friends, I'm afraid my age and infirmities prevent me from joining you this night. This 'tea party' you're planning should make quite a surprise for the British. I'm glad I have this shop for you to meet in. You should be safe here for getting ready. I'll be waiting for your return, so you can tell me how it went for you. Godspeed to you all."

Side-coaching (as needed)

(Start record player.) "Your strategies and plans for the "tea party" seem well thought out. I hope there are enough costumes and makeup for all. It's good it's dark tonight so you will be able to sneak on board without being seen. Some of you look anxious to get started. Be careful." (Now you can talk to yourself as if they have all left.) "It's too dark to see the harbor from here. I hope all goes well. Though I'm sure there will be a few difficulties, even if small ones. But these "Sons of Liberty" are a determined lot. I'm sure they'll be strong enough to get through any problems. Ah, it appears that some have accomplished their mission already and are returning. I see some others in the distance headed back this way, though others appear to have ridden off on horseback. I'm anxious to hear all about it. (Fade out record as groups end their playing.)

If class is divided into two groups, let second group play before going to the verbal acitvity.

Followup Discussion

"After the 'Tea Party,' the English closed the port of Boston. Many dockworkers as well as others in the city were out of work, and many goods and supplies were at a premium. Suppose some people, who are not that sympathetic to the revolutionary cause, have a chance to question those of you who were a part of the 'Tea Party.' You will probably be asked to defend your position. How would you answer for your actions?"

Set up a character panel discussion and let six to eight persons be the "Sons of Liberty." Others are Bostonians who ask questions. Switch sides.

(*Variations*: Divide the class half and half for the debate. Make out instruction cards for some of the questioners and/or the panel, giving their roles and their various points of view.)

Quieting Activity

Narrate/sidecoach a paragraph about a large bag of tea being tossed into Boston Harbor. They are to become the bags of tea. They float for a few moments on top of the water and then slowly sink into the ocean, down, down, until they come to their final resting place on the floor of the ocean.

10 Story Dramatization: Circle Stories

The term *story dramatization* refers to the process of creating an informal play from a story, improvisationally and with the leader's guidance. Generally the procedure includes:

a. sharing a story or other piece of literature with a group of students,

b. planning the characters, scenes and events,

c. playing,

d. evaluating, and

e. replaying.

After much interchanging of roles and experimenting with ideas, the story/play can be "set" much like a rehearsed play.

The process, however, has been the improvisational method. No script is memorized. No one student is cast in or "owns" any one role. And the play is the result of the group's work, facilitated by the leader.

Within this general framework, there can still be many ways to dramatize any given story. We will take several approaches, giving you many lesson plan samples to select from, and eventually you will decide for yourself what methods you want to use.

SOME PRELIMINARY CONSIDERATIONS

SELECTING THE STORY

First, you will need to select a story of good, literary quality. (Many sample lessons are included to help you get started with an additional bibliography at the end of this chapter for those who are ready to make your own lesson plans.) The story should also be one that appeals to you as well as to the students.

There should be plenty of interesting *action* in the story that can be played without elaborate staging. The *dialogue* should be interesting, but not so difficult that the students become frustrated in their attempts to improvise from it.

The characters should be believable. There should also be enough characters (or the possibility of adding characters) so that a significant number of students, if not the entire class, can be involved in the playing.

PRESENTING THE STORY

You may wish to read the story or tell it in your own words. You will probably want to share picture books visually with the students. There may even be times when you will want to share filmed versions or audio recordings of a story.

Simple folk tales should be shared orally, if possible, since they were originally told rather than read or recorded. Besides, oral telling allows you to maintain eye contact with the audience, helping you judge how the students are reacting to it.

PRESENTING THE DIALOGUE

Presenting the dialogue in the story is important. Students listen closely to the dialogue and repeat much of it in their playing.

Sometimes it is helpful to add dialogue to a story that is too simply told. For example, a line might say, "The King told the Royal Cook to prepare a special feast." You can help the students visualize this scene if you say, for example, "The King said to the Royal Cook, 'Prepare a feast. I want only the best!'"

Simplify dialogue that is too complicated. Otherwise, students might be frustrated trying to remember it. Even if you encourage them to "tell it in your own words," they may feel compelled to recreate the original wording and experience failure in the attempt. For example, when I tell the story of *Bartholomew and the Oobleck*,

I omit the Magicians' lengthy, poetic chant and simply say, "While they mixed the oobleck, they said their magical chants."

CASTING THE STORY

Because you will be playing the story several times, and because you will want each playing to build on the previous one, it will be important to establish a solid beginning. The following suggestions should help.

a. Cast the most competent students for the first playing in order to establish an appropriate model for the rest of the class to build on. Shy or slower students can benefit from seeing the story enacted by others before they undertake it themselves.

b. Double and even triple casting (two or three students playing one character) will also be useful. It will allow more students to play the story and will provide the security needed for improvising freely. "What one can't think of to say, the other one usually can."

c. You may need to assist with the main role, particularly in first playings, even with some of the most competent students. This allows you to "walk the students through the a story," mapping out the playing areas as you go along. By using the technique of double and triple casting, you can easily "tag along," often unnoticed, and still be available to help as needed.

AIDS FOR ORGANIZATION

One of your main concerns with story dramatization will be, "How will I keep things organized?" It is a legitimate concern, but with some careful planning, many problems and difficulties can be alleviated.

Following are a number of organizational suggestions for you to consider. All of them have been utilized in the lesson plans included, so you need not be overwhelmed by them. In fact, they are designed to help you remember the storyline you are playing and to avoid having students all moving and talking at the same time. The techniques usually evolve quite logically as you work with the stories. In time, you will find the techniques that work best for you and for your students as well as for the stories that will become your particular favorites.

a. Organize space carefully. Usually you will want to have the major scenes take place in the middle of the playing circle or in front of the classroom. However, other areas of the room, such as the corners, will be useful for additional scenes. It is particularly helpful to place the scenes around the circle or the room, sequencing them in the same order that they appear in the story.

You will need to think this organization through ahead of time. Later, as you feel more comfortable, you will want to consult the students about their ideas on mapping out the scenes. Sometimes it is helpful to create specific locations using classroom furnishings. For example, your teacher's chair can become "the King's throne" or your desk might become "a banquet table."

b. Use the students desks/tables whenever possible. Often these can be "homes" for the citizens of the town, "stores" for shopkeepers, or horses for the King's army. Try also to keep at least some students at their desks until "their scene" is ready to be played. During these "sitting out" periods, you can refer to the students as the *audience* so they will not feel left out or neglected.

c. Look for the natural controls within the story. Often the characters take a nap or rest. Sometimes characters are in an immobile position due to enchantment or other reasons. Often characters "return to their homes," or desks. Capitalize upon these moments to give legitimate quiet periods.

d. Designate characters in some way so that you—and they—can remember who is playing which part. An easy method is to make simple nametags or use simple costuming with hats, props, and pieces of fabric. Since the latter will take more time, you may wish to add these after initial playings when you are sure the students are interested enough in the story to continue playing. Separating and grouping students in various parts of the classroom, as well as using the nametags and costumes, will help you (and them) see the layout of the story and remember the characters in groups.

ORGANIZATION THROUGH NARRATION AND CHARACTER ROLE (REVIEW)

Two additional techniques (both of which have been discussed in previous sections) will be indispensible to you in dramatizing a story. They are *narration* and *playing a character role*. Narration will help you guide the dramatization from outside the story. If you play a character role in the story, you can guide the playing from within. And, you can use both techniques interchangeably in the same story dramatization.

Ways to Guide Using Narration

1. Open the story.
"Once upon a time there was. . . ."

2. Guide the story if it lags or if the students forget the sequence of events.
"And then the traveler set off on his way again."

3. Control the action if problems arise.
   "Finally the townspeople decided to stop arguing with each other and returned to their homes."

4. Add pantomime ideas if the students need suggestions.
   "The weavers set up their imaginary looms with great care, making sure each part was adjusted to their satisfaction. They impressed everyone with their attention to detail as they busily squared the corners, tightened the bolts, tied the threads, and began weaving the imaginary cloth."

5. Provide transitions for scenes, indicating passage of time or change of environment.
   "The next day, the boy went out to the field to see if the magic beans had grown during the night."

6. Close the story.
   "And they rode out of town and never bothered the people again."

Ways to Guide by Playing a Character Role
What Role Do I Play?

a. You can play the main role, either by yourself or with perhaps one or two students. This technique can be useful with shy students or those who need considerable assistance. Even when students are experienced in story dramatization, you may be able to help revitalize a story by playing a character role yourself.

b. You may choose to play a secondary role, such as a king's prime minister or a friend to the central character. If these roles do not already exist in the story itself, they can usually be easily added.

c. You may step into a scene in a spontaneously invented role and assist if students have forgotten the sequence of events or to reactivate the students' involvement if the playing is becoming perfunctory.

What You Can Do in a Character Role

1. Carry the dialogue, initiating the interactions.
   "I believe I've lost my way. Can you give me directions to get to the nearest town?" Or, if playing a role with students, "We're trying to move this cart out of the way. Can you help us?"

2. Give directions and assistance in character to help the story along.
   "Well, I don't believe these people can help us at all. Over there's someone else who may be able to." "I don't know about you, but I'm awfully tired. I think I'll rest a bit by the side of the road here."

Leader can assist students in dialogue by playing a character role.

3. Control the action and discipline.

   "As the King's prime minister, I must remind you that you cannot go into the throne room until you are quiet. And you must bow to the King before you speak. Are you ready?"

4. Reactivate involvement, offering new situations for students to react to and new challenges for them to solve.

   "This letter just arrived, and it's addressed to you. I'm sure everyone here would like you to read it aloud."

   "As the Mayor of the town, I must insist that you explain your presence. If you don't give me a good reason for your being here, I shall have to ask you to leave."

Now, let us look at a very simple way to play easy stories.

SIMPLE STORY DRAMATIZATION WITH "CIRCLE STORIES"

Many simple stories can be dramatized very easily and quickly. For many groups this will be desirable, especially if the students are eager to see immediate progress in their efforts at making a play.

One useful technique I call "Circle Stories." With "Circle Stories," the focus is on the easiest and most orderly methods to involve all the students in a playing

The Magicians work long into the night, creating "oobleck," for King Derwin of Didd.

of the action or basic story line. This technique is more like organizing a game since little emphasis is given to characterization, emotion, and sensory awareness. (You will learn these other procedures in the next chapter.) The method is also useful for run-through playing in order to set a framework to build on in replayings.

With "circle stories" you visualize a story being dramatized in a circle. The circle may be seats in a circle, students sitting in a circle on a carpeted area, or a circle around the outer aisles of the room. Even the most active students understand and sense an orderliness about a circle and will usually be most cooperative. You and they will also quickly learn the procedure and will be able to adapt it yourselves to other stories.

Generally, stories that fit this method best have characters and an indefinite number of people in a group. For example, in some of the stories there are "villagers" or "people of the kingdom." The number of people is flexible and can accommodate an entire class.

Other stories that fit this method best have one or two main characters and a series of different characters who are met. The dialogue is simple and usually repetitive. Often these stories are called "cumulative." "Sody Sallyraytus" is a classic example of this type. Even the Dr. Seuss story *Bartholomew and the Oobleck* is similar in structure to the cumulative story, especially when Bartholomew goes off in search of a solution to the oobleck problem.

In playing "Circle Stories," you, with perhaps one or two other students, will play the main part initially. This gives you the opportunity to move the story along, to initiate dialogue, and to role model the playing. You will often alternate between being a narrator and playing your role. The rest of the children will sit in a circle and become the other characters when they appear in the story.

Following are lesson plans for several circle stories, with some added hints on playing them. Feel free to add your own touches and additions to the suggested instructions and to adapt the methods to similar and favorite stories of your own.

SAMPLE LESSON PLANS
FOR CIRCLE STORIES
Bartholomew and the Oobleck
Dr. Seuss. New York: Random House, 1949

Synopsis

King Derwin of Didd complains to his page boy, Bartholomew, that he is bored with the weather. The problem is turned over to the Magicians who suggest that ''oobleck'' would be a good solution, though they have never made it before. As the ''oobleck'' begins to fall the following morning, the King is delighted and declares a holiday. But the joyousness is shortlived when it is discovered that the oobleck is green, sticky, and falling in greater abundance hourly. Only the King's magic words, ''I'm sorry,'' stop the oobleck and restore sanity to the Kingdom once again.

1. Casting:

    a. Two students can play Bartholomew so more can have opportunity for this role. I use a boy and a girl to stress that many parts are interchangeable and not limited to one sex.

    b. Three to five students can play the Magicians, the Bell Ringer, the Trumpet Blower, and the Captain of the Guard.

    c. There can be a King and a Prime Minister or a King and Queen. You may also want to have guards stationed at the sides of the throne room. They can pretend to have crossed spears that they uncross whenever anyone enters or exits the throne room.

    d. The rest of the students can be divided into townspeople and people in the palace. The book's illustrations show various occupations in the kingdom and mention is made specifically of musicians, the laundress, and a cook in the palace. Students should be given specific jobs (or should choose occupations) that are appropriate to the time period. They will be acting out their routine tasks when they become stuck in the oobleck.

I find this story works with both younger and older students. Therefore, it is also included in *Creative Drama Resource Book K–3*. There are some modifications here to reflect the abilities of older students. But they should also have the opportunity to repeat at least one story they may have played before in order to see how much more they can add to it now that they are more mature.

2. *Action:*

a. Before starting the story, place the students around the room in the circular pattern. The throne room is at the front of the classroom. On the King's right (as he sits on his throne) are the Magicians in the corner as if "offstage." On the King's left are the three Bell Ringers. In the back corners of the room are the three Trumpet Blowers and the three Captains of the Guard. Seated at the back desks are the people of the kingdom and at the front desks are the people of the palace.

b. In the opening scene the King complains about how boring the weather is. You can narrate a brief opening like, "Once upon a time, in the Kingdom of Didd, there lived King Derwin who was always bored with the weather. One day he was overheard complaining about the weather to his pages."

c. If the King doesn't remember to call the Magicians, you (as Bartholomew) can suggest it. The pages can also legitimately escort them to the palace with the admonition to be sure to bow before speaking to the King. The dialogue here is simple enough, but if needed, you can tell the Magicians what it is the King wants. The Magicians can be escorted back to their workplace.

d. Here you can narrate how the Magicians work late into the night; if they need help thinking of actions to perform, you can sidecoach/narrate how they take down bottles from the shelves, pour and stir the different ingredients, whisper magic chants, and so forth. Narrate/sidecoach that everyone in the kingdom goes to sleep, including the King and Bartholomew. Finally, the Magicians, too, are finished with their task and go to sleep.

Trumpet blowers try to get the "oobleck" out of their instruments.

"I'll show you I'm not afraid," says the Captain of the Guard. (triplecasting of one character)

e. (Continue narrating) "The following morning, the King got up early and looked out the window and was delighted with what he saw. But Bartholomew woke up, looked out the window, and wasn't sure how to react. Small little green specks dotted the sky. It was the oobleck. Bartholomew went to the King to see how things were going." This should be enough narration to let the King and Bartholomew pick up their dialogue and for the King to declare the holiday, sending Bartholomew off to the Bell Ringers.

f. The Bell Ringers will not be able to ring the bell because of the oobleck, and now Bartholomew realizes that there is no cause for a holiday. Instead, he must warn the people of the Kingdom.

g. The two Bartholomew pages go to the Trumpet Blowers and then to the Captains of the Guard, Students usually remember what to do and say as the characters in **f** and **g.**

h. You may need to help by narrating, "The pages decided that they'd better return to the palace. But on their way they saw many people of the kingdom. Bartholomew stopped and talked briefly to each one in order to find out just how bad the situation was." Here the pages should talk to those students seated in the back desks.

i.   As the pages approach the front desks, you may need to narrate, "And as the pages approached the castle, they saw the people of the palace also stuck in oobleck. Again, they stopped to talk briefly.

j.   As the pages enter the throne room (front of classroom) they find that the guards, the King (and Prime Minister or Queen) will also be stuck. You can narrate these facts if you need to. Here there is an important exchange of dialogue. If the King has trouble remembering, you may need to narrate, "And, if you listened closely, you could hear the King say very softly, 'I'm sorry.'"

k.   Narrate an ending like, "And no one knows why, but as soon as those magic words were spoken, the oobleck began to melt, until it finally disappeared altogether. And then there was cause to celebrate. The bells rang, the trumpets blew, and the guards marched and everyone cheered ('Hip, hip, hooray!') in honor of the day the oobleck came *and left*." Lead the class in applause for themselves and return to seats.

3.   *Dialogue:*

a.   The King complains about the weather; calls for Magicians; declares a holiday; and says "I'm sorry."

b.   The Magicians usually have no trouble remembering to suggest oobleck and the fact that they have never made it before.

c.   The Bell Ringers, Trumpet Blowers, and Captains of the Guard usually have no trouble remembering their difficulties with the oobleck.

d.   The dialogue with the people of the Kingdom and the people in the palace need not be lengthy, but it is useful in establishing the extent of the problem oobleck has created for the entire kingdom. It also gives more importance to the additional character roles.

Additional Considerations

If the students feel comfortable with the plot of the story, you probably will not need to narrate at all. Sometimes in subsequent playings students have wanted to keep the narration in but ask to do it themselves. Encourage any show of independence and readiness to take over production aspects.

After the students become familiar with the story they may want to add a little more dialogue or a few more characters. Encourage this, too, as long as the plot of the story does not lose its focus. You can treat it as an "experiment," letting the students see for themselves which ideas work best. Even professional playwrights have to test out their ideas with actors on a stage, so this will give them an excellent opportunity to find out how it is really done.

"THE GOLDEN GOOSE"
The Brothers Grimm (3), (57)

Additional Sources:

"The Golden Goose," Andrew Lang in *The Red Fairy Book,* edited by Brian Anderson. New York Viking, 1978.

The Golden Goose, illustrated by Diane Paterson. Mahwah, N.J.: Troll Associates, 1981. See variation: "Taper Tom," Gudrun Thorne-Thomsen (40).

Synopsis

A man and wife who have three sons, treat the two older sons well. But, as is the case in many folktales, the youngest receives little attention and is considered a simpleton.* The oldest son goes off to cut wood, but refuses to share his fine lunch with a little old man he meets. When cutting the wood, he is injured (the old man's revenge) and has to return home. The same happens to the second son. The youngest, however, shares his meager lunch. As a reward for his generosity, the old man shows him where to find a goose of pure gold. The young man sets off with the goose under his arm, and everyone he meets tries to take a feather from it. But they all stick fast to the goose, creating a bizarre parade. When they pass the castle, the princess, who never smiles, bursts into laughter. And, as the King has promised her in marriage to anyone who can make her laugh, the young man wins a bride. (This is an appropriate ending although in some versions the king puts the man through other tasks.)

1. Casting:

a. If necessary for the first playing, you can be the young man with one other student. The story is easy enough to play that you may prefer just to cast a competent student as the young man from the very first playing.

b. Two students are needed for mother and father. Two are needed for the two older sons. All four can return at the end of the story to see the young son's success, cheering with him or being remorseful at their earlier treatment of him.

c. One person is needed for the old man, though this part can easily be doubled. The old man also return at the end of the story to see the results of his gift to the young man.

d. Four people are needed for the innkeeper and his three daughters.

e. The parson, sexton, and two laborers add four more to the parade.

f. The king and the princess are needed. You can add a queen and other courtiers as well.

g. The rest of the class can be additional people who add to the parade. Since they are all stuck together, a large number can be controlled. Encourage the students to think of additional people with definitive characters or identities.

---

*In most versions, the youngest is called "Dummling." It is better to give him a more respectful name, such as "Hans."

2. *Action:*

a. Before playing the story, place the students around the room in the circular pattern and in the order of their appearance in the story. (Or, they may be seated in a circle with the scenes being played in the middle.)

b. The young man's home can be at the front of the room.

c. You may want to pretend to "change scenes" (perhaps turn the lights off to signify the deep, dark woods) when the brothers go off into the forest and meet the little old man. If so, these scenes can also be played at the front of the room. Or, you can have the first brother's scene take place at the right side of the room, and the second brother's scene at the left side of the room. Each returns home, of course.

d. The young man's scene can be played at one of the back corners of the room, as if he had to travel farther into the forest. When he goes to the inn, he can go to the opposite back corner of the room.

e. As the young man leaves the inn with the innkeeper's daughters attached to the goose, he can lead them up and down the rows of the class where the other invented characters can add on. In addition to encouraging the children to consider who they are, they should also consider what they are doing when they see the strange parade.

f. The castle can be the front of the room, with the king and queen, princess, and optional courtiers. The parade passes by; the princess laughs; and the king gives her to the young man. Now the people can be unstuck from each other and the family and the little old man can appear to congratulate the young man and his bride.

3. *Dialogue:*

a. The dialogue scenes between the brothers and their parents can be brief. With replaying, additional dialogue can be invented.

b. The two brothers' dialogue with the little man is also easily done.

c. The young man's dialogue with the little old man is only a little more involved with the addition of the reward of the golden goose.

d. The scene at the inn can be a little more involved, giving attention to the three daughters.

e. As the parade goes by, the parson scolds the girls for chasing after the young man; the sexton reminds the parson of a christening; and two laborers try to help the people get unstuck.

f. For the invented characters who are added on, encourage students to make them definitive. In addition to the questions in 2e, students should also consider what dialogue they might add. What different greeting might each have or what suggestions might they have for getting the people unstuck?

g. The princess need only laugh; the people can become unstuck and express their relief; the king (and queen) can rush in delightfully and announce that the young man has won the hand of the princess.

h. A simple cheering scene, with everyone present, can end the story.

i. After students have played the story, they may begin adding a little more dialogue to each of the scenes. They might decide they want to have a first scene showing the king and queen in despair over their daughter's inability to laugh. A "meanwhile, in a small hut at the edge of the woods," introduction can open the next scene.

"The King's Tower"
Harold Courlander

From *Ride With the Sun*. New York: McGraw-Hill, 1955.*

Synopsis

A very foolish king desires to reach the moon and commands a carpenter to build a tower to reach the sky. The carpenter knows the task is impossible and has no idea how to satisfy the King. After a number of weeks with no results, the King tells the carpenter he has three days to complete the task or he will be executed. The carpenter says he has a plan, but asks to be the first to climb the tower. The King insists that he will be the one to have the honor. Everyone in the city is ordered to stack boxes and crates to build the tower. When the boxes and crates are all used up, trees must cut down to build more boxes. The King climbs to the top, only to discover that the tower is not quite tall enough. All he needs is one more box. But the carpenter says there are no more boxes; indeed, there are no more trees. The King's solution is to take one from the bottom. "But, your majesty . . ." He insists. Of course, the inevitable happens.

1. Casting

    a. Students usually want to play the King. If the role is double cast, it is best to invent an equally stupid counselor to the King so that both are "done in" by their own foolishness.

    b. As I tell the story, I add some wise persons who are called on to come up with a plan for getting to the moon and then cast perhaps five in this role. This is optional, but does give a few more people a specifically named role to play.

    c. Two people can be cast as the carpenter and you can become their assistant.

    d. Everyone else is a subject of the king at his/her desk or home. The seats or desks can be in a circle, or you may use your usual classroom arrangement.

2. Action

    a. After the initial dialogue scenes, the carpenters (with some assistance from you) can organize the people of the city. First,

*This Latin American folk tale is also found in *Folk Tales of Latin America*, edited by Shirlee P. Newman. Indianapolis, IN: Bobbs-Merrill, 1962.

there is the collecting of the "boxes." The three carpenters can go around to the "homes" (desks of other students), gathering up boxes and stacking them in the center of the circle or in front of the classroom. (I usually model this first by knocking on a student's desk top, as if it is a door to a house, having a brief conversation with the occupant, and then asking for any contributions. The other carpenters and I then go quickly around to everyone, collecting and stacking boxes.)

b. Next, the people are asked to cut down all the trees in their "yard" (desk area) and to construct all manner of boxes and crates.

c. Then they need to go out to the countryside to cut more trees. (For this action they can move a couple feet from their desks to signify going a distance from home.)

d. When all the boxes are made and stacked and there are no more trees, it is time to have the King and Counselor test the tower. You might allow them to stand on a piano bench or a sturdy table for this scene. Of course all the people are on hand to see the big event, so all students are still part of the story even though the majority remain at their seats.

e. The King's fall must be in slow motion along with the crowd's reaction. (You count slowly to 5.) You may wish to call "Freeze" just before any final "collapse," the way many films and television shows frequently do. For me, it is the most effective, and safest, ending to such a story. If students wish to carry action further, they will need to decide whether the ending is catastrophic (everyone gets killed or injured) or whether they wish to have a comic ending (the only thing hurt is the king's dignity and pride.)

3. Dialogue

a. You may want to open with a brief narration: "Once upon a time there was a foolish King who wanted to go to the moon. One day he discussed it with his equally foolish counselor." Pause for any possible dialogue the students may want to try out. They may decide to call in the five wise advisors. If not, you can narrate, "Finally they decided to ask five wise advisors for their opinions."

b. You can briefly play a guard or other role to escort the advisors in and out of the throne room. In replayings, a student will probably want to play this role now that you have introduced it.

c. After the advisors leave, you can narrate that carpenters are called in and ordered to do the task. This scene is played briefly.

d. With the carpenters you can discuss how you do not know what to do. Eventually narrate that the King and his counselor come to check on your progress and then play this brief scene quickly.

e. After the King and counselor leave to return to the palace, you and the carpenters hit upon your plan of building the tower.

f. As you prepare to go around to the people's homes, you can announce these commands as if you are a messenger from the King ("Hear ye, hear ye, the King wishes to go to the moon. The royal carpenters are building a tower and all citizens are commanded to cooperate . . .") Or, you may narrate the actions.

g. When it is time to test the tower, you can narrate: "At last the day arrived when all the boxes had been gathered and all the trees had been cut and the tower was completed. For such an occasion, the entire kingdom was on hand. The King and counselor arrived in splendor." Now you help with the simple interaction between the carpenters and the King and counselor. Eventually they will ask for the box from the bottom. Your attempts to talk the King and Counselor out of their decision will fail. And the final fall will end the story.

Optional: In subsequent playings, you may wish to add a small parade (with music) before the King and Counselor climb the tower. Students may have ideas for other festivities (jugglers, acrobats, food concessions, souvenir sales, and so forth) to make the day a real event. Everyone should stop to watch the climb, however.

The Legend of the Bluebonnet
Tomie dePaola. New York: G. P. Putnam's Sons, 1983
Synopsis

Years ago, a Comanche Indian tribe was in the midst of a famine. In spite of their prayers to the Great Spirits, the land remained parched. A shaman goes to speak to the Spirits and is told that, because the people have been selfish and taken the Earth's gifts without giving anything back, they must sacrifice. A burnt offering of a most valued possession must be made to the Spirits and the ashes strewn about. No one comes forth with a sacrifice except a little orphan girl who has a beloved warrior doll, the only possession left from her family. She sacrifices the doll in the fire and scatters the ashes. The next morning she awakens to find that the ground is covered with beautiful blue flowers, a sign of forgiveness from the Great Spirits. The little girl's name is changed from She-Who-Is-Alone to One-Who-Dearly-Loved-Her-People. And in the land now known as Texas, the bluebonnet blooms each spring as a remembrance of the unselfish sacrifice of a little girl.

1. Casting

   a. For me, the story is most effectively played with one student as the little girl.

   b. One student should play the shaman, one the runer-messenger, and three or four can be the Great Spirits. (dePaola explains that the Comanches revered many spirits.)

   c. (Optional) Four students can play the spirits or shadows of the little girl's parents and grandparents. A simple dance movement, perhaps with pieces of gray gauze covering their bodies, can be an effective addition to the story.

   d. The rest of the students play the dancers and the people of the tribe. Two (or more) may be designated as those who indicate their unwillingness to sacrifice, if dialogue is being encouraged.

   e. You, or a student who is an excellent reader, will need to narrate. The reading should be slow and stately.

2. Action

   a. Place the dancers/tribe in a circle. Their seats are their "tee-pees." The front of the classroom can be used for the little girl's scenes and can also be the place where the Great Spirits reside.

 b. The narrator reads the story as it is written, including dialogue.

 c. A dance can be done in a circle at the opening. This can be done simply and with a muffled drum beat. This fades out (dancers/tribe sit with heads bowed) as the scene focuses on the little girl. She mimes her speech with her doll as the narrator reads it.

 d. A brief pause can allow some time for the shadows of the parents and grandparents to enter briefly and depart.

 e. As the shaman tells (mimes) the message from the Great Spirits, the tribe looks to the shaman to indicate that they have gathered in a circle. The Great Spirits can mime their explanation as the shaman "tells" it. The tribe can mime (or dance) their song of thanks.

 f. The little girl's scene of sacrifice can be narrated and mimed. Here the Great Spirits could watch and indicate their forgiveness.

 g. A final simple dance could enfold the little girl into the center of the circle, perhaps led by the shaman, as the narrator ends the story.

3. *Dialogue*

 a. Dialogue is unnecessary for this story as described above unless students wish to add it. If so, you may also wish to add a brief scene of the shaman visiting the Great Spirits.

 b. You may choose to have different voices reading the dialogue. For example, one voice might be used for the tribe's opening speech, another voice for the little girl's dialogue, and another for the shaman.

Optional Additions: Research into costumes, masks, dance, music, and poetry of the Comanche could enrich the background of this story and provide ideas for enhancing the drama.

"SODY SALLYRAYTUS"*
Richard Chase

From *Grandfather Tales*. Boston, MA: Houghton-Mifflin   Company, 1948.

Synopsis:

An old woman wants to make biscuits but has no "sody sallyraytus" or "baking soda." She sends the little boy to the store. On his way home a bear under a bridge "swallers" him up. The same happens with all the other family members. The pet squirrel finally goes off to find them, and when he meets the bear, he scurries up a tree. The bear follows, falls, splits wide open and everyone comes out.

Variations:

"The Cat and the Parrot," Sara Cone Bryant (3)(35). A greedy cat eats a parrot and everyone else in sight before he meets his match.

Fat Cat, by Jack Kent (New York: Parents, 1971). This is a modern illustrated version of "The Cat and the Parrot" with the same plot but different characters.

The Greedy Fat Old Man, Paul Goldone (New York: Clarion, 1983). Called an American tale, a fat old man replaces the cat in "The Cat and the Parrot" and the bear in "Sody Sallyraytus" and different characters are eaten.

The Terrible Tiger, Jack Prelutsky (New York: Macmillan, 1970). In this rhymed tale and illustrated picturebook, a tiger eats a grocer, a baker, a farmer, and a tailor.

1. Casting

    a. The old woman and the old man and squirrel are best played by one person each. The boy and girl could each be double-cast. The storekeeper could have a wife or an assistant.

    b. Several students together can play the bear and encircle, holding hands, the family members when they are eaten.

    c. It is interesting to have students play the bridge and react to what it sees happening, as if it were a person.

    d. Additional characters could be people in the store, playing

*This is an Appalachian story similar to "The Cat and the Parrot" circle story in *Creative Drama Resource Book for Kindergarten Through Grade 3,* the companion volume to this text. The timing and the dry humor in this story make it a more sophisticated version, one that older students can handle better than younger. It would be particularly interesting for older students to share this with younger grades who are familiar with "The Cat and the Parrot." They will recognize the similar plot and should find it entertaining.

checkers, whittling, or some other activities to pass the time of day.

2. Action

a. The story can be played in a circle with the house on one side and the store on the other.

b. The bridge and the bear can be in the center of the circle. For variety, the characters can alternate their path to the store by sometimes going around the circle one way and sometimes the other. On the return trip, they come through the center of the circle.

c. The bridge and the bear should remain low to the floor until the people arrive. As they rise, it is as if they suddenly loom into sight. The swallowed people must follow the bear's actions.

d. The squirrel will need to pantomime climbing up in the tree, or perhaps it can look as if he is climbing the side of the bridge.

3. Dialogue

a. The dialogue is repetitive, with the bear's threats and cumulative listing of all the people it has eaten. One person can speak this, or all the people as the bear can speak the lines together.

b. The people who go off to buy the sody can chant, as the little boy does, "Sody, sody, sody sallyraytus!"

c. The storekeeper tells all who inquire that someone has been there before them.

d. The squirrel "squarked a time or two," the story says, so it should be fun to have a little gibberish conversation with the store-keeper.

e. When they all step out of the bear at the end, the old woman asks where the sody is and the boy hands it to her saying, "Here."

f. It is fun to add a little dialogue in some of the scenes, but take care to keep the simplicity of the story.

Optional:

For sharing the story with an audience, you might want to use a large piece of lightweight cloth over the bear.

It might also be helpful to play the story a few times as a narrative pantomime so you can follow the wonderful speech and rhythm of the story. You might even want to keep a narrator in your final version, telling parts of the story in between the dialogue.

"The Wise Old Woman"
adapted by Yoshiko Uchida (36)

Synopsis

In this Japanese folktale, a cruel lord banishes anyone over seventy-one from his village. But a young farmer disobeys and hides his mother. In time, the village is threatened by another cruel lord who wants to conquer the village. He will spare the people if certain riddles can be solved. The wisdom of the old woman solves each riddle, and eventually the son reveals her existence. The repentant ruler reverses his decree, now realizing that the elderly deserve respect and honor.

1. Casting

a. A student plays the ruler. To double cast, his or her associate may be added.

b. Another student plays the young farmer. If double cast, you may want to add a wife.

c. The wise old woman may be double cast with a husband and become "wise parents" in the telling of the story.

d. The second cruel lord (Lord Higa) may have perhaps three guards or soldiers accompany him.

e. Several (three to five) wise counselors are needed for the first lord.

f. The rest of the students are the villagers. They should think of at least a general character for themselves: what is their age, their occupation, their personality?

2. Action

a. The two lords can have their respective palaces on either side of the front of the classroom. The farmer's house may be closer to the "audience," so that the secretive nature of their actions can be enhanced. The trip to the mountain may go around one side of the classroom to the mountain at the back and the return trip on the opposite side. Villagers may sit in a semi-circle to indicate they are at their homes or farms and at work. When they are called by the lord, they may come closer to the front of the classroom, but still in their semi-circle positioning.

b. The opening sentence may be narrated with the addition: "One day he called all the people of the village together to make an announcement." If the lord forgets to call the villagers together or to dismiss them, you may simply narrate this.

c. Narration again picks up after the opening scene and moves quickly to the focus on the farmer and his mother. The action will be tighter if the old woman is already seventy-one years old, the age for banishment and the farmer is forced to carry out the law on the same day it is given. You can narrate the walk to the mountain and back, as well as the digging of the hiding place under the kitchen floor.

d. Narration can also introduce Lord Higa with his soldiers and set a scene in the first lord's castle where Lord Higa announces his takeover unless the riddle can be solved.

e. The first lord calls his wise counselors, then posts a notice for the villagers.

f. Encourage the villagers to think of their characters' role or work and what actions they might be pantomiming as they are called to hear the lord's announcement.

g. The action returns to the young farmer and his mother (parents) who solves the riddle. The farmer rushes to the first lord to tell him.

h. The action in c, d, and e repeats two more times.

i. In the final scene the lord finds out about the mother. I like to change the ending to have the lord ask to see the mother and then make his announcement to the village of his change of heart.

j. If needed, a few words of narration can end the drama.

3. *Dialogue*

a. The dialogue is usually easy for students to remember since they are impressed with the riddles and their solutions.

b. The first lord must be intimidating to the villagers, while Lord Higa intimidates the first lord and everyone else. Note that Lord Higa is also impressed at the end with the wisdom of the people and is convinced that they should be allowed to live in peace. The student playing this part will probably wish to make this statement at the end.

c. The mother and son dialogue of caring is also impressive to students and usually easily remembered. Having four students in these scenes may be helpful to the dialogue, too. The riddles are repeated in the mother/son scenes.

d. The villagers really do more responding and commenting to each other than speaking aloud with specific dialogue. Their part is important, however, as it enhances the dramatic impact of an entire village being under domination. In replayings, you may want to encourage students to consider their particular characters and what comments they might make that would fit their characters. Then specify certain ones to speak a sentence or two aloud for an audience to hear.

CIRCLE STORY AS PART
OF LONGER LESSON PLAN

There may be times when you will want to make a circle story part of a more extended lesson plan. Two lesson plans of popular folktales are presented here for your use, "The Bremen Town Musicians" and *Stone Soup*. (Note: Each of these stories is also included in the next chapter using the "Segmented Story" method so you can compare the two methods. "The Bremen Town Musicians 2" begins on p. 192 and *Stone Soup 2* begins on p. 210.

Bremen Town Musicians 1

Sources:

The Bremen Town Musicians, Ilse Plume. Garden City, N.Y.: Doubleday, 1980. This is a Caldecott honor book, but the pictures are small.

The Bremen Town Musicians, Paul Galdone. New York: McGraw-Hill, 1968. Students will like the pictures of the robbers, burly and with missing teeth.

The Traveling Musicians, Hans Fischer. New York: Harcourt Brace & Co., 1955. The pictures are rather whimsical, but large enough to show to the class.

"Jack and the Robbers," Richard C. Chase in *Jack Tales*. Boston: Houghton-Mifflin, 1943. This is an Appalachian version.

Synopsis:

Four farm animals, a donkey, dog, cat, and rooster, whose masters consider them too old to be kept anymore, join forces to go to Bremen and become traveling musicians. On the way, they stumble on a house that has been taken over by robbers. They frighten the robbers away and take the house for themselves. The robbers return to fight for the house, but are frightened once again. The animals are now secure and live to a ripe old age.

Introduction

Discuss aging and some of the stereotyped views people hold of older people. "When is a person too old to work any more? Is the age the same for all people? How are the elderly treated in different countries or cultures?"

Warmup

"What can happen to our bodies as they age? How might people walk or move differently because of age?" (Encourage realistic discussion rather than allowing students to go to extremes in portraying age.) You might also tie this discussion in with health information about nutrition, bone density, arthritis, or other ailments which have an effect on aging, too.

Have students pretend to do different tasks at their desks first as a very young person and then as an older person. How might they read a book as a young person (who may not even know how to read yet) and an older person (who might need glasses or even a magnifying glass)? How might they stand up and sit back down again as a very young and as an older person? You can try other activities at the side of the desk like jogging. With each beat of a drum, they can pretend to age 10 more years.

Presenting the Story

Tell or read your favorite version of the story.

Playing a Circle Story

1. Casting

    a.   Four animals are needed. They may be double cast, but this is not recommended if your students are overly active or tend to get out of control easily. Caution them that they are not to touch the two robbers who return to the house.

    b.   Four masters, one for each of the animals, can also be cast. If you like, in later playings you can cast two family members for the owners of each animal and expand upon those scenes.

    c.   Four or five robbers will probably be as many as you can manage. You may wish to number them 1, 2, and so on, and instruct them that they are to run out of the house in the scare scene as you call their numbers. Designate which robbers (double cast) should be the ones to return to the house. Place chairs for robbers at front of classroom.

    d.   The rest of the class become the trees in the forest. Several can form the house (4 to mark the corners), including door (1 student) and window (2 students). Much can be made of these parts if you and the students use your imagination. The trees, for example, can bend and wave their branches ominously, frightening the animals as they journey through the woods. (No touching of animals is allowed.) The door can creak open, and so forth.

    e.   Because the characters are so distinct in this story, it is best for you to narrate rather than trying to play one role throughout. Be prepared to step in as another animal or another robber, if students seem to need assistance.

2. *Action*

a.   Play the story in a circle around the classroom. Place the four animals and their masters in the four corners. (Everyone else is seated.) Narrate a couple of opening lines to begin the donkey's scene with his master. Narrate to open the dog's scene: "While the donkey was being thrown out of his house, nearby a dog was experiencing the same treatment."

b.   After each animal is thrown out, go back to the donkey and narrate him down the road to meet the dog, the cat, and finally the rooster.

c.   Now the animals make their way through the woods (up and down the aisles of the classroom where the remaining students are the trees.) While this is happening, the house is formed by students in front of the classroom, and the robbers take their place in the house. Narrate: "And now the animals see a light through the woods. It's the robbers' house, but they don't know it. They move closer. They see the robbers eating a big meal and counting their money. They suddenly think of a plan to take over the house." (Pause here for the animals to organize themselves for the scare scene.)

d.   If you have numbered the robbers, be ready to call out the numbers so they can run back to their seats in orderly fashion. Pause to let the robbers make a few comments to each other.

e.   Narrate: "The animals took over the house and ate the meal the robbers left. Then they went to bed—the donkey on some straw in the yard, the dog on a mat behind the door, the cat by the fireplace, and the rooster on top of the house. (You might allow the rooster to stand on a chair.) But two of the robbers, who were bolder than the others, decided to return to the house. They looked through the window and saw that everything was still. They went carefully through the door. Then they saw the cat's eyes glowing in the dark. They thought the eyes were live coals and tried to light a candle from them. But the cat sprang at them and hissed and scratched them. They ran to the door, but the dog bit them. They ran out into the yard where the donkey kicked them. And the rooster, who had been awakened by the noise, crowed loudly."

f.   "But the robbers ran back to the other robbers and had quite a different story to tell." (Pause and let the robbers talk.)

g.   (Narrate ending) "And so the robbers never dared to return to the house. And the animals decided to stay there. And, if I'm not mistaken, they're living there to this day."

Evaluation

If time permits, they will probably want to repeat the playing and switch parts. Check for trouble spots. See if they have other ideas for the students playing the house and the trees.

Replaying

Consider doublecasting the animals for a second playing, even if you did not do it on the first playing. Now that they have seen the story, they may be able to handle eight animals instead of four.

Quieting Activity

A good narrative pantomime poem to use is "Sunning," by James Tippett (4)(33). It is about an old dog sleeping on a porch in the sun.

Stone Soup 1

Source

Stone Soup, Marcia Brown. New York: Scribner's, 1947, 1975.

Synopsis

Three war-weary soldiers, tired and hungry, come upon a village where they hope to find food. The villagers, fearful of strangers, hide the food they have and pretend they have nothing to give. The soldiers then suggest soup by boiling stones. The villagers are intrigued enough to "add a few more ingredients for just a bit more flavor." Eventually, of course, a real soup is created, though the villagers still think the stones have made all the difference.

Introduction

Option A.   Discuss army occupation in war or peace time. Discuss necessity in some countries and some periods of time to house and feed soldiers; hence, a possible explanation for the reluctance of the villagers in the story to feed the three soldiers who come to the town asking for food.

Option B.   Discuss the concept of "making something out of nothing." What examples can the students think of? Expand to the concept of "recycling" or finding new uses for previously useless materials.

Warmup

Option A.   You might wish to narrate/sidecoach an experience of soldiers' basic training. You might even play the part of the drill instructor or the sergeant. You can begin with morning reveille, dressing, making bed, morning exercises, eating in mess hall, doing particular chores and duties (even k.p.!), and end with a chance to sit down before the noon meal.

Option B.   Try out some pantomimes of eating various foods that are eaten in distinctive ways: corn on the cob, slice of watermelon, spaghetti, cotton candy, ice cream cone, and so forth. Challenge them to make it as real as possible. (You might even want to show students the famous scene from Charlie Chaplin's film *The Gold Rush*. In it the starving Charlie cooks a shoe and eats it with such care and relish (shoelaces are spaghetti, the sole is a steak, the nails are like small fishbones) you are convinced it must be delicious.)

Presenting the Story

Tell or read your favorite version of the story.

Playing a Circle Story

1. Casting

a. Three soldiers may be cast. You may play one of the three or become a fourth.

b. Cast the priest, barber, and mayor.

c. The rest of the students may be cast as various family groups around the circle. Designate which ones will be visited by the soldiers and which ones are responsible for bringing which foods to the soup kettle when they are called for. Also, what job (pantomime) will each family do to get the feast table ready? (This may be listed on a chalkboard for reference.)

2. Action

a. Narrate a couple of opening lines to introduce the three soldiers who can walk around the circle once and then enter the town (circle). Soldiers may want to talk here. If not, go on.

b. Narrate that the soldiers look about the town but the villagers, upon seeing them, hide their food.

c. Soldiers visit designated homes.

d. After the soldiers are denied food but allowed to make stone soup, the pot (you might use a wastebasket) is brought to the center of town and a fire started under it. The villagers bring the additional food for the stone soup as the soldiers ask for it. They interact with the soldiers, but can be seated again after they have made their contribution.

d. When the soup is finished, you can narrate what each family does to help set up the feast table. It is easiest just to move the soup kettle aside and pretend the table is circular so the family groups can do their tasks near their seats. When everyone sits down to eat, they are each at their desks. (One family's task might be to bring extra chairs for the soldiers.)

e. After the feasting, the singing and dancing can take place in the circle formation. The number of dancers may need to be limited. A simple dance such as a polka may be taught beforehand.

f. The soldiers ask to sleep over and each goes to a different house. This may be narrated.

g. In the morning, after the townspeople have thanked them, the soldiers can leave, walking around the outside of the circle once more. You can narrate a couple of closing sentences from the book.

3. *Dialogue:*

a. By playing one of the soldiers, you can help the interaction of of meeting the townspeople. The list on the board can help soldiers taking turns asking for various foods to add to the soup.

b. A folk song may be incorporated into the feasting scene.

c. You may wish to designate someone as spokesperson for the town, perhaps the mayor, who can, on behalf of the villagers, thank the soldiers at the end.

Evaluation

If time permits, they will probably want to repeat the playing and switch parts. Have a brief discussion of what worked the best. Check for trouble spots.

Replaying

Most students will probably want to be the soldiers, but as the playing evolves, they may also see equally interesting characters developing in the villagers as well. Encourage this individuality of personality in the replayings in order to keep the story growing and taking more interesting shape.

Quieting Activity

All students return to their seats. They may be the flickering flames of the fire under the soup kettle, slowly dying out after the big feast. Or they may be the villagers, going to sleep after a delicious feast. Or, they may be the soldiers, sleeping out under the stars at night, with full bellies for the first time in days and happy memories of people who became friendly after they thought they got something for nothing.

11 Story Dramatization: Segmented Stories

In the last chapter you learned about story dramatization with "circle stories." In this chapter, another method (I call them "segmented stories") is used.

For segmented stories, a story or even a book, becomes a stimulus for creating numerous separate (or segmented) drama activities. Both pantomime and verbal activities are considered. Each of these categories is then divided into solo and group activities. All the various kinds of activities in the sample lesson plans provided will be familiar to you, since they have already been explained in the preceding chapters.

Once you have created your list of activities, you simply select ones which would be most meaningful for your group to try out. Since there are far more activities than you would play in one session, you can pick and choose, as from a menu. Each story will thus give you several lesson possibilities, should you care to try all the activities.

You can begin the lesson with some solo activities, both pantomime and verbal, at the desk. For pantomime solo activities, the students all play simultaneously. For verbal solos, call on as many volunteers as you wish. If there are more volunteers than you have time for, you can pair the students and let them share their ideas with each other.

Then you can move to the group pantomimes and finally to the group dialogue scenes. For these, divide the class into small groups. You may wish to assign one activity to each group, though students will probably want to play them all eventually. In the pair and group verbal activities you will want to let students rehearse a bit and then share the scenes as in the method described on page 133. Some classes will eventually want to try their hand at playing these scenes spontaneously, without rehearsing. To end the lesson, you can return to one of the desk activities for a quieting activity.

Notice that many of the activities extend beyond the original storyline and may introduce new characters or new situations. Often students get so interested in the uniqueness of these activities that they do not even consider "putting the story together." The exploration into the various aspects of the story is often satisfying by itself.

But, it is also true that you have really rehearsed the story in bits and pieces after playing the various activities. So, then it is very easy to select the ones you and the students like best, arrange them chronologically as they appear in the original story, and use them as a basis for creating your own improvised play from beginning to end. Either way you choose, you are bound to have much fun!

Bremen Town Musicians 2

Sources

The Bremen Town Musicians, Ilse Plume. Garden City, N.Y.: Doubleday, 1980. This is a Caldecott honor book, but the pictures are small.

The Bremen Town Musicians, Paul Galdone. New York: Mc-Graw-Hill, 1968. Students will like the pictures of the robbers, burly and with missing teeth.

The Traveling Musicians, Hans Fischer. New York: Harcourt Brace & Co, 1955. The pictures are rather whimsical, but large enough to show to the class.

"Jack and the Robbers" Richard C. Chase in *Jack Tales.* Boston: Houghton-Mifflin, 1943. This is an Appalachian version.

Pantomime (solo at desks)

1. "Let's pretend you're the robber who got chased out of the house by the animals. You were frightened by 1. cat's eyes shining in the dark and the cat spitting and scratching you, 2. the dog biting, 3. donkey kicking, and 4. the rooster crowing. I'll count to 4 slowly and you react to each experience." ("1, the cat . . . 2, the dog," and so on.)

2. "You are the donkey whose master wants to get rid of you because you can't do the work you used to do. Think about three things you can still do that make you a useful animal. As I count to three, be the donkey doing these three things."

3. Do the above with the other animals: dog, cat, and rooster.

4. "You are a sneaky robber. I'll give you some tasks to do, and let's see how sneaky you can be. First, count your money and hide it. Now you're eating a meal, but you know someone is watching you. Now try to take a little nap, knowing that other person is still watching your every move."

5. "Give a big yawn the way the cat would and then slowly curl up into a big ball in front of a warm, cozy fireplace and go to sleep." (This can also serve as a quieting activity at the end.)

Verbal (solo at desks)

1. "You're one of the animals in the story. Make the sound of the animal you want to be (so we'll know who you are), and then tell us why you're leaving home."

2. "You're the robber who got chased out of the house by the animals. You run back to the other robbers excitedly and tell us

what happened, even though you're so scared you can hardly talk.''

3. ''You're one of the animals looking in the house the robbers are in. Tell us what you see inside, and we'll try to guess which animal you are by the sound of your voice.''

4. ''Suppose a police officer investigates the incident at the house the following morning. As one of the animals, you tell the story so it appears that you are the hero.''

5. ''You are the anchorperson on the local late-night television news. You are reporting on the story of the animals who captured the bank robbers. How will you present your story?''

Pantomime in Pairs and Groups

1. Groups of five. ''Create a frozen picture of the robbers, showing how tough and mean they look. Now create a second picture, showing how they looked after they were all frightened by the 'monster.' ''

2. In pairs. ''One of you is a mouse that can easily get away from the cat. It's a game to you, so you laugh and tease her. Cat, you will try to catch the mouse; but you become frustrated and finally stop. Then mouse, you realize it's no fun anymore; and you stop also. There will be no touching. I will count slowly to ten while you do this.'' (Perhaps only three or four pairs should do this, so you can check their self control.)

3. Count Freeze pantomime (see p. 100) of the animals. ''We'll guess which animal you are.''

4. Groups of five. ''You're the robbers. Create a pantomime story, showing where you got your money from and how you found the hideout in the woods.'' (See ''Creating Stories'' in Chapter 9).

5. Groups of five. ''Four of you are the animals in the house. The one robber returns and you each frighten him as in the story. Line up so the robber can pass by you one at a time. I'll count to four to indicate when you interact with the next animal. Absolutely no touching allowed. You must create the illusion of attack.'' (Use one or two trustworthy groups to model this before allowing entire class to try it.)

6. Groups of four. ''Pretend you are the animals who have been travelling all day and are very tired. Let's see how tired you are first. Then on my signal (light switch or bell) you can rest and take a nap.''

7. Groups of four. ''The animals wanted to become musicians. Decide which animal you want to be and what instrument you want to play. As I play the music, you pretend to be your animal, playing your instrument. Keep in time to the music.'' (March music played by a small band will probably work best.)

8. Groups of four (or add extras). "The Bremen Town Musicians have become a famous group and have just released their latest T.V. video for a number called _____. "(You can select an appropriate title from records you or the students have. Classic Beatles' songs like "It's Been a Hard Day's Night," or "When I'm Sixty-Four" are suggested.) "In your group, create an appropriate video for the song. Then, as the music plays in the background, act it out for us."

Verbal in Pairs and Groups

1. In pairs. "One of you is the owner of the rooster, talking with your cook about how to make soup of him. Let us hear you making your plans in the kitchen."

2. In pairs. "One of you is the farmer who owns the donkey and wants to get rid of him. Your partner is a family member who wants to keep him. Give your reasons."

3. "In groups of four, everyone be one of the animals. Find a way to create the 'monster' you all were when you decided to scare the robbers away. First create a frozen picture. Then, as I walk by each group and give you the signal from the sound arrow, you may make your sound all together."

4. In groups of four. "You are the animals talking over your plans to scare the robbers and take over the house. You will have to talk quietly so the robbers don't hear you, but you'll need to make sure the rest of us (audience) can hear at least some of your plans. When I walk by your group, you can let us overhear your ideas."

5. "The Bremen Town Musicians have become so famous they now have souvenirs to sell. Six of you (panel in front of class) are the promoters of these souvenirs; the rest of the class will be an audience of various people interested in knowing more about your line of goods."

6. "Because you are rich and famous, you are able to hire your owner to work for you! With a partner, decide which animal you want to be and enact the scene of you having the owner wait on you and do other chores. The owner/servant will probably not be happy, but enjoys getting the good pay, so grudgingly continues to work for you."

"The Doughnuts"

Robert McCloskey
From *Homer Price*
New York: Viking Press, 1943

Synopsis

Homer's Uncle Ulysses, who is fond of labor-saving devices, one day purchases a doughnut machine for his lunchroom. When young Homer is left in charge, a rich woman customer offers to make doughnut batter for the machine. But after a number of doughnuts are made, Homer cannot get the machine to stop and the lunchroom is soon "flooded" with doughnuts. The woman returns, looking for her lost bracelet that dropped in the batter. A reward is offered to anyone who can find the bracelet in one of the doughnuts, a marketing technique that luckily gets rid of all the doughnut surplus.

Pantomime (solo at desks)

1. "Roll into the shape of a ball of dough. As I count to ten, expand into a big doughnut. Be light and fluffy."

2. "You are the lady from the big, shiny black car, mixing up a batch of doughnuts. As I play the music, you put in all the ingredients, carefully measuring and mixing each one." (Sidecoach some of the ingredients.)

3. "You are Homer trying to stop the doughnut machine. Think of three things he would do to try to make it stop. As I count to three, you act out your three ideas, becoming more frustrated with each unsuccessful try. At the end, sit down exhausted."

4. "You are one of the townspeople having doughnuts and milk, trying to find the lost diamond bracelet. You need to eat quickly, but also carefully."

5. "You are Rupert, the young man who discovers the diamond bracelet. Let's see what happens as you eat doughnuts and suddenly make your find." (Count to five).

Verbal (solo at desks)

1. "You are Uncle Ulysses. Tell about one of the other labor saving device you have in your lunchroom, explaining how it works, where you got it, how much it cost, why you think you needed it."

2. "You're the rich lady who made the doughnuts. I understand it was a special recipe, handed down in your family. Please tell us the recipe."

3. "You're Mr. Gabby, the man with the sandwich board advertising. What is your sales pitch to get the folks to come and buy the doughnuts?"

4. "You're a townsperson who's trying to win the $100 reward for finding the bracelet. Who are you and what would you do with the money?"

Pantomime in Pairs and Groups

1. "In groups of eight, create the doughnut machine." (Show picture from text for those who want to see it.) "Decide which parts you will be and then become the machine. The machine will begin operating when I play the music. Unlike the one in the book, this one stops when the music ends."

2. "In groups of five, create a frozen picture of the townspeople watching the doughnut machine outside the lunchroom window. You're all pressed against the window trying to get a close look. Be sure we see one pane of glass."

3. "In groups of five, pose for a picture for the local newspaper. Decide which characters from the story you want to be and we'll try to guess who you are."

Verbal in Pairs and Groups

1. "In pairs be Aunt Agnes and Uncle Ulysses. She wants to get rid of all the labor saving devices, and he tries to convince her they're necessary."

2. "In pairs be the Sheriff and Uncle Ulysses. You discuss how nothing exciting ever happens in Centerburg. End the scene after Homer calls to tell you about the doughnut machine."

3. "In groups of five, you are townspeople gathered for some purpose. Decide who you are and what you're meeting about. I'll tell you the news about the doughnut machine, and after I 'leave,' you gossip about the incident."

4. "Be a salesperson trying to sell Uncle Ulysses a new labor saving device. Explain what it is and how it works. Why does Uncle Ulysses need it? It's the day after the doughnut incident, and Uncle Ulysses is having second thoughts about investing in any more machines."

Duffy and the Devil

Harve and Margot Zemach.
New York: Farrar, Straus and Giroux, 1973

Synopsis

A young woman, Duffy, is fired from her job for laziness. She claims to be a fine knitter and spinner, so Squire Lovel of Trove hires her. When the housekeeper, Jone, tells Duffy to spin and knit, Duffy exclaims that the devil can do it. The devil does, and Squire Lovel is so pleased with what he thinks is Duffy's work that he marries her. But the devil has made a bargain that Duffy will belong to him if she cannot guess his name. Old Jone helps the remorseful Duffy learn that the Devil's name is Tarroway, and all ends happily. (Note: In the 1800's, players (mummers) in Cornwall, England went from door to door at Christmas time performing this story as a play.)

Pantomime (solo at desks)

1. "Duffy doesn't know anything about spinning or how a spinning wheel works. Pretend you're Duffy trying to figure out this contraption."

2. "Be Old Jone carrying the heavy keg up the cellar steps. I'll count to ten for each of the ten steps. I'm sure the keg gets heavier as Old Jone gets near the top, so I'll slow the counting down toward the end. You may set the keg down carefully at the top step, and you, too, can sit down."

3. "Squire Lovel has to squeeze through a 'fuggy-hole' that leads to the underground cavern. It was probably a tight squeeze, and he must have gotten pretty dirty. On the count of ten, do this the way you think the Squire would have done it."

4. "When Duffy guessed the devil's name, he became very upset. Let's see how he looks expressing his rage in slow motion. Now in fast motion." (Count to 10 for each).

5. "Squire Lovel was out on the moors when his clothes suddenly vanished. It was very cold and the wind was piercing. Be the Squire in this situation and then think of three ways he might have solved his problem in order to get back home safely. I'll play some music and as I call out numbers 1, 2, and 3, you act out your solution to your problem. Let's do this in fast motion, since it's so cold and you probably don't want anyone to see you."

6. "Old Jone has poor eyesight, yet she still does the cooking and cleaning for the Squire. Let's see her at work while the music plays."

7. "Let's see how the devil can spin and knit with fast flying fingers. As I play the music at fast speed, you spin and knit an entire wardrobe for the Squire." (You can use "Spinning Song.")

Verbal (solo at desks)

1. "One day, with tears in her eyes, Duffy tells Old Jone the story of her spinning and how the devil has helped her. Be Duffy tearfully explaining what happened. I'll pretend to be Jone listening to you."
2. "Be Squire Lovel after being chased home by the witches. You're out of breath and exhausted. Tell Duffy what you saw and heard tonight."
3. "You're the devil singing your song. (Have words on the chalkboard or a chart.) Make up a tune to go with the words."

Pantomime in Pairs and Groups

1. Groups of five. "While Duffy tried to figure out how to spin, the spinning wheel fell apart and parts rolled on the floor. Create the spinning wheel and fall apart on my signal in slow motion."
2. "Build a Place" (see Chapter 7) "Create the cavern. Then add some of the people and animals and play the game. 'One at a Time' " (see Chapter 4).
3. "In groups of five, create the fire in the cavern. Be the fire burning and glowing. Fade away and then flare up again. Follow the rhythm and intensity of the music." (Try Moussorgsky's "Night on Bald Mountain." It might be fun to add red, orange, or yellow scarves or crepe paper streamers.)
4. "In pairs, show how Squire Lovel and Duffy looked as they jogged off on the squire's horse. Remember Duffy sits 'ladylike' behind him. You'll have to imagine the horse."
5. "After Duffy became Lady Duffy Lovel of Trove and wore satin gowns, laces, and red-heeled shoes from France, she danced on the green with other ladies of the community. As I play the music, in threes, dance the way you think Duffy and her friends might have out in the field."
6. "Create a frozen picture of the witches in the cavern, each riding on something different." (Groups of five to eight.)
7. "Jone played the fiddle while the devil and the witches danced faster and faster around the fire. In groups of seven, make a circle of five witches with the devil in the center and Jone off at the side playing the fiddle. As I play the music, you create this scene." (Play "Danse Macabre" by Saint Saëns and switch to

fast speed halfway through. Students move only when music is playing.

8. "Build a Place" (See Chapter 7). "Create a room in the Squire's castle."

Verbal in Pairs and Groups

1. "Create a frozen picture of Squire Lovel with his new stockings on outside the church, with the members of the community admiring them. On my signal, while still frozen, let's hear some of the comments the people might have made."

2. "Duffy was chased out of her first place of employment. The old woman with the broom declared that Duffy was lazy. Duffy insisted that she did superior work and wasn't appreciated. Let's hear the argument between the two." (Leader may play Squire Lovel entering the scene and asking questions.)

3. "In pairs, one be the devil and one be Duffy. The devil is making his bargain with Duffy, convincing her, while Duffy isn't so sure she should go ahead. What does the devil say to convince her and what are Duffy's initial arguments against the plan?"

4. "When Duffy was introduced to Old Jone, they talked and got acquainted. The book doesn't tell what they talked about. In pairs act out the getting acquainted scene as you think it might have taken place."

5. "After Squire Lovel told Duffy the devil's secret name, she laughed and made the Squire laugh. Then they both laughed until they couldn't laugh any more. In pairs, act out this scene." (They can also try this silently and in slow motion.)

The Emperor's New Clothes

Hans Christian Andersen

Sources

The Emperor's New Clothes, Erik Blegvad, translator and illustrator. New York: Doubleday and Co., 1974. Small ink drawings, alternating black and white pictures with full color ones.

    The Emperor's New Clothes, illustrated by Monika Laimgruber. Reading, Massachusetts: Addison-Wesley, 1973. This book received the *New York Times* Choice of Best Illustrated Children's Book of the Year.

    The Emperor's New Clothes, Jack and Irene Delano. New York: Random House, 1971. The Delanos explain that this is a folktale that did not originate with Andersen. Their illustrations present a Puerto Rican setting.

Synopsis

A vain emperor, who is particularly fond of his wardrobe, is visited by two rogues posing as weavers. They claim to be able to weave fabric invisible to those unworthy of the office they hold. Of course, everyone pretends to see the imaginary fabric in order not to lose their jobs. A parade is held to show off the Emperor's new clothes, but only when a small child innocently calls out, "But the King has nothing on!" do the people finally realize the swindle and their own gullibility.

Pantomime (solo at desks)

1. "You are the Emperor who loves clothes and you are posing for your latest portrait. How will you pose to show off all the new garments you're wearing?"

2. "You are the Emperor, proudly walking in the procession, listening to all the appreciative comments of the admiring crowd. Then you hear the voice of the child saying you have no clothes on. You freeze. How will you look? I'll play processional music. After you've paraded a few moments (in place), I'll say the child's line and stop the music. That will be your cue to freeze."

3. "The rogues wove their cloth at night by candlelight. Be one of the candles slowly melting and then burning out as daybreak approaches." (This may serve as a quieting activity.)

4. "Suppose that when the Emperor doesn't get his way, he throws

a temper tantrum. Demonstrate one of his temper tantrums—
silently and in slow motion as I count to 10.''

5. ''The Emperor returns to his palace after the procession. Think
of how he must feel, and then think of three things he might do.
As I count to three, pantomime each of your three ideas.'' (You
can also do this as a Count Freeze Pantomime, see p. 100.)

Verbal (solo at desks)

1. ''Suppose the Emperor has a young son or daughter. What
Christmas or birthday present are you getting for your dad this
year. How do you know he'll like it?''

2. ''Suppose you're the Emperor's mother or father. How did your
son get so interested in clothes? Has he always been like this?''

3. ''You're the parade marshall who is planning the procession. Who
will be in it, what will be the parade route, and what will be the
order of people in the procession?''

4. ''You are one of the rogues, giving your description of the fabric
you have woven. You might include comments on the lovely patterns, the careful attention to detail, the unusual color combinations, and so forth. Give us your sales pitch.''

Pantomime for Pairs and Groups

1. ''You are the two swindlers setting up your loom. You're un-
packing it and setting it up carefully for this special job. The court
is watching you, so look professional.''

2. ''In groups of eight-ten, create and become the special loom on
which the marvelous fabric is to be woven.''

3. ''You are the swindlers putting on a good show of how diligently
and carefully you work at weaving, cutting out and sewing these
garments. As the music plays, put on your best performance.''

4. ''You are the rogues when you are certain that no one is watching you work. What will you do to pass the time and to entertain
yourself, locked up in the workroom?''

5. (Groups of six.) ''The Emperor is being dressed for the great
procession by the two rogues. Mirror this activity.''

6. ''In groups of ten, create a frozen picture of the procession. Decide who each of you is and we'll see if the rest of us can guess.''

7. ''The band is rehearsing for the procession. A conductor leads
as you each play a different instrument. Use groups of six: one
conductor and five band members.'' (March music like Elgar's
''Pomp and Circumstance'' might be used.)

Verbal in Pairs and Groups

1. Groups of three. "The Emperor has learned his lesson about listening to clothes swindlers. But today new swindlers come to town. What will they try to sell to the Emperor? Will it have unusual qualities as the special cloth did? Remember that the Emperor may be harder to convince than last time."

2. Groups of three. "You are the old Minister visiting the rogues. When you can't see the material you make up excuses. What are they? You'd like to leave but the rogues keep showing you more things for you to admire. How will you finally get away from them?"

3. Pairs. "You are an official who is to visit the weavers and see how the work is coming along. You don't trust them and you don't really believe their story, but you don't want to say so to the Emperor. What else will you use as your excuse to him to get out of going on this mission."

4. "Suppose you are the emperor's wife (or brother) who is given a meager supply of funds for clothing. You'd like a new outfit and you're trying to get money from the Minister of Finance who claims no more money is available. Show him your pitiful wardrobe as evidence that you need a bigger clothes allowance. What other arguments can you give to make your case?"

5. "You are the citizens of the kingdom where the Emperor spends huge sums on clothing. There are a number of community projects that need tending to. You go as a committee to the Emperor to present your case on behalf of the kingdom. The Emperor and his advisors reluctantly decide to fund one of the projects. Let's play the scene and find out how the Emperor decides which project will be funded."

6. Groups of three. "The rogues have received an order of knighthood to wear in their buttonholes and the title of "Gentlemen Weavers." Now that they have left the kingdom, they would like to sell this prize. They bargain with a used goods merchant for the best price they can get for this medal."

7. Pairs. "The Emperor has spent the entire kindgom's treasury on clothes for himself. Now he must go to the bank for a loan. He must try to convince the bank president that he will be a good credit risk. The bank president is a shrewd operator."

8. Groups of five. "The kingdom's garment workers are exhausted from trying to keep up with all the new clothes orders the Emperor demands. We hear them complaining as they work. The scene ends when they decide to go on strike."

9. "You are a clothing designer who has just designed a new outfit for the Emperor to wear. It is the most unusual design the Emperor has ever seen. Convince the Emperor to order this outfit

from you, even though the Emperor is not sure it's suited to him.''

10. ''The Emperor holds a press conference some time after the incident with the rogues. Reporters still have questions about what happened, but they must be diplomatic in asking them so as not to embarass or anger the Emperor. The Emperor may enlist the aid of his Minister or other officials in answering the questions.'' Set up as a Character Panel Discussion, p. 134.

Johnny Tremain

Esther Forbes. Boston:
Houghton Mifflin Company, 1943

Synopsis

Johnny, a gifted apprentice to a silversmith in Boston in 1773, has a superior attitude with his peers. When a crucible of molten silver breaks and Johnny's hand is crippled from the severe burns, his future as a silversmith seems virtually ended. After a series of unfortunate events, Johnny becomes a dispatch rider for a political newspaper and comes in contact with John Hancock, John and Samuel Adams, and other Boston patriots. Johnny becomes involved in the Boston Tea Party and the Battle of Lexington and makes friends with a doctor who is sure he will be able to restore Johnny's hand to usefulness again.

Pantomime (solo at desks)

1. "You're Johnny doing your work in the silversmith shop. What tasks do you do and how do you do them? (arrogantly, determinedly) Select three tasks and as I count to three, do each task. Now you're Johnny after burning your hand and you are doing ordinary household tasks. What will the tasks be and how will you do them?" (bitterly, restlessly) Count again to three.

2. "You're Cilla at work in the Lapham household or Lavinia Lyte in her home. Choose three things to do that will show a difference in their station in life in the 1700's." Count or play music.

3. "Be Johnny practicing chopping wood in the backyard with your injured hand in order to be prepared to chop open the tea chests for the Boston Tea Party. How frustrated he must have been!"

4. "Be Johnny disguising himself in Pumpkin's uniform to look like a British soldier in order to slip through enemy territory to find Dr. Warren and Rab."

Verbal (solo at desks)

1. "You are Dove. Why did you give Johnny the cracked crucible to use? What were you thinking at the time? How do you feel about it now that Johnny's hand is crippled?"

2. "Mrs. Lapham says Isannah is "hardly worth the bother" she is to raise. You're Mrs. Lapham. Would you explain what you mean by that?"

3. "You're John Hancock. Why did you give silver money to Johnny

when you wouldn't hire him? What are your impressions of this boy?''

4. ''You're Merchant Lyte. Why don't you believe Johnny's story about being a relative of yours? Isn't it possible that this story could be true?''

5. ''You're Rab. Tell us your view of Mr. Lyte, particularly his political leanings.''

6. ''You're Mrs. Lapham. Lavinia Light has just asked to take Isannah to raise. What answer will you give and why?''

7. ''You're Dove, after being given ale and brandy, telling Rab and Johnny some of the secrets of the British that you know about. Remember, also, how grateful you are for their friendship when others have treated you unkindly. Let us overhear a little of what you tell Rab and Johnny.''

8. ''Rab never really tells Johnny how he feels about him. Suppose he had written a letter to Johnny, sealed it, and asked that it be opened in the event of his death. Now that he is gone, the letter is discovered. Johnny asks Cilla (or Dr. Warren) to read it. You're Cilla or Dr. Warren. Begin reading the letter. Another Cilla or Dr. Warren will pick up where you leave off.''

Pantomime in Pairs and Groups

1. ''Do a Count Freeze (p. 100) of various occupations held by residents of Boston in the second half of the 1700's.'' (Consider cooper, printer, gunsmith, shipwright, weaver, butcher, clock maker, and so forth.)

2. Create a frozen picture of such scenes as:

   Johnny being burned by the hot silver

   Courtroom scene when Johnny is accused of stealing Mr. Lye's silver cup

   Any of the secret meetings of the Boston Observers or other groups

   Boston Tea Party when Dove is caught stealing tea

   Uncle Lorne hiding in the feather bed while British soldiers search

3. Create, as a group narrative pantomime, the courtroom scene from Chapter IV, Section 5. Major characters are: Mr. Justice Dana, Johnny, Mr. Quincy (Johnny's lawyer), Mr. Lyte, Lavinia Lyte, Sewall, Rab, Cilla, Isannah. The bakeress can be included, as well as other people appearing before the Justice. For the lines of dialogue, other students might read the voices. Once the actions are gone through, dialogue may be added. (See Activity 4 in the next section).

4. Build a Place (p. 105) ''Create Mr. Lapham's silversmith shop.

You may expand to other kinds of occupations and shops mentioned in the book.''

5. Build a Place. ''Create a room (or larger area) of Mr. Lyte's house, recalling the descriptions given.''

Verbal in Pairs and Groups

1. ''In pairs, pretend one person is Johnny and one person is Dove. Try to get information about the British from your partner in the same manipulative ways that Johnny does from Dove. See if the rest of us can figure out exactly what information you're trying to discover.''

2. Divide the class into two groups: Whigs and Tories. Teacher moderates the discussion. Alternate comments from each side. Whigs try to convince Tories to join them in their stand against England on the matter of taxation. Tories explain their loyalties and chide the Whigs. (*Note*: You may wish to have students choose to be certain characters in the story. They identify themselves before they speak.)

3. A number of interesting vocabulary words appear in the novel, some that are now seldom used. After locating and defining the words, do a session of round-robin storytelling (see p. 124), using them. As students become familiar with usage, place words on cards. Students draw the words they are to use in the storytelling. (Consider: crucible, cheeky, knave, tankard, indenture, Sabbath-breaking, yokel, brackish, indenture, atrophy, and so forth.)

4. After playing the Courtroom Scene in Chapter 4, Section 5 as a group pantomime (See Activity 3 in the above section), try enacting the scene adding dialogue, expanding on the indirect dialogue given.

5. ''In pairs, be Dr. Warren and the old midwife, Gran' Hopper, having a difference of opinion on how Johnny's hand should have been treated.''

Many Moons

James Thurber. New York: Harcourt, Brace, Jovanovich, 1971

Synopsis:

Princess Lenore is ill from eating too many raspberry tarts but can be cured, she says, if she can have the moon. The King, who is determined to get it for her, consults all the wise men of the Kingdom, but they have no answer. Only the court jester is able to find the solution. When he asks the princess to tell him about the moon, she says it is gold and as big as her thumbnail. So a small, golden globe on a chain is made for her to wear around her neck, and she is perfectly satisfied. Even when she sees the moon again in the sky, she happily explains that when she loses a tooth, another grows in its place.

Pantomime (solo at desks)

1. "You are the little Princess who has just eaten too many raspberry tarts. Demonstrate how you feel as you get into bed and pull the covers up."
2. "You are the Royal Wizard doing three of your magic tricks. As I count slowly to three you will do the following: squeeze blood out of a turnip; produce doves from nowhere; and top it off with a cloak of invisibility which you will put on to demonstrate that it works."
3. "Demonstrate one of the King's rages—silently and in slow motion."
4. "Be the Royal Goldsmith making the little gold moon for the Princess. Be very careful to make it just a little smaller than her thumbnail. Now put it on a delicate golden chain."

Verbal (solo at desks)

1. "You are the Queen. Tell us how you feel about all the things the King has the Wizard and the Lord High Chamberlain find for him. The palace must be pretty cluttered. I'm particularly curious about the blue poodles. The King doesn't even remember getting those!"
2. "You are the Court Jester. Why did you become a jester? Do you enjoy it? What makes you so wise and able to solve problems the so-called wise men cannot solve?"

3. "Decide whether you want to be the Royal Wizard, the Lord High Chamberlain, or the Royal Mathematician. Tell us some of the things you've done for the King. You may read from your prepared list."

4. "You are the Princess, who is growing weaker by the minute waiting for someone to bring the moon to her. Tell us about the moon, if it wouldn't tire you too much, the way you described it to the Court Jester."

Pantomime in Pairs and Groups

1. "In groups of four, create the moon rising slowly in the sky, getting larger, then getting tangled in the branches of the tree, and finally freeing itself. At your highest point in the sky, wink back at the Jester."

2. Groups of six. "Let's see a royal portrait of the King, the Royal Physician, the Royal Wizard, the Lord High Chamberlain, the Royal Magician, and the Court Jester. Be sure we can tell who's who."

3. Build a Place (see Chapter 7). "Suppose the king has a storage room for all the things his wise men have brought to him over the years. Create that room so we can see some of those very unusual objects."

4. "In groups of eight, create the fireworks the Royal Mathematician suggested having in order to hide the moon from the Princess. Decide what kind of fireworks you will be (fountain, waterfall, and so forth)."

5. Do in threes. "You are two page boys who must look after the King's robe (it has a very long train) and make sure it is always in place. But the King is so distressed today that he keeps moving about, pacing, going into rages, and so on. As I play some music, the King will go through a part of his day while the two page boys try to keep the robe properly adjusted."

Verbal in Pairs and Groups

1. "All the wise men are worried they may lose their jobs if they can't do what the King wants. They are discussing their fears together, and each one tries to help the other think of other kinds of employment. Alas, they don't seem to be suited for any of the suggestions."

2. Groups of five. "Various groups of servants about the palace and the gardens are discussing the problems. They all have their own ideas and suggestions to make as well as complaining about the money the King spends on things he doesn't really need. Decide

what kind of servants you want to be, where you are, what you are doing, and let us listen in on some of your discussion and argument.''

3. ''Suppose other people are called or invited in to give advice to the King. Decide who you are and come into the throne room to offer your ideas. The King and Queen and the Wise Men will be there waiting for you. You may wish to have someone accompany you. The King has been warned by the Queen not to fly into a rage when visitors are present, so you needn't be afraid of him. Remember, though, to be very polite and on your best behavior or you will be sent away immediately. The King might even decide to give you a reward for your efforts.''

*Stone Soup 2**

**Marcia Brown. New York:
Scribner's, 1947, 1975**

Synopsis

Three war-weary soldiers, tired and hungry, come upon a village where they hope to find food. The villagers, fearful of strangers, hide the food they have and pretend they have nothing to give. The soldiers then suggest making soup by boiling stones. The villagers are intrigued enough to "add a few more ingredients for just a bit more flavor." Eventually, of course, a real soup is created, though the villagers still think the stones have made all the difference.

Pantomime (solo at desks)

1. "You're one of the peasants in the village. Think of three places to hide your food from the soldiers. By the way you handle it, we should be able to tell what the food is and where you're hiding it. I'll count a slow three."

2. "The peasants looked as hungry as they could to convince the soldiers they didn't even have enough food for themselves. Show how you would look, trying to convince someone you hadn't had much to eat and were hungry yourself."

3. "You're in charge of stirring the pot of soup. It's a very large one, the spoon is taller than you, and the fire under the pot is getting very hot. Besides that, more ingredients are being added every few minutes, so the soup is getting thicker and heavier. Show how you would stir at the beginning through to the end when you're more than ready to quit. I'll count to 10."

4. "The story says the peasants eyes "grew round" as they watched the stones being dropped into the pot. How can you make your eyes "grow round" and your face show the amazement the peasants felt?"

5. "The peasants brought food for the stone soup. Pretend to bring three different foods to the pot. What will they be? How will you get them, carry them, and prepare them for the soup? I'll count to three slowly."

6. "After the feast everyone sang and danced. Think of three different people you might be and how they might look as they dance. I'll play music and count to three. Let's see those three different people."

*Compare this method of playing *Stone Soup* with the method on page 187.

Verbal (solo at desks)

1. "You're the mayor of the town. On behalf of the village, make a small speech of thanks to the three soldiers."

2. "You're one of the soldiers. Where have you been in your travels and what have you been doing so that you've had nothing to eat in the last two days? Try to get me to feel sorry for you."

3. "After the feast, the villagers were more than willing to let the soldiers spend the night in their homes. Pretend you're someone who would like to have one of the soldiers stay in your home. There are so many offers, you'll have to make your home sound better than the rest in order to entice a soldier to stay. What will you say?"

Pantomime for Pairs and Groups

1. Build a Place (see p. 105). "Create the peasant village in the story. What kind of buildings will there be? Is there a small courtyard or village square in the middle?"

2. Count Freeze Pantomime (see p. 100). "Act out the occupations of some of the people of the village for the rest of the class to guess."

3. "In pairs, two soldiers mirror each others putting on a soldier's uniform of the historical period in Marcia Brown's illustrations. Add any other gear that you think these soldiers might have had."

4. "In threes, be the soldiers as if posed for a picture. First, pose as you might look at the beginning of the story, tired and hungry, then as you might look at the end of the story."

5. "In groups of five, plan how your group would get things ready for the feast described in the story. Remember to get the additional food ready, set up tables, light the torches, and so forth. As I count to ten slowly, you pantomime how your group would get the feast organized."

6. "It took many buckets of water to fill the pot. Make a bucket brigade from the town well to the pot and keep the buckets coming faster and faster. Be careful not to drop anything. Keep in time to the music and move only when the music plays." (Play music and switch to faster speeds.)

Verbal for Pairs and Groups

1. "In groups of six, create the scene where the soldiers go to the home of a villager and ask for food. You will be refused, but what

will the family's excuses be? What reasons might you give to persuade the family?''

2. ''After the feast, the people sang far into the night. In your group, think of a song that the peasants might have sung, and then let's hear you sing some of the song.''

3. ''Suppose the three soldiers go to another town and play a new trick on the people there. What might they try to do this time? Work out your ideas and share them in a short skit.'' (Groups of 5–8).

4. ''News of the stone soup has spread far and wide. Suppose a king hears of the story and calls in the three soldiers for an interview. What questions will he and other people of the palace ask and how will the soldiers answer them in a believable way?'' (Set up like ''Panel of Experts'' p. 127.)

Tales of a Fourth Grade Nothing

Judy Blume. New York: E. P. Dutton, 1972

Synopsis

Peter Hatcher, a fourth grader, feels much put upon by his two-year old brother. So much attention is paid to baby brother, (Farley Drexel) Fudge, that Peter sometimes wonders if he really belongs to the family. The final straw is when Fudge eats Peter's pet turtle, Dribble. After a stay in the hospital, during which time the turtle is expelled, Fudge returns home. Peter is given a dog for being a "good sport" about everything.

Pantomime (solo at desks)

1. "Fudge has temper tantrums when he gets mad. Show silently, and in slow motion, a temper tantrum. You will become exhausted and then fall asleep, the way Fudge does, sucking four fingers on your left hand. I'll count to ten slowly."

2. "For Peter's birthday, he receives a surprise present. It's an imaginary box on the desk in front of you. Open it and find out what it is. I'll probably know what it is by the way you handle it."

3. "You're Fudge doing three naughty things while the Yarbys are visiting. I'll count to three while you act out three naughty things."

Verbal (solo at desks)

1. "You're Mr. or Mrs. Hatcher or Peter. Tell us how your little brother Fudge got his name."

2. "Peter's mother wants to get a wind-up fire truck with real siren for Fudge for Christmas. You're Peter and you don't think this is a good gift for your brother. What are your reasons?"

3. "You're Peter and you're beginning to think that you don't really belong to the Hatcher family. What are your reasons?"

4. "You're Mr. Hatcher. Mr. Yarby has just taken away his advertising account from you because of Fudge's actions when they were visiting. How do you feel about this?"

Pantomime in Pairs and Groups

1. Count Freeze (see Chapter 7) of the games played at Peter's birthday party.

2. Build a Place (see Chapter 7). "Create an aquarium, the size it would be if you were a fish (or other creature) living in it. What different things would be in it—plants, figurines, and so on?"

3. "Fudge does only the things Peter shows him how to do. Play the mirror game with Peter teaching Fudge how to do different tasks—tying a shoelace, eating certain foods, brushing teeth, or whatever else you think Fudge should know."

4. "Create a frozen picture of something that happened during the weekend Peter, Fudge, and Mr. Hatcher spent together." (See Chapter 7.)

Verbal in Pairs and Groups

1. "Peter has just brought home the turtle he has won at school. But his mother isn't very happy about having a pet in the apartment. In pairs, be Peter and his mother having a difference of opinion about turtles as pets."

2. "There is a scene in the shoe store. In pairs, there will be a shopper and a salesperson. The customer only likes the shoes that don't fit. The salesperson keeps trying to find a pair that the customer likes that do fit. Let's see some of that scene."

3. "In pairs, you're Mrs. Hatcher trying to get Fudge to eat at dinner. Let us hear how this scene might sound."

4. Experts' Panel of five child psychologists. The rest of the class are any of the characters from the book who have a question to ask about child rearing, including appropriate punishments.

5. Groups of five. "Peter's father is in advertising and one of his clients is Juicy-O. Create a television commercial for Juicy-O."

STORY BIBLIOGRAPHY

The following stories are arranged in alphabetical order according to title. Suggested grade levels are in the left-hand margin. Numbers in parentheses refer to numbered anthologies in the bibliography at the end of this text.

5–6 "Aladdin and the Wonderful Lamp," (4) (35). This well-known tale from one of the greatest collections of short stories in existence, *Arabian Nights,* recounts the adventures of an idle tailor's boy who becomes a sultan. Finding himself the possessor of an oil lamp and a genie who grants his every wish, Aladdin gains great wealth and status amid magic and intrigue.

4–5 "Anansi and the Fish Country," Philip Sherlock. (2) Anansi tries to trick fish by pretending to be a doctor.

4–5 "Anansi Plays Dead," Harold Courlander and Albert Kofi Prempeh. (22) Anansi pretends to die so that he will not have to be prosecuted for a crime. But the villagers trick him into revealing himself.

5–6 "The Case of the Sensational Scent," Robert McCloskey. (78) Robbers, a suitcase with $2,000, a skunk, and after-shave lotion create an unusual adventure for Homer Price.

5–6 *The Clown of God.* Thomas Anthony dePaola. New York: Harcourt Brace Jovanovich, 1978. A once-famous juggler gives his final performance before the statue of Mary and the Child. For mature groups.

4 *The Cuckoo's Reward*, Daisy Kouzel and Earl Thollander. Garden City, N.Y.: Doubleday, 1977. A cuckoo helps save the grain from fire in this Mexican folktale.

6 *The Devil's Bridge*, Charles Scribner, Jr. New York: Charles Scribner's, 1978. The Devil promises a French town that he will build them a bridge for the price of a human soul.

5–6 *Everyone Knows What a Dragon Looks Like*, Jay Williams. New York: Four Winds Press, 1976. Only the road sweeper believes the old man who claims to be a dragon and offers to save the city from the Wild Horsemen of the North. For the boy's sake, the dragon comes to the rescue. This has a Chinese setting and demonstrates that things are not always what they seem.

4 *The Fence*, Jan Balet. New York: Delacorte, 1969. A poor family in Mexico is taken to court by a rich family because the former sniffed the delicious aromas from the kitchen of the rich family's house.

5–6 *Finzel the Farsighted*, Paul Fleishman. New York: E. P. Dutton, 1983. Finzel is a fortune teller who can see into the future with great accuracy. But he is nearsighted in dealing with the present. Nevertheless, he cleverly outwits a thief who robs him.

6 *The Golem: A Jewish Legend*, Beverly McDermott. Philadelphia: J. B. Lippincott, 1976. A rabbi in Prague creates a clay figure to help suppress an uprising against the Jewish community.

4–6 *Granny and the Desperadoes*, Peggy Parish. New York: Macmillan, 1970. Granny captures some desperadoes and turns them over to the sheriff, but not before she gets them to do chores for her.

5–6 *Harald and the Giant Knight,* Donald Carrick. New York: Clarion, 1982. A group of knights decide to use Harald's father's farm to train. Father cannot plant and will not have food or money to pay his rent to the Baron. Harald, who once admired the knights, now has the idea of how to scare knights away by weaving a huge reed knight. This has a medieval setting.

4 *Horton Hatches the Egg*, Dr. Seuss. New York: Random House, 1940. Horton the elephant hatches an egg for lazy Maizie.

4 "How Jahdu Took Care of Trouble," Virginia Hamilton. (50) Jahdu tricks Trouble and frees everyone from the huge barrel they have been caught in.

5–6 "How Pa Learned to Grow Hot Peppers," Ellis Credle. (57) Pa is too easygoing to be able to raise peppers with zip in them, so the family has to find a way to get him fired up.

4–5 "How the Animals Got Their Fur Coats," Hilda Mary Hooke. (48) All the animals get lovely new coats except Moose, who gets the leftovers. Charming characters appear in this Canadian Indian legend.

4–5 "How the Birds Got Their Colors," Hilda Mary Hooke. (48) This is a delightfully funny tale of how all the birds get colorful feathers except the Sapsucker. It is a Canadian Indian legend.

4 "How the Little Owl's Name Was Changed," Charles E. Gillham. (5) Brave Little Owl takes fire away from evil men in this Alaskan Eskimo folktale.

4 *How the Sun Made a Promise and Kept It*. Margery Bernstein. New York: Charles Scribner's, 1974. In this retelling of a Canadian myth, the sun is captured and the animals attempt to free it.

4–5 *Jim and the Beanstalk*, Raymond Briggs. Reading, MA: Addison-Wesley, 1970. In this new version of an old tale, the Giant wants eyeglasses, false teeth, and a red wig.

6 *Joco and the Fishbone*, William Wiesner. New York: Viking, 1966. Joco the Hunchback chokes on a fishbone and everyone tries to get rid of the body. Joco eventually coughs up the bone. A retelling of a tale from *The Arabian Nights*. Compare with "Old Dry Frye" in this bibliography.

4–6 *Kassim's Shoes*, Harold Berson. New York: Crown Publishers, 1977. Kassim finally agrees to throw out his old shoes, but then has trouble getting rid of them because everyone keeps returning them.

4–5 *The King's Stilts*, Dr. Seuss. New York: Random House, 1939. When the King's stilts are stolen by the evil Lord Droon, he becomes too depressed to protect the kingdom from its main enemy: large birds called Nizzards. Eric, the pageboy, comes to the rescue.

6 "The Legend of the Moor's Legacy," Washington Irving. (40) A humble water carrier inherits a secret passport to a cave of riches.

4 *The Magician Who Lost His Magic*, David McKee. New York: Abelard-Schuman, 1970. Melric loses his magic because he misused it by helping people do things they should do for themselves. He gets the magic back just in time to save the day for the King.

6 *The Nightingale*, Eva Le Gallienne, trans. New York: Harper & Row, Pub., 1965. This is the Hans Christian Andersen tale of the Emperor of China who orders the nightingale to stay in court and sing his beau-

tiful song. When he receives a gift of a mechanical bird that sings very well, the nightingale is banished. The nightingale returns to save the depressed Emperor from Death's grasp. The beauty of nature is extolled.

4–6 *Of Cobblers and Kings*, Aure Sheldon. New York: Parents', 1978. Because of his common sense, a cobbler rises from one important position to another until he becomes Grand Chancellor. Then he notices that the people of the kingdom have no shoes.

6 "Old Dry Frye," Richard Chase. (20) An old preacher accidentally dies and everyone tries to get rid of the body, afraid they will be accused of his murder. This Appalachian folk tale is derived from one that goes back to *The Arabian Nights*. Compare with *Joco and the Fishbone* in this bibliography.

4–6 "Old One Eye," Richard Chase. (20) An old lady unwittingly frightens robbers who plan to steal her money. It is fun to add a general store scene in the beginning where the robbers hear about the old lady's riches. It is an Appalachian tale.
(*Note*: Excellent music for these two tales are on an album by Richard Chase entitled "Instrumental Music of the Southern Appalachians." Tradition Records, TLP 1007.)

4–5 *Once Upon a Dinkelshühl*, Patricia Lee Gauch. New York: Putnam's, 1977. In a retelling of a medieval German legend, the city's gate keeper's daughter and her friends confront the invading soldiers and save the town from being plundered and burned.

Pairs of sixth graders practice moving the dead body in the Grandfather Tale "Old Dry Frye."

6 *Petronella*, Jay Williams. New York: Parents', 1973. A princess rescues a prince in this turnabout tale.

4–6 *The Pied Piper of Hamelin*, Tony Ross. New York: Lothrop, Lee & Shepard, 1977. This is Robert Browning's poem of the piper who rids the town of rats but who gets his revenge when the town refuses to pay.

5–6 "A Portrait Which Suited Everyone and Pleased No One," M. A. Jagendorf. (40) Tyll Ulenspiegel is commissioned to paint the court portrait, but each member wants a flattering picture of himself. This is one of the many tales about this legendary German prankster.

4–6 *Princess Rosetta and the Popcorn Man*, retold by Ellin Greene. New York: Lothrop, Lee & Shepard, 1971. When the Princess Rosetta of Romalia is stolen by a neighboring kingdom, only the popcorn man's solution works.

5–6 *Punch and the Magic Fish*, Emanuele Luzzati. New York: Pantheon, n.d. In a dream Punch experiences the story of "The Fisherman and His Wife" with Punch and Judy as well as modern touches. There are five children and a cat in addition to the fish and several minor characters.

6 *The Rabbi and the Twenty-Nine Witches: A Talmudic Legend*, Marilyn Hirsh. New York: Holiday House, 1976. A rabbi notices that troublesome witches do not appear on rainy days. When he tricks them out into the rain, they shrink into nothing.

6 "Rip Van Winkle," Washington Irving. (40) This is the American tale of a man who falls asleep for twenty years to return to a world that has forgotten him.

6 "Robin Hood's Merry Adventure with the Miller," Howard Pyle. (93) Robin Hood and the Miller fight for the right of way on a log.

5–6 "Saltin' the Pudding," B. A. Botkin. (57) Ma does not have time to salt the pudding. So, without checking with each other, everyone else in the family adds his or her pinch. This is an American folk tale.

6 *The Sorcerer's Scrapbook*, Michael Berenstain. New York: Random, 1981. A wizard, a sorcerer school dropout, tells his story of how he came to help a duke capture a unicorn. Told in a humorous way, the story gives some of the lore and myths of medieval times.

4–6 *Six Companions Find Fortune*, Katya Sheppard. Garden City, NY: Doubleday, 1969. A retired soldier finds a strong man, a hunter, a blower, a runner, and a frost maker to help him win a race. The King does not give the promised reward and tries to get rid of them in various ways. But each plan is foiled by the specific skills of each man.

5–6 *The Squire's Bride*, P. C. Asbjornsen. New York: Atheneum, 1975. An old squire decides to marry a young woman who has other ideas. She fools the squire's servants into taking a donkey to be dressed for the wedding.

4–6 *The Stone in the Road*, Stephen Seskin. New York: D. Van Nostrand, 1968. Efforts to find gold under a huge stone present this story's conflict. It has a medieval setting.

4–6 *A Story—A Story*, Gail E. Haley. New York: Atheneum, 1970. The African tale of how all stories came to be Anansi's, the spider man. Anansi must capture and give to the Sky God a leopard, hornets, and a dancing fairy whom men never see.

4–6 *Striding Slippers*, Mirra Ginsburg. New York: Macmillan, 1978. A shepherd makes magical striding slippers to help him in his work, but those who steal them seem not to be able to control them. Students will love pretending that their shoes are walking where they themselves do not want to go.

6 *Three Strong Women*, Claus Stamm. New York: Viking, 1962. A wrestler meets his match with a strong family of women. They train him and he becomes the champion in this Japanese tall tale.

6 "Urashima Taro and the Princess of the Sea," Yoshiko Uchida. (12) Urashima is enticed to live in the sea and spends much more time there than he imagines. When he returns home, he finds how much time has lapsed. This Japanese folktale compares with "Rip Van Winkle."

4–6 *The Vinananee and the Tree Toad: a Liberian Tale*, Verna Aardema. New York: Frederick Warne, 1983. A little tree toad is able to capture the bothersome Vinananee. This story presents another possibility for masks.

4–6 *The Wave*, Margaret Hodges. Boston: Houghton Mifflin, 1964. There is a small earthquake, and Grandfather knows a tidal wave will follow. The villagers are unaware of the danger, and Grandfather decides to burn his rice fields to warn them. This has a Japanese setting.

4–6 *When Noodlehead Went to the Fair*, Kathryn Hitte. New York: Parents', 1968. This old tale is told in the classic fashion of Noodlehead's adventure which begins with a carrot and ends with the capture of two robbers. Plan out carefully the running at the end, using techniques explained on pp. 146–47.

4 *When the Drum Sang*, Anne Rockwell. New York: Parents', 1970. A little girl, who sings beautiful songs, is kidnapped by a man who hides her in a drum and forces her to sing. Her parents discover her and must trick the man to release her from the drum in this African folktale.

5–6 *When the Porcupine Moved In*, Cora Annett. New York: Franklin Watts, 1971. Porcupine moves in with Rabbit. He demands his own way, even when Rabbit's wishes differ. Porcupine's talkative relatives even move in. Finally Rabbit uses reverse psychology and outwits Porcupine. It has wonderful characters and plenty of opportunity for dialogue and presents a good lesson in solving interpersonal conflicts.

6 *The Woodcutter's Duck*, Krystyna Turska. New York: Macmillan, 1972. Bartek outwits the army commander who wants the young man's pet duck in this Polish folktale.

6 "The Youth Who Wanted to Shiver," Eric Carle. (14) A young man wonders what shivering is and goes through some harrowing experiences in order to find out. But only when he is doused with minnows and cold water in his warm bed does he understand!

Extended Drama Lesson Planning 12

Throughout this resource guide you have been given many ideas for drama activities and even some lesson plans. As you have seen, single activities can be incorporated into your classroom teaching at any time and with various curricular subjects. Lesson plans for some of the longer activities can range from fifteen or twenty minutes to forty-five minutes. Sometimes it has been recommended that a lesson plan cover two class periods.

You may find that you want to take a given topic or theme and create an extended drama lesson around it. Perhaps you would like an extended lesson plan to last over a few days' time, spending about twenty to thirty minutes each day on an activity. This chapter is designed to help you in this planning.

1. Our first consideration is the theme or topic which will tie the activities together in a unified plan. Like most teachers, you are probably pressed for time, and will want your drama lessons to fit other areas of the curriculum. Perhaps you want to cover explorers, pilgrim life, or biographies. Or, perhaps your class has a particular interest in motorcycles, occupations, or a favorite author and you would like to center a lesson on a topic of high appeal.

2. Next consider your goals and objectives. No doubt you will want to emphasize, as often as possible, the three goals identified at the outset: drama, personal development, and subject matter.

3. You then might make a list of possible activities you could do, trying to include as wide a range as possible: beginning activities, narrative pantomime, verbal activities, creative stories, and so forth.

4. Now you are ready to sequence the activities.

    a. The first activity is generally a warmup. This material should not be overly challenging in order to put the class in a relaxed mood and ready for further work together. If students are easily excited, the opening material will need to be highly structured and controlled. It may also be helpful to use an activity that expends students' excess energy in order to calm them down and focus on the task.

    b. As the activities progress, they should become more challenging. To analyze the level of difficulty, consider the sequence chart on p. 13.

        For example, you might choose to do a pantomime game from the many listed in Chapter 7. According to Variable 3 on the chart, pantomimes are easy activities compared to verbal ones. But, they are also advanced, according to Variable 8, since they require an audience of guessers. At the same time, it would probably be easier for students to perform a pantomime of their favorite sport in a Count Freeze Pantomime (p. 100) than it would be to participate in creating a Group Frozen Picture (p. 102) of a current event. The former relies on the students' individual and personal interests (Variable 4: solo playing) and something they are familiar with (Variable 7: informational content), while the latter requires group decision making (Variable 4: pair and group work) and a knowledge of current events (Variable 7: higher data content). Each activity is a pantomime for guessing, but the other variables change the levels of difficulty.

        While you need not slavishly adhere to a thorough analysis of each activity you choose to do, an overall consideration will help you sequence your activities so that students will experience maximum success.

    c. Finally you end with a relaxing or quieting activity.

    d. (optional) As a personal preference, I like to include some alternative possibilities to my activities so that I have more flexibility to make changes as I see the group's response.

On the following pages are several extended lesson plans for you to begin on, adapt from, or simply use as stimulus for your own ideas.

EXTENDED LESSON PLAN
Abraham Lincoln
Objectives

a. Gain an understanding of some of the events in the life of an important American historical figure and recall information previously studied.

b. Experience pantomiming and interpret pantomime of occupations of Lincoln's time.

c. Enact dialogue situations appropriate to circumstances of Lincoln's presidency.

d. Dramatize in groups an interpretation of an episode in Lincoln's life demonstrating personal characteristic of honesty.

Preparation and Materials

a. Copies of Abraham Lincoln biographies. Suggestions:

d'Aulaire, Ingri and Edgar Parin, *Abraham Lincoln.* Garden City, N.J.: Doubleday and Co., Inc., 1939.

Judson, Clara Ingram, *Abraham Lincoln, Friend of the People.* Chicago: Wilcox and Follett Co., 1950.

McGovern, Ann, . . . *If You Grew Up with Abraham Lincoln.* New York: Four Winds, Press, 1966.

b. Picture of the Lincoln Memorial in Washington, D.C., or other Lincoln statues.

c. (optional) Other pictures of Lincoln which might motivate or illustrate points in the lesson.

d. Length of unit: Lessons of approximately 30 to 40 minutes each on four separate days. (Time will vary according to how familiar students are with the information. The activities may be used to stimulate interest in the information and motivate further research.)

Warmup Activity

Count Freeze Pantomimes (p. 100) of Jobs Lincoln Held (use front of classroom)

a. Review the various jobs held by Lincoln during his lifetime, if needed. (rail splitter, postmaster, carpenter, peddler, surveyor, sawmiller, lawyer, storekeeper, farmer, riverboat driver, and president).

b. Several students at a time will act out one of these occupations for guessing.

Option: Build a Place pantomime (p. 105) of Lincoln's log cabin in Indiana or a general store where Lincoln worked. Refer to texts above for data and illustrations.

Option: Frozen Pictures (p. 102) of famous scenes in Lincoln's life.

Group Scene
"Honest Abe"

a. Review or read to the class some of the stories or legends about how Lincoln got the nickname "Honest Abe." There are several stories including his walking six miles to return six pennies to a woman who overpaid him for some cloth, or the amount of time he spent working to pay off a library book he inadvertently damaged, and so forth.

b. Students may reenact one of these scenes, showing their version of what they think might have happened. Or, students might create a new story, based on data they know about Lincoln and the time period in which he lived, to demonstrate how someone might come to be known as a particularly honest person.

c. Groups of approximately five students each discuss and plan a scene. Share scenes in front of the classroom. Scenes may be in pantomime or may include dialogue.

Dialogue Scene
"Open Door Policy" (two days)

a. Review or read about Abraham Lincoln's concern that everyone should have a right to talk to the President. There were always crowds of people to see him, and he made every effort to see as many as possible.

b. Discuss: What kinds of people would come to see the President and what reasons would they have? How would Lincoln be able to talk to so many people?

c. Students decide who they are and what their reason for seeing the President might be. If students work in pairs and groups, more would have a chance to participate. Alternative plan: Have person's (or group's) role and reason for visit written on cards for students to select.

d. Set the scene in the White House (front of classroom) and the waiting room (students' desks.) You may want to set a time limit on each person's visit.

e. You may need to play Lincoln at first in order to guide the playing. The drama can be enhanced if you introduce others into the scene: "Let me get Mrs. Lincoln, who will want to meet you, since you've come all the way from Illinois . . . " or "Here's my son Tad who's just about your age . . . " and draw volunteers from the "audience." You will need to find ways to end each visit tactfully, diplomatically, and appropriately.

f. If, or when, you turn over Lincoln's role to a student, you can play a presidential aide and be on hand to assist when needed. In this role you can monitor the "crowd" and introduce those who are waiting to see the President. In this role, you can also introduce additional people into the scene: for example, a photographer who wants to get a picture of the many people who come to see the president. (Frozen Pictures, p. 102) Note: You may need to help students with information about cameras of the period.

g. Eventually students will take the presidential aide role themselves. Then you may choose to introduce other kinds of tension or problems by entering a scene as, for example, the Secretary of State, who says Lincoln is late for a Cabinet meeting. The Secretary might also be upset over Lincoln's spending so much time with people, which should encourage the student playing Lincoln, as well as others, to defend this policy.

Quieting Activity

Lincoln Statue (May be used whenever needed after other activities.)

a. Show class a picture of the Lincoln Memorial or other Lincoln statue.

b. On a slow count of ten, the students very slowly transform themselves into the statue.

EXTENDED LESSON PLAN
Pecos Bill and Slue-Foot Sue

Objectives

a. Gain an understanding of tall tales and of the particular stories surrounding one tall tale character.

b. Experience pantomime and group work in dramatic activities related to topic.

c. Experience verbal activities in panel discussions related to topic.

d. Have the opportunity to retell some of the tall tales surrounding Pecos Bill as well as inventing other episodes in the manner of the tall tale genre.

e. Have the opportunity to play some of the characters in the Pecos Bill tall tales.

Preparation and Materials

a. Students should be familiar with some of the stories surrounding the life of Pecos Bill. Suggested sources:

Bowman, James Cloyd, *Pecos Bill*. Chicago: Albert Whitman, 1937.

Felton, Harold W., *Pecos Bill: Texas Cowpuncher*. New York: Alfred A. Knopf, 1958.

Stoutenberg, Adrien, *American Tall Tales*. New York: Viking, 1966.

b. Record player and recording of cowboy songs or guitar or harmonica instrumental record.

c. (Optional) Pictures and illustrations of Pecos Bill, some of the legends, and/or other suitable cowboy activities related to the drama activities below.

d. Length of unit: Lessons of approximately 30 to 40 minutes each which may be played on several days. Some may also be replayed by switching roles. (Length of playing will vary according to how familiar the students are with the material.) The activities may also be used to stimulate interest in the information and motivate further reading.

Warmup Activity

Narrative pantomime of Pecos Bill riding a cyclone. Condense the section from Bowman's book, Chapter XIV (or other suitable source) that begins when Bill actually meets the cyclone and ropes it. Edit out the sections that do not pertain to the action of the ride itself. End when the cyclone dumps him and creates Death Valley.

Since he is sore from the ride, he can just rest here, happily waiting for the coyotes to get him back to the ranch. The students' desks can be Widow Maker, Pecos Bill's horse. When he rides the cyclone, they can pantomime this at the side of their desks. When the cyclone dumps him, they can be seated again at the desk for the quieting close of the narrative.

Optional activity: Using *Pecos Bill* by Ariane Dewey, New York: Greenwillow, 1983, create a solo narrative pantomime. This simple text rapidly covers all of Pecos Bill's life, and with a bit of editing, can serve nicely.

Frozen Pictures of Events in Pecos Bill's Life

Students work in groups of five or six. They create a frozen picture of their favorite event from one of the stories about Pecos Bill. Scenes may include falling out of the family's covered wagon; being raised by the coyotes; inventing the lariat, chaps, modern cowpunching, and so forth; the wedding with bouncing bride, Slue-Foot Sue; or any other scene they like. Rest of class guesses the scene, the events surrounding the scene, and identifies as many characters as possible.

Perpetual Motion Ranch as a Machine

Students work in groups of about eight each to create a picture of Pecos Bill's Perpetual Motion Ranch (or Circle Mountain Ranch), which was able to "run itself." Since the ranch supposedly runs like clockwork, the movements can be mechanical. Students will have to decide how they will show the parts of the ranch they think most important—the mountain, the animals with short legs on one side, how the cattle grazed, how the post holes were dug, what the cowboys do while the ranch takes care of itself, and so forth. They may also add whatever else they think might have been part of such a ranch. Then, on a signal from you, (counting or music cues), each group will demonstrate its version of the activities.

Panel of Experts on the Life and Times of Pecos Bill

Several students are selected to serve on the panel. They should be familiar with the stories and incidents in the life of Pecos Bill. The audience may question about particular details, or they may ask new questions about Bill. Panel participants can recall stories or make up new data and answers to the audience's questions. Change panel participants so that all who wish can have a chance, though this may take more than one or two playings to accomplish.

Debate on the Validity of the Pecos Bill Legends
This discussion is geared to be a little more demanding than the one above. In this case, we suppose that the character of Pecos Bill is being called into question. Some are claiming that the stories are exaggerated and untrue for the most part. Others are claiming that the stories have both truth and logic. The panel participants may be themselves, or they may choose to be characters from the stories, or they may be newly invented characters. The audience may be allowed to take on roles, too. Someone may wish to ask a question as Slue-Foot Sue, Gun Smith, Bill's human or coyote family, or even Pecos Bill's horse, Widow Maker. (Note: It is best not to have someone play Pecos Bill, since it is always easier to talk about people when they are not present.) The final chapter of Felton's book may be helpful in getting into the spirit of this kind of discussion.

Pecos Bill and Slue-Foot Sue Debate on Raising Coyotes
According to Stoutenberg, Sue and Bill had many children and lived a happy life. Their only quarrel was when Bill wanted to adopt coyotes to raise as children. Sue said humans could not raise "varmints," but Bill argued that the varmints had raised him. He argued so much that Sue finally gave in, but there is no record of the argument itself. Students can argue in pairs to explore this debate. (See Debate Method II, p. 133.)

Quieting Activities
(May be used whenever needed after other activities.)

1. Be cowboys going to sleep under the stars or resting around the campfire at night listening to quiet strumming of a guitar (or harmonica) or perhaps roundup songs supposedly written by Pecos Bill.

2. Pecos Bill, it is said, once met an Eastern dude who asked about the *doggies* in the song "Git Along Little Dogies." Bill laughed so hard he laughed himself to death, according to one legend. Have students demonstrate "laughing to death" silently and in slow motion to a slow count of 10.

EXTENDED LESSON PLAN
Greek Mythology
Objectives

a. Gain an understanding of Greek mythology, particular Greek myths, and various mythological characters.

b. Participate in dramatic activities, both pantomime and verbal, individually, and in pairs and groups, related to the topic of Greek mythology.

Preparation and Materials

a. Students should be familiar with the myths included in this lesson. (The activities may also be modified to fit other myths you prefer to teach.) Suggested sources:

Coolidge, Olivia, *Greek Myths.* Boston: Houghton Mifflin, 1949.

d'Aulaire, Ingri and Edgar Parin d'Aulaire. *Book of Greek Myths.* Garden City: Doubleday, 1962.

Fadiman, Clifton, *The Adventures of Hercules.* New York: Random House, 1960.

Graves, Robert, *Greek Gods and Heroes.* Garden City: Doubleday, 1960.

b. Copies of the various versions of the legend of Pandora for use in the trial activity.

c. Stories selected for the skits activity, with copies available for the groups.

d. Length of unit. Activities vary from 30 minutes in length to an hour, depending on students' familiarity with the myths and how much review and discussion is necessary. The activity requiring the longest amount of time will probably be the group skits. These may need to be planned and rehearsed one day and shared on another day.

Warmup Activity: Paired Narrative of Daedalus and Icarus
Review of the story and how King Minos of Crete imprisoned the master architect, Daedalus, and his son, Icarus, in a tower on an island. They escape prison, but find it impossible to leave the island, since the ships are too well guarded.

Pair (one plays Daedalus and one Icarus) the class for the following narrative pantomime:

"One day, Daedalus notices the seagulls flying and thinks of a plan for escape. The two of them gather all the feathers they can find. Then they fasten them with thread and mold them in place with wax in order to make a pair of wings. Daedalus fits them to his shoulders and waves his arms like a bird waves its wings. He tries several times and then finally manages to lift himself off the ground while Icarus watches in disbelief. Daedalus wavers with the wind, but soon manages to learn to fly. He returns to Icarus, and they make a second pair of wings for the son. The wings are fitted on, and Daedalus shows him how to use them. But he warns Icarus to be careful not to get too near the sun. Icarus pays no attention because he is so eager to escape the island and to fly.

"At last the day arrives when the winds seem just right for flying. Daedalus flies up first and watches to see that Icarus is able to follow him. They are excited to be leaving the hated island of Crete and, as they fly higher and higher, they are pleased to see the island slowly become smaller and smaller until it is lost from view. Soon they are flying so high their heads are dizzy. A great wind fills their wings and they fly like birds soaring in space. Soon Icarus forgets everything but the joy of the flight itself. He stretches his arms up to the sky and takes off for the heavens above. Daedalus turns his head to see Icarus doing what he has been warned not to do, and in fear flies back toward Icarus. As Icarus flies higher and higher toward the sun, the air grows warmer and warmer. His wings seem to droop, and he cannot make them fly. Then in terror he remembers Daedalus' warning and realizes that the wax is melting and the feathers are slowly dropping from the wings. Now he is like a leaf being tossed by the wind as he falls. Daedalus arrives just as Icarus falls below into the sea and drowns. Daedalus circles the place where Icarus has dropped but can find only the feathers floating on the water. He flies sorrowfully to the temple of Apollo and lands there. Kneeling, head bowed, he hangs up his wings as an offering to the gods and never attempts to fly again." (Daedalus names an island near to Crete "Icaria," in honor of his son.)

Pantomime Spelling of Greek Mythological Characters
In groups, students will spell out the words of various Greek mythological characters by pantomiming words beginning with the appropriate letters. Categories of words pantomimed (occupations, foods, animals, and so on) may be of the students' choosing,

but only one category per word may be used. The number of students in a group will be determined by the number of letters in the Greek name. Hera, for example, may be spelled out by four students using the category of animals: H-horse, E-elephant, R-rhinoceros, and A-alligator.

The "Trial" of Pandora

Review legend of Prometheus giving fire to mortals. Zeus punishes Prometheus and, to punish the mortals, too, creates a scheme and Pandora to carry it out. Prometheus has given Epimetheus a container of all the ills of the world and asks him to keep it hidden and not open it. Epimetheus marries Pandora, and one day she discovers the container. Upon her opening it, all manner of winged things called envy, greed, sickness, vice, and so forth, fly out and inhabit the earth to plague mortals. One creature, Hope, flies out last of all and makes the ills tolerable. *Important:* Try to read or make available as many versions of the story as possible so that students see various interpretations.

For this activity, the characters of Prometheus, Zeus, Epimetheus, and Pandora take seats at the front of the classroom. (You may wish to double-cast each character so that a panel of eight is selected.) Use nametags or nameplates so that everyone can remember who is playing which part. You may also need to indicate that while the "court" recognizes that Prometheus and Zeus are gods, they have no particular power in this courtroom and will come under the same law as any mortal. This precaution may be necessary in order to keep "Zeus" from doing away with everyone in the room!

Panel members will probably feel that the other is to blame, and this will be the fuel for the discussion. It should also be noted that the various stories or accounts are like witnesses' evidence. Are there biases in the stories? Who do the authors seem to "blame"?

Allow audience members (who are the humans who have suffered from the events that have taken place in the story) to question the panel members. As the audience begins to take sides, you may want to ask at some point if anyone wishes to make a short speech of defense or accusation of any of the characters. (This role will be similar to that of prosecuting attorney or a lawyer for the defense.)

If you wish, you can let the audience be the "jury" and take a vote to decide if Pandora is guilty or innocent—or rank order all four according to degree of guilt. But once the vote is taken, usually the discussion is ended. Students may want to have another trial on another day, exchanging roles. This may produce a different vote, particularly if new evidence (new story versions) are introduced or if the speakers and questioners raise new points or speak persuasively for their points of view.

Obviously, there will be no one outcome to this discussion nor should there be. If students feel their viewpoint is slighted or not recognized, you may wish to let the class write their opinions. This may even be done in small groups as "position papers."

Skits of Greek Myths

Since there are so many versions, interpretations, and descriptions of the myths, they lend themselves nicely to short, group skits. Brief synopses may be duplicated for groups to read and prepare their own versions from. The skits may be told in pantomime or may include dialogue.

Suggested myths: King Midas and the Golden Touch, Baucis and Philemon, Arachne, Orpheus and Eurydice, Medusa's Head, Atalanta's Race, Theseus and the Minotaur, or one of the labors of Hercules.

Quieting Activity

(May be used whenever needed after other activities.)

Students may be one of the feathers from the wings of Icarus, slowly becoming unstuck from the wax and wafting down slowly to the sea, where it floats calmly and quietly in the water.

LESSON PLAN REFERENCE CHART

Following is a list of some of the topics or themes covered by the various materials and activities in this book. The left-hand column gives the topics and titles, the center column lists the type of drama activity they are, and the final column gives the page references.

The intent of the chart is to help you begin to make a variety of lesson plans by presenting some possible themes and then listing some of the activities and materials under that heading that are found in this book. In some cases the listing is only a reference; in other cases lesson plans (*) are provided.

No attempt has been made to include every reference in this text, nor is the chart designed to provide an inclusive list of themes for each activity or literary selection.

Puppets, Shadow Plays, and Masks 13

Saying the word "puppets" today probably conjures up the image of the "Muppets" in the minds of most people. The popularity of *Sesame Street* Muppets, as well as the Muppet television show and the Muppet films, have made Jim Henson's creations a household word and one that is almost synonymous with puppets.

But puppets are as ancient and as varied as history itself. Different cultures have evolved their own kinds of puppets, many of which have been passed down from generation to generation and are still in existence today. There are puppets manipulated by strings, by rods, and by hand. They may require only two fingers on the hand of one person, or they may require the manipulator's entire body or the cooperative manipulation of several puppeteers. They may be a "found object" (a wooden spoon, a feather), the hand by itself, or a person in a costume. Their size can range from being larger than the average person to being as small as a finger puppet. And, of course, they can represent abstract beings as well as humans and animals. In short, their versatility knows no bounds.

But basic to all puppets is the puppeteer/manipulator or actor. While actors usually do not consider themselves puppeteers, puppeteers consider themselves actors—in disguise. Although the attention is on the puppet during the performance and even after, it is the actor manipulating the puppet who is the real performer and theatre artist. Even though we adults may recognize Jim Henson's voice when Kermit speaks or Frank Oz as Miss Piggy, we still think of the two puppets as people in their own right. The puppeteer/actor has created that magical illusion of character creation for us.

It is this aspect of puppetry magic that makes the fascination of puppets so universal and appealing to all ages. The puppeteer's power to do this magic may also explain why the motivation for creating theatre with puppets is so strong. It also helps to explain why many children can play with puppets, making them say and do things they would be too shy or too inhibited to express on their own. The therapeutic and educational value is almost a given. Who can ignore these personages who seem to have a life of their own? No one, it seems. And, least of all, your students.

HOW TO BEGIN

There is no one way to begin working with puppets. In fact, you may find yourself choosing one method for one class and taking a totally different approach with another. It is important for you to feel free to experiment with the method you use. Therefore, several approaches will be mentioned so that you will begin to see some of the choices available to you.

There are some *cautions*. First, be sure that you do not spend more time making the puppets than you and the children spend using them. Frequently puppet-making is used as an art project, but that is often where it stops. But a puppet is not a puppet

A "Puppet Tree" collection awaits sixth grade actors to bring them to life.

until someone brings it to life. For this reason, some teachers prefer to purchase, collect, or make puppets and have them ready for students to use.

If you take the above approach and buy or make your own puppets, be sure they are not just the toy variety you stick your hand into but cannot manipulate very well. Puppets should fit the hand to create the illusion of reality rather than being just a doll that bounces up and down. Obviously, the more durable the puppets are, the more use you will get from them.

It is also useful to think in terms of a cast of characters as you collect or make your puppets. If you have three pigs and a wolf, for example, a simple story is ready and more likely to be played out. Or, a king, queen, and various other court characters might inspire the enactment of "Sleeping Beauty" or "Thurber's *Many Moons*. Familiar stories are almost always easier for students to enact than is the creation of originals, though that, too, is possible.

PUPPETS AND MOVEMENT

Once students have experienced many of the previous creative drama activities and are more aware of what their own bodies can communicate, they will more readily enjoy trying some of the same ideas with puppets. Most puppets are very limited, in comparison to the human body, in their ability to move in a variety of ways. Yet, by experimenting with their own pantomime skills first and then translating these ideas to the puppet's body, it can be quite amazing what discoveries your students can make.

WHAT CAN THE HANDS DO?

One beginning approach is to focus on the puppeteer/actor and explore various ways to create puppets with the hands. How might the hands dance to some music? Play a record and let the students explore ways to dance their hands on their desk tops. Or, try some actions and emotions. Can a hand bow? How might it sneeze? Or show anger?

FOUND MATERIALS

Now you might find objects to turn into puppets. What sorts of characters might they suggest and what might they do? How might they walk, dance, or perform other actions? What character is suggested by a pencil, a feather, a small scarf, or a stapler?

REHEARSAL PUPPET

Some puppeteers advocate the making of rehearsal puppets so that the emphasis can be on exploring movement. This approach is rather like an actor or dancer working in rehearsal clothes before putting on costume and makeup. A simple rehearsal puppet can be made of a styrofoam ball for the head, a hollowed portion in one end for the finger, and a thumbtack for the nose. No eyes are indicated in order that students will be encouraged to make puppets "look" in appropriate directions. With this basic puppet shape, the beginning puppeteer is ready to explore head movements, hand movements, and, the most challenging, leg movements. Students at their desks can explore:

Head:
looking up, down, side to side.

> *Seeing*: watching birds fly overhead, looking for something lost on the ground, watching a parade going by.
> *Hearing*: a telephone ringing, a clock striking 3:00, being bothered by a pesky mosquito.
> *Smelling*: a skunk, freshly baked pie, smoke (something's on fire!)
> *Tasting*: pantomiming eating a lemon, chewing bubble gum, tasting bitter medicine.

Hands:
clapping, waving, pointing, scratching.

> *Touch*: sit on something hot, cold, pantomime petting a dog.

Waist or Torso:
bow, rotate, do exercises.

Legs:
(If you turn the puppet body slightly from one side to the other, you can create the illusion of the puppet going from one foot to the other.)

> *Pretend to*: walk, jump, stamp, tiptoe, skate, march.
> Pantomime aerobic dancing, lifting weights, riding a bicycle.

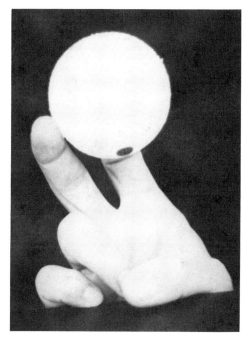

Rehearsal puppet listens to phone ringing.

At this point you may want to have students explore the variety of movements presented in some of the stories or poems listed under "Narrative Pantomimes for Solo Playing" in Chapter 5. Let them share with each other the ideas and techniques they discover. You can eventually try the narrative pantomimes for paired playing and work up to the group stories. When students are satisfied they have done the best work they can with the rehearsal puppet, the fully dressed puppet can take the stage for a pantomime show.

SIMPLE PUPPET STAGE

Once students have seen the puppet as an actor, they will realize how the puppet itself commands its own attention. Hiding behind a stage in order to create the illusion of reality will now seem less important. For the pantomime show, however, students may want a little more formality. The simplest and most satisfactory of puppet stages at this point is a table with a cloth draped over the front or a table turned on its side. In either case, the puppeteers can kneel or sit on low stools behind the table.

A table turned on its side is all you need for a puppet stage.

REHEARSAL PUPPET WITH PROPS

After exploring some basic movements with the puppet, students will want to see what their little actor can do with props. At their desks, students can discover ways to show their puppets doing a variety of activities listed below. They will need to remember that their one hand must do all the actions. Try as much solo work as possible. Then do the same activities with students acting in pairs.

> *Writing with a pencil and paper.* (Using regular sized paper and pencil, the puppet will appear to be like a small child maneuvering giant objects.) Try writing, erasing, folding the paper, putting on a "stamp," and sealing it.
>
> *Reading a book.* Open book, turn pages, show "reading," react to what is written.
>
> *Cleaning the desk top as if it were a floor.* Use a paper cup as a bucket and a piece of paper tissue as a rag. Scrub the desk, finding trouble spots.
>
> *Taking a bath or shower or washing hair.* Use paper cup as a bucket, paper tissue as washcloth and towel, paper clip or rubber eraser as bar of soap.

In pairs:

> Cut a piece of paper into a certain shape. One holds the paper, the other cuts.
>
> Play "Tug of War" with a piece of string; seesaw on a ruler placed over a book; unwrap a piece of gum or candy; open box of paints, crayons.

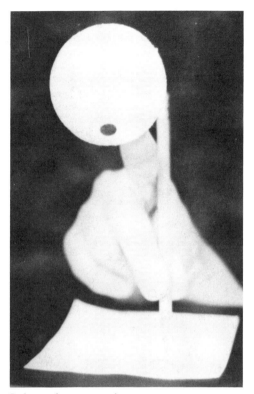

Rehearsal puppet writes . . .

reads a book . . .

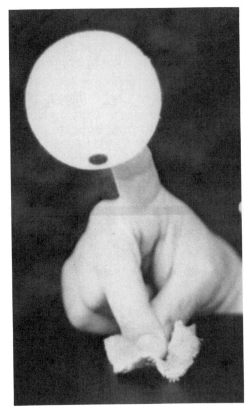

. . . and scrubs a desk.

Let two puppets clean out your desk, carrying books, dusting items, and so forth.

See if two puppets can take a wristwatch off your arm, roll up a shirt sleeve, or tie a shoe.

PUPPETS AND DIALOGUE

When you are ready to work with speech and dialogue with the puppets, it will be important to recognize that the puppet can say a great deal nonverbally. That is, even if a puppet does not have a mouth, it will still be able to convey a variety of emotions and speech related behaviors. For example, it can move its head up and down to indicate "yes." And, if you move the head up and down quickly, it will show an eagerness to the yes response. The puppet may also be able to point to indicate "There." Or, it may be able to clap its hands to show a joyful reaction or to scratch its head as if thinking. All of these communicative responses can be explored by themselves so that students can explore their little actors' capabilities. The following exercises can be fun to try:

a. *Movements for the Head*. What does the puppet appear to be "saying" if the head drops forward? (tired, bashful, sad) If the head moves to one side? (listening, thinking) If the head rotates all around in a circle? (dizzy, overwhelmed)

b. *Movements for the Hands*. Clapping, waving, pointing, scratching, rubbing together, patting stomach, hand to mouth, hand to cheek, hand behind ear. What might these gestures "say"?

PUPPETS WITH MOVEABLE MOUTHS

In focusing on dialogue, you may also want to work with puppets that have moveable mouths. The following suggestions are made:

a. **Paper envelope puppets** are easy to make and to manipulate. The flap is tucked inside, and the hand is placed inside the envelope with the fingers in one of the bottom ends and the thumb in the other. Then tuck and bend into the middle of the bottom of the envelope to form a sort of beak. This can become a rehearsal mouth to explore with. And, if desired, a sturdy envelope can be decorated and painted to create a full puppet.

b. **Paper bag puppets** are also useful for focusing on a moveable mouth. Since paper bags come in a variety of sizes and styles and are easily obtained, they provide a quick and inexpensive way to get started on a cast of characters. Like the envelope puppet, they are also easy for young children to manipulate. You need a bag that

Puppets with moveable mouths.

has a flat bottom. When that is folded over at its natural crease, and the fingers are enclosed inside, the bottom becomes the upper jaw of the puppet, which moves up and down against the thumb or palm of the hand for speech. This "mouth" is enhanced by painting or gluing teeth, tongue, and other human or animal features to the upper and lower jaw. The rest of the puppet can be decorated to any extent desired.

c. **Sock puppets** also allow for moveable mouths. Put the sock on your hand and put the fingers in the toe and the thumb in the heel. Again, the mouth features can be enhanced as above. The rest of the puppet can also be decorated to any extent desired. Unlike the bag puppet, however, you can more readily sew the sock puppet, adding pieces of fabric, buttons, yarn, and so forth. A sock puppet is also more durable and can, if care is used, be made washable.

With puppets that have moveable mouths, students can focus on additional dialogue exercises like the ones listed below. Students should not try to keep the puppet's mouth moving incessantly when speaking. The illusion of speaking will be created if the mouth opens only now and then. A mouth that appears to be constantly "yapping" will only distract from what it is the puppet is "saying."

DIALOGUE EXERCISES FOR PUPPETS

a. Try the verbal Sequence Games from Literature (See Chapter 8) using puppets. Students should raise the puppet high enough for the class to see "it" speaking the lines.

b. Also in Chapter 8 the students might want to try the One Liners, Ad Talks, and/or Storytelling with puppets.

c. Consider also the Verbal Games from Chapter 8. A panel of puppets ("on stage," if desired) may be questioned by students; puppets may question a panel of students; or the entire game may be played with puppets.

PUPPETS AND CHARACTERIZATION

Characterization is determined by a variety of things: physical features such as size, age, the sound of the voice, and the manner of movement. One way to begin thinking about characterization is by using found objects for puppets. Again, as before, we might take the pencil and think about it as a puppet character. How does it sound when it talks, what personality might it have, and how would it describe itself? Now compare other found objects like a wooden spoon, a feather, an egg beater, and so on to each other. How do they sound or behave differently? Try giving them names. Let them interview each other. Let them tell a story about themselves. These kinds of activities will be helpful to the students in creating uniqueness of character for the puppets.

STORY DRAMATIZATION WITH PUPPETS

Eventually, students will want to work with entire stories, turning them into puppet plays. Since puppet plays usually have only a few characters in them, it may be necessary to select several stories and to create several groups of students to work on their own play. In addition, if a puppet play is presented on a puppet stage, there will be a limited amount of space for puppeteers as well as puppets.

On the other hand, if an entire class wishes to be involved in a single story, it is possible to expand a stage. A sheet, tightly secured at each end and at an appropriate height, can hide a number of puppeteers. Stories with numerous characters (large crowd scenes, for example) can then be dramatized.

You may find it helpful to have students dramatize a story on their own, using methods suggested in the section "Story Dramatization," before trying the same story with puppets. It is also possible to use the same methods of story dramatization with puppets. Using rehearsal puppets, for example, exercises can be tried and scenes can be played out as before. Again, we must remember that the puppeteers are, first and foremost, actors. The puppeteers, through the puppets, develop themselves as the actor does. They are actors in diguise.

PUPPET REFERENCES

Currell, David, *Learning with Puppets.* Boston: Plays, Inc., 1980. In addition to puppet construction and techniques, Durrell discusses uses of puppetry in specific areas of the curriculum.

Hanford, Robert Ten Eyck, *The Complete Book of Puppets and Puppeteering.* New York: Sterling Publishing Co, 1981. Along with a history of puppetry, Hanford discusses all aspects of puppet making and production of plays as well as some tips from the pros.

Latshaw, George, *Puppetry: The Ultimate Disguise.* New York: Richards Rosen Press, 1978. Latshaw documents his work as a puppeteer and also presents many of his exercises from workshops he does with teachers and students. Many of the activities above are adapted from this valuable text by a gifted artist and teacher.

SHADOW PLAY

Shadow plays work on the same principle of making shadow pictures with your hands on a wall. Instead of a wall, however, we will suggest two different shadow play methods.

METHOD I

Shadow puppetry is easiest to do by using an overhead projector. The cutouts of the puppets are made and then laid flat on the glass surface of the projector. The shadows of the puppets are then projected on the screen. This method is easy for children to do and also allows them to see their work. This latter fact can be important for children who are not yet able to envision how things look from the audience's viewpoint. There will be some confusion at first since it is a little like working with a mirror image.

METHOD II

A second method for older children involves using a screen of thin, white fabric. An old sheet does nicely. This may be stretched tightly over a frame. Behind the screen (away from the audience) and shining on it is a very bright light. The puppets are flat and, when pressed against the screen, create a strong shadow outline or silhouette.

Tug-of-war shadow drama behind a sheet with a back light.

The screen is elevated, often on a table, so that the puppet operators can stay below it. (You want to see the puppets' shadows, not the shadows of the puppeteers.)

MAKING THE PUPPETS

The puppets are black paper cutouts which are attached to a stick or rod. Several of the group stories in the Narrative Pantomime chapter can be made into shadow plays. Since most of these group stories come from picturebooks, the illustrations will give you many ideas for interpretation.

If you make a number of cutouts of each character similar to the various positions of the characters on different pages of the book, you will have additional movement and a more interesting presentation of your play. You can also turn the puppet over so it can be shown facing the opposite direction.

You can make groups of people or animals as one large puppet. This makes it much simpler to perform stories with many characters.

If you use thick or dark cardboard for your puppets, they will appear as a very solid, black shadow. This can be very effective and dramatic. But you may also want to cut away some of the cardboard so that light can show through and create simple facial features or bits of costuming. If you then cover the cut out areas with colored tissue or cellophane, you will get color in your puppets.

If you wish more color, you can use light-weight cardboard or a heavy paper and apply the color you wish. Then, to stiffen it and

Authentic Asian shadow puppets made of animal hide.

protect it, cover it with several thicknesses of clear, plastic adhesive paper. This creates an almost translucent puppet, similar to those made of thin animal skins centuries ago in many countries of the world.

ATTACHING THE RODS

To hold the puppet, you will need a rod or stick. Thin wires from craft stores work well. Rods can also be made from coat-hanger wire, although these are a little heavier. If you tape the end of the wire or attach a bit of foam rubber, you can make a handle that will be easier to hold.

The wires are attached to the puppet either in a flat position or in a hinged position. If the wire is flat, you will have to hold it directly against the screen. If you bend the wire a bit and attach it to the puppet with thick clear vinyl tape, then you can hold the puppet against the screen even though you are standing several inches away. This allows you to have a bit of shelf space on your table to lay the puppets on when they are not "on stage."

More elaborate puppets are hinged to enable more sophisticated

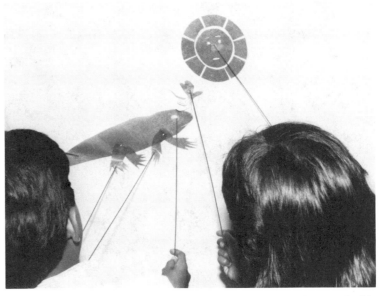

These shadow puppets are made of colored tissue paper and covered with several thicknesses of plastic adhesive paper. (*Why Mosquitoes Buzz in People's Ears,* Verna Aardema)

movements. Generally, it is the arms and legs of the puppet that are made to move. Simply cut legs and arms to overlap the torso or body of the puppet. Then make a small hole and thread a string through, knotting it on each side so the arms and legs are free to move. Sometimes the arms and legs are simply allowed to dangle or move of their own accord. Older children may wish to attach rods to the arms and legs and control these movements.

SCENERY

For Method I

When using the overhead projector, you can draw scenery on overhead transparencies with a felt pen. The transparencies come in different colors which can give you some variety of mood and setting.

For Method II

You can also create scenery for shadow plays that use the sheet screen and light. Again, you can trace what is in the picture book, or you can create your own. However, you do not want to clutter the screen up with too many extraneous details. Remember that the puppets are the most important part of your play. Also, if the story changes scenes frequently, you will spend all your time changing the scenery rather than operating the puppets.

Scenery can be very simple and, if possible, put in place prior to the showing of the play. A "ground row," for example, can be a horizontal strip of cardboard taped along the bottom of the screen. It is shaped to look like grass, a hill, a floor, or whatever is needed. At the side might be a tree, or at the top might be a sun, clouds, and so forth. If these are taped or attached to the frame of the screen, they will leave the center of the screen free for the puppets' actions.

DRAMATIZATION WITH SHADOW PUPPETS

Since shadow plays are so versatile, it is possible to use a variety of sources. The following selections are suggested because of the many pictorial images they utilize.

4–6 *Bringing the Rain to Kapiti Plain*, Verna Aardema. New York: Dial Press, 1981. A Nandi tale from Africa about how the herdsman Kipat helped end the drought is told in the style of "The House that Jack Built."

4–6 *The Desert is Theirs*, Byrd Baylor. New York: Charles Scribner's, 1975. This is a description of the many animals, plants, and people who inhabit the desert. Movement can be shown of the plants growing and the animal's daily activities. Simple pastel drawings form the pictorial basis of this subtle, quiet drama. It is an excellent nature lesson as well as sociological study.

4–6 *The Gift of the Sacred Dog*, Paul Goble. Scarsdale, NY: Bradbury Press, 1980. Horses (called by some Indians "sacred dogs") are given to the Indians by the Great Spirit.

4–6 *The Girl Who Loved Wild Horses*, Paul Goble. Scarsdale, NY: Bradbury Press, 1978. An Indian girl, though she loves her people, prefers to live among the wild horses and eventually becomes one of them.

4–6 *Hailstones and Halibut Bones,* Mary O'Neill. Garden City, NY: Doubleday, 1961. This contains poetry about various colors, the things they portray and symbolize.

4–6 *Hansel and Gretel*, William Wiesner. New York: Seabury Press, 1971. This is a shadow puppet picture book that includes instructions for staging the story as a shadow puppet play.

4–6 *Harriet and the Promised Land*, Jacob Lawrence. New York: Windmill, 1968. The story of Harriet Tubman is beautifully but starkly illustrated in woodcuts.

4–6 *Inspector Mouse*, Bernard Stone and Ralph Steadman. New York: Holt, Rinehart, and Winston, 1980. Inspector Mouse, with his friend Toothy, finds the culprit who stole the Mayor's cheese. There is sophisticated humor in this picture book, with references to Humphrey Bogart and to jazz musicians. Vivid pictures inspire a clever shadow play.

4–6 *Once a Mouse*, Marcia Brown. New York: Charles Scribner's Sons, 1961. An East Indian hermit/magician befriends a mouse. To save the mouse's life, the man turns him into progressively larger, more powerful animals until the mouse becomes too arrogant and is returned to his former state.

4–6 *One Wide River to Cross*, Barbara Emberley. Englewood Cliffs, N.J.: Prentice-Hall, 1966. An old folk song of Noah and the Ark is brought to life. Because black woodcuts are used in this book, reading it is almost like watching a shadow play.

4–6 *Paul Revere's Ride*, Henry Wadsworth Longfellow. New York: Greenwillow, 1985. The dramatic setting and mission of this poem lends itself to shadow puppetry.

4–6 *Peter and the Wolf*, Erna Voight. New York: David R. Godine, 1980. This beautifully illustrated musical story of a young boy's adventure with a duck, a cat, a bird, and a wolf can be narrated with Serge Prokofieff's music in the background.

Shadow play of Emberley's *One Wide River to Cross* behind the scenes and from audience's viewpoint.

4–6 *The Rooster's Horns: A Chinese Puppet Play to Make and Perform*, Ed Young with Hilary Beckett. New York: Collins and World, 1978. This is a story and instructions to children for making and performing their own shadow puppet play. It includes puppet pieces to trace.

4–6 *Shadow*, Marcia Brown. New York: Charles Scribner's, 1982. This is a poetic description of shadows. It begs to be done as a shadow play.

4–6 *Sometimes I Dance Mountains*, Byrd Baylor. New York: Charles Scribner's, 1973. This is a dance poem that is very effective choreographed as a live shadow play. It is long enough that several dancers can take turns interpreting different sections. Add colored lighting and simple instruments for a highly theatrical piece.

4–6 *The Stonecutter*, Gerald McDermott. New York: Viking, 1975. A Japanese folktale is simply told with an artistry that calls for a shadow play interpretation.

4–6 "The Strange Visitor," Joseph Jacobs in *English Fairy Tales*. New York: G. P. Putnam's, 1892. An old woman sits spinning and wishing for company. A visitor arrives, but the body parts enter one at a time.

4–6 *Why Mosquitos Buzz in People's Ears*, Verna Aardema. New York: Dial, 1975. This is an imaginatively illustrated retelling of an African folk tale that explains the mosquito's behavior.

REFERENCES ON SHADOW PUPPETRY

Currell, David, *Learning with Puppets*. Boston: Plays, Inc., 1980. Shadow puppet construction is detailed on pp. 110–119.

Lynch-Watson, Janet, *The Shadow Puppet Book.* New York: Sterling Publishing Co., 1980. Extensive treatment of this one type of puppetry is presented.

Mendoza, George, *Shadowplay.* New York: Holt, Rinehart and Winston, 1974. Black and white photographs show the hands of Prasanna Rao of India, a foremost shadowplay artist, creating shadow images from swans to witches. Although not about shadow puppetry, this fascinating book explains a related art form that will be of interest to children as well as adults.

Ormai, Stella, *Shadow Magic.* New York: Lothrop, Lee & Shepard, 1985. This tells of shadow entertainment as well as many science concepts about light.

MASKS

Because children enjoy making and wearing them, and because they can be used effectively in many dramatizations, we include a few words here about masks.

Masks and dramatic rituals and plays have had a long history. Masks were believed to give power to the wearer by allowing him or her to be someone else. Perhaps the wearer might be an animal to be killed in some future hunt and the wearer/hunter would have power over the animal. Or, perhaps the mask symbolized some god or superior entity or being.

Students, of course, associate masks with Halloween and with other sorts of dress-up events like a costume ball. But, similar to the experience of manipulating a puppet, wearing a mask can also hide a person and encourage expression anonymously. Shy students or those who need self confidence for other reasons may find mask wearing a particularly satisfying activity.

Also, many of the stories we have suggested can be extended artistically and dramatically by the addition of masks. Masks can be humorous or they can lend a very formalistic or ritualistic atmosphere. Since the mood of a story can be greatly affected by the use of masks, it will be important to match the story and the type of mask wisely in order to achieve the desired mood and effect. Students will be able to assist in this decision making process.

MAKING MASKS

Masks can be made in a variety of ways. We shall focus on the most simple ways. As with puppets, for drama experiences it is more important to make use of the mask than to spend inordinate amounts of time making them only as art projects to be looked at or hung on a wall.

Paper Bag Mask

a. This type is worn over the head, with places for the eyes, nose, and mouth cut out.

b. The mask should be of a size to fit snugly so that it can turn when the students move their heads. It may be helpful to cut slits in the bottom four corners of the bag or as a fringe all around so that it will fit down over the students' heads.

c. Now the bag can be decorated in any manner the students wish.

d. You may want to cut out the bottom half of the bag so that the face is covered only as far as the mouth in order to make speaking easier, should that be desirable.

Paper Plate Mask

a. These masks are made simply by attaching a stick or other type of holder to the edge of the plate so that the mask can be held up in front of the face. Eye holes are cut in the appropriate places. Because these masks are held far enough away from the mouth that they usually do not muffle the voice, it is possible to speak without having to make a mouth hole.

b. If you wish to attach the mask to the head, then you will want to cut nose and mouth holes. Some students will want to put their own noses through the nose hole in order to get a three dimensional effect.

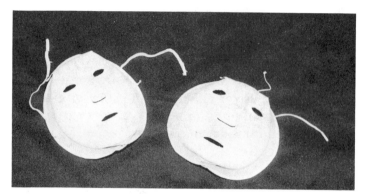

Masks made of paper plates, with stapled darts for chin and forehead, and string or elastic for ties.

c. To attach the mask to the face, make holes in the paper plate near the ears. Then knot a length of heavy string in each hole and tie in back of the head. You can also use rubber bands or pipe cleaners (curved over the ears like a pair of glasses).

d. If you want to shape the paper plate, just make slits in the edges of the paper plate, overlap the pieces and staple together as if you are making darts or tucks in clothing. A two inch dart for the chin and three inch dart for the forehead is suggested.

e. Now you can decorate the paper plate any way you wish. Extra noses and ears, horns, or fringed hair make interesting extensions in the masks. Covering the mask with aluminum foil can create interesting robot-type characters or masks for medieval knights.

Grief and surprise—expressing emotions with expressionless masks.

Paper Plate Half Masks

a. You can also shape half masks from half a paper plate. These can also have sticks attached to them to hold or can attach to the head.

b. Students may think of a woman wearing such a mask at the opera or at a costume ball or of the Lone Ranger. But with extensions and various decorations, these masks can also be made fearsome and humorous.

DRAMATIZATION WITH MASKS

You and the students will have your own ideas for ways to use the masks. Here are a few to get you started. Animal masks can be used for any of the stories with animal characters such as "How the Birds Got Their Colors" or *Horton Hatches the Egg.* Other types of masks may be inspired by the stories listed below.

4 *The Funny Little Woman*, Arlene Mosel. New York: E. P. Dutton, 1972. A giggling little Japanese woman chases a rice dumpling past some Jizos (statues of gods) to the wicked onis (troll-like creatures). Masks can be used for the Jizos and the onis.

5–6 *Harald and the Giant Knight*, Donald Carrick. New York: Clarion, 1982. The knights, as they practice in the fields, can use masks covered with aluminum foil.

4–6 *The Hobyahs*, Simon Stern. Englewood Cliffs, N.J.: Prentice-Hall, 1977. Masks can be used for the little hobyah creatures, and may be interpreted in any fashion the students wish. I find the characters funny, but you and your students may wish to make them scary.

4–6 *The Loon's Necklace*, William Toye. New York: Oxford University Press, 1977. An illustrated retelling of an Indian legend involving a loon and a medicine man. Authentic Indian masks are used to dramatize the story in a film by Encyclopedia Brittanica, Chicago, Ill. Color, ten minutes.

4–6 *The Musicians of Bremen*, many editions. Masks can be used for both the robbers and for the animals. (See lesson plans in Chapters 10 and 11.)

4–6 "Urashima Taro and the Princess of the Sea," Yoshika Uchida. (12) For the creatures of the underwater, masks could be most effective.

4–6 *Who's in Rabbit's House?* Verna Aardema. New York: Dial, 1977. This picturebook shows all the characters in animal masks performing a play. Students can use the pictures as a model or may create their own designs.

A grocery bag makes an oni character for *The Funny Little Woman* by Arlene Mosel.

SELECTED REFERENCES

Alkema, Chester J., *Mask Making*. New York: Sterling Press, 1981. This contains extensive instructions for making a variety of masks.

Hunt, Kari and Bernice Carlson, *Masks and Mask Makers*. New York: Abingdon Press, 1961. Many unusual masks are illustrated in this book for students.

Price, Christine, *The Mystery of Masks*. New York: Charles Scribner's Sons, 1978. The author describes for student readers the many purposes masks have served in ancient times and still today. It is extensive, but readable. Documentation is accompanied by detailed pencil illustrations.

Going to the Theatre 14

For many children in today's world, going to the theatre is a unique experience. No doubt, your students have spent many more hours in front of a television screen or even attending films than they have in going to the theatre. And, in fact, the same is probably true of most adults.

There are several obvious similarities between live theatre performances and television and film performances. For example, what appears on film and television screens is what has traditionally been performed live. Many artists do their work in all three media. There are scripts used in all three. There are actors involved as characters in dramatic situations, and directors who supervise the actors' work.

But the differences between a live theatre performance and television and film performances are quite significant. The theatre is live actors performing in front of an audience. Many students who have never seen a play before will comment on and be amazed by the realization that there are "real people up there." Sometimes after a children's play, the actors, in their costumes and makeup, will form a receiving line in the theatre lobby so the children can meet them. This makes children even more aware of the aliveness of the performers.

Most importantly, theatre performers develop a communication with the audience. They can hear the laughter, the gasping, and the other responses of the audience. This feedback stimulates the performers, helping them know if the audience is understanding the play and the dramatic situations in it. On the other hand, when films are made, usually only the other actors and film crew are watching. The per-

Simple, but effective, costumes used in formal plays can give you ideas for classroom use. This dragon's costume can be imitated with a decorated grocery bag (stuffed with newspaper), three yardsticks (crosspiece at top), and a large strip of material. (Kalamazoo Junior Civic Youth Theatre)

formers never know what an audience's response will be until they sit in the audience themselves, watching themselves on screen in the completed film. Television sometimes has studio audiences and shows that are "taped before a live audience," but these are rare and only a sample of the audience that will eventually see the show. Frequently, professional actors and actresses comment on their desire for the live audience contact that is missed when they perform in film and television. And it is the reason many actors and actresses go back to acting in a play from time to time in order to renew the feeling of communicating with a live audience.

It is this communication between the performers and the audience in a live theatre performance that students need to be made aware of, particularly if their experiences have been limited to television and film. There is a theatre etiquette that is demanded, or everyone's enjoyment of the event will be spoiled. The following list will be a starter for you to discuss with your students.

THEATRE ETIQUETTE

a.   One should arrive on time for the scheduled theatre performance. (If your school is going to the theatre by bus or walking, departure and arrival times must be carefully coordinated.)

b.   Going to the bathroom and getting drinks of water while a performance is in progress are both difficult and disturbing for others. Children need to understand the

A well-produced children's theatre play can bring children's literature alive. (The whitewashing scene from *The Trial of Tom Sawyer* by Virginia Koste. Kalamazoo Junior Civic Youth Theatre)

importance of having this taken care of before the play begins. (Most children's plays are short enough to make intermissions unnecessary.)

c. One should be considerate of others in the theatre audience. Talking during the performance disturbs the actors as well as the rest of the audience. Before the performance begins, the audience may talk quietly, but it is not acceptable to walk around in the theatre, play punching games, fuss with seats and clothing, kick the seats in front of you, or engage in other such behaviors.

d. Unlike television or film viewing, neither food nor drink is allowed in the theatre.

e. A theatre audience shows respect and appreciation for the performance by giving their full attention to the play and by applauding at the end. Loud whistling and shouting may be appropriate at a ball game outdoors, but is not acceptable in a theatre auditorium.

f. Dimming of house lights and blackouts of stage lighting are often a part of many performances. Children should understand this theatrical technique and remain calm when the lights go out.

The Prince Street Players, a professional touring children's theatre company, performs their musical version of *Pinocchio*.

g.   When the performance is over, the audience does not rush to the exits but patiently waits its turn to leave the theatre.

THEATRICAL CONVENTIONS

Theatrical "conventions" are those common practices in the theatre which are accepted by all in attendance. "Conventions" may also be the devices the theatre uses to encourage the audience to accept the play as reality. Many of these conventions are traditionally accepted by the audience, even children, without question. Some may need explaining or discussion. Following is a list of some of the more common conventions:

PERFORMANCE SPACE

Performers are always physically separated in some way from the audience. Often they perform on a stage, on platforms, or in some

Sir Gawain and the Green Knight performed by Western Michigan University Theatre.

other specifically defined area. The audience sits outside that area. (In some plays, the actors will come into the aisles of the theatre or may even interact with the audience. But they are still characters in the play, and if they encourage responses from the audience, they do it in accordance with their character.)

USE OF CURTAIN

In most cases, if a play is in an auditorium on a stage, a curtain raising or opening is the signal that the performance has begun. When it is lowered or closed, either the play has ended or an intermission is indicated.

INTERMISSION

An intermission is a pause in the performance, lasting anywhere from five to fifteen minutes, during which time the audience members may stand up, go to the bathroom, get a drink of water, or talk quietly. Many children's plays are short enough in length so that an intermission is unnecessary.

USE OF LIGHTS

a. Blinking of auditorium lights is a signal for the audience to take their seats and that the play will begin in about five minutes.

b. Dimming of auditorium lights is a signal that the play is about to begin. As soon as the house lights go down, the stage lights go on and the curtain is opened or raised.

c. Blackouts (all lights out briefly) are used as a special effect or to show the passing of time at the end of a scene or an act.

APPLAUSE

In the theatre, the audience shows its appreciation of the performance by a polite clapping of hands. Usually applause comes at the end of scenes, acts, the end of the play, and for the curtain call. If a particularly exciting moment or special effect occurs during the play, an audience may spontaneously applaud.

PROGRAM

A theatre program gives written information about the production. It lists the cast of characters as well as an acknowledgement of the playwright, director, actors, designers, and technicians. It may also include an explanation of the plot. A program is also a souvenir. (Some children's theatre companies have a practice of not distributing programs for fear that the child audience will not be able to handle them quietly.)

CURTAIN CALL

At the end of the performance, all the actors come back on stage to take their bows and acknowledge the audience's applause.

STUDY GUIDES

Most children's theatre companies provide study guides for their productions. These guides vary considerably, but most will contain some or all of the following:

plot summary
information about the script, source of material, theme
information about the author, cast, the producing company

discussion of play setting, historical period, style, staging techniques
pre- and post-discussion questions
pre- and post-activities
bibliography

Often the experiences related to the play will incorporate creative drama as well as music, visual art, creative writing, or creative movement activities. There may also be a number of suggestions for integrating the play into other areas of the curriculum such as science, language arts, or social studies.

THEATRE, TELEVISION AND FILM

At first, children may be confused with the differences between theatre and other entertainment forms like film and television. This chapter has discussed some of the conventions of theatre and why children's behavior in a theatre audience has restrictions on it. The chief difference, of course, is that theatre is **live.** Although a play has been rehearsed for many days and weeks, it is happening at the very moment the audience is seeing it.

The theatre is an ancient art form that has been a part of every culture in the world since the beginning of time. Film and television are relatively new when compared to the centuries that theatre has been in existence. They are part of what is called the "electronic media," dependent upon highly developed technology to make them available to audiences.

Unlike the theatre, film and television use cameras to select and record what the audience eventually sees. Film, which is a little older than television, is literally **moving pictures** or **"movies."** The series of pictures on film, when run through a projector, actually create the movement of the actors on the screen. Cartoon films are drawn or "animated" pictures. The more movement that is drawn in the pictures, the more movement there will be when the film is projected. Of course, the more animation in the pictures, the more the film will cost.

When live action films are made, they are "shot" in a studio on a "set" or "on location." The "set" is much like the scenery in the theatre. "On location" means the place the film crew go to in order to create, as realistically as possible, special scenes that are needed: a desert, mountains, city, or a farm, for example. These scenes would be too difficult to recreate in a studio.

Many scenes are shot and reshot during the filming period. Sometimes dozens and even hundreds of "takes" of one particular scene may be shot before the director and other artists feel satisfied. After the film is developed, it is previewed and the best scenes are selected for the final copy. Sometimes as much as half to ninety percent of the film is rejected. This fact, plus the many other expenses involved, is the reason that film budgets of well-publicized films that children hear about are so costly.

In the early days of television, the shows were performed "live;" that is, they were actually happening as the home audience watched. Many mistakes would be seen although the performers often "covered," or made up for, the errors so the audience would not be as aware of them. Now most shows are pre-recorded or filmed for later viewing. "Live" shows today are very rare.

Sometimes live studio audiences watch the videotaping being done. Often it is this audience's response and laughter that we hear in the background when the tape is eventually "aired" or played for the home audience. If a show does not have a live audience, sometimes "canned laughter" will be added to the tape. This artificially-reproduced laughter is supposed to encourage the audience to respond appropriately. Viewers who are watching at home alone are helped to feel that they are part of a larger audience, the way one would feel at a theatrical performance or in a movie theatre. Depending on the careful selection of "canned laughter," it sometimes adds to the show. Often it seems unnatural and quite phoney.

While there are many other similarities and differences in theatre, film, and television, it is the "live" audience aspect that is the most significant and notable in any comparison. In the theatre the audience gives an immediate response; in film and television it is often delayed. But it is usually the audience's reaction, over time, that eventually determines the success or failure of all material produced by these three entertainment forms.

SUGGESTED CLASS ACTIVITIES FOR DEVELOPING AWARENESS OF DIFFERENCES IN THEATRE, FILM, AND TELEVISION

1. Saturday morning television cartoons often have less animation than cartoon "specials" (*Peanuts,* for example) shown in the evening. Have the class watch a Saturday morning cartoon and compare it with an animated special shown in the early evening or with an animated film you show in class. Have them discuss the differences they note in the amount of movement that was drawn for the pictures. What are their reactions to each?

2. Ask at your local library or at a camera store for a section of old film or a piece of filmstrip. Use regular household bleach to remove the old pictures and make it transparent. Now the film can be colored with markers to make interesting patterns. Show the film or filmstrip with some background music to see how it can create an interesting mood. Experiment with as many ideas as the children express an interest in.

3. Show students the film *Gene Deitch: The Picture Book Animated* (Weston Woods, 25 min. live-action, color). In it, Deitch, a renowned American film animator now living in Prague, Czechoslovakia, shows how he turns well-known children's picture books into animated films for Weston Woods. It is both fascinating and informative.

4. Take a field trip to a local television station or a cable access station and let children see first-hand how television shows are made.

5. Check with your school or local library for children's books describing film, television, and theatre, particularly those that show people engaged in careers in these fields.

6. Have class watch a particular television show that you know uses "canned laughter." Afterwards have them discuss how they reacted to it. When did it seem realistic and when did it disrupt?

7. Check with students to see if they or someone they know makes films or has a video camera. Invite these resource people into the classroom to explain their hobby or work to the class.

8. Have students select a television show or even a televised film and watch it with the sound turned off. Have them focus on the camera shots to see what the "eye of the camera" lets the audience see.

9. If a video or a film camera is available to you, use it to record creative drama activities. It will be particularly interesting to videotape skits and story dramatizations although students will probably also want to see themselves doing pantomime and other short activities. Let students view their work and evaluate. Compare the differences they see in watching the activities "live" and on tape. If you are fortunate enough to have more then one camera, use it to videotape at the same time from a different angle. Show both videotapes at the same time, studying them to see how "cuts" could be made from one tape to another to achieve the best picture and best variety.

10. Many students are already familiar with terms like, "quiet on the set," "lights, camera, action!" Try using them in conducting drama activities for establishing a professional atmosphere.

SELECTED READINGS FOR CHILDREN ON THE THEATRE

There are a number of books for children which focus in some way on theatre. You may wish to make them available to your class for independent reading.

4 *Backstage*, Robert Maiorano and Rachel Isadora. New York: Greenwillow, 1978. A young girl, whose mother is a ballerina, goes backstage in the theatre during a rehearsal of Tchaikovsky's *The Nutcracker* ballet, taking the reader with her through the pictures. Although the performance is a ballet, the backstage details are similar to those for theatre.

4 *The Bionic Bunny Show*, Marc Brown and Laurene Krasny Brown. Boston: Little, Brown, 1984. This is a humorous behind-the-scenes look at how a fictitious television show, "The Bionic Bunny," is made. Focus is particularly on showing how the star, a rather ordinary bunny, is made to look heroic. The book cleverly cuts from what is seen on

the television screen to what is seen on the actual television set. A glossary of television terms is included.

4–6 *Circus in a Suitcase,* Reg Bolton. Rowayton, CT: New Plays, 1982. This is not a book about the theatre but about the circus, circus tricks, and clowning. It is informative and geared to both children and adults.

4 *The Duck with Squeaky Feet*, Denys Cazet. Scarsdale, NY: Bradbury Press, 1980. This is a humorous story about a mouse who tries to write a play for a duck with squeaky feet, a toothless alligator, and other assorted animals who keep appearing on stage. But the play turns out to be too silly for words.

5–6 *Exploring Mime*, Mark Stolzenberg. New York: Sterling Publishing Company, 1979. This is a fascinating and informative look at stylized mime for beginners. It is interesting to read and guaranteed to get some interested students trying out this art form.

4 *Hattie the Backstage Bat*, Don Freeman. New York: Viking, 1970. Hattie, a bat who lives in the theatre, makes a dull mystery play exciting when she flies out of hiding and into the lights casting a huge shadow. The illustrations show scenery being built, stage lighting, the back of a set and stage relationship to the auditorium.

4–5 *Here Come the Purim Players*, Barbara Cohen. New York: Lothrop, Lee & Shepard, 1984. Purim players in Prague, in medieval tradition, perform the Biblical story of Queen Esther's bravery.

4 *Jesse and Abe*, Rachel Isadora. New York: Greenwillow, 1981. Set in the 1920's, Jesse's grandfather is a doorman at Brown's Variety Theatre. Every night Jesse gets to watch the theatrical acts from the wings. This gives a glimpse at an era when vaudeville was at its peak.

4 *The Little Moon Theatre,* Irene Haas. New York: Atheneum, 1981. A caravan theatre travels all around giving tailor-made performances and meeting an assortment of people, including a fairy godmother. Though whimsical in treatment, the book does give an interesting look into the traveling show.

4–6 *The Marcel Marceau Alphabet Book*, George Mendoza. New York: Doubleday, 1970. This is an interesting look at a famous mimist who recreates the alphabet in this book of photographs. It gives children an exposure to the art of stylized mime. For older students, the photos are, of course, more interesting than the alphabet.

6 *Master Rosiland*, John and Patricia Beatty. New York: William Morrow, 1974. A young woman disguises herself as a young boy in order to play the female roles (a traditional practice) in Shakespearean plays in the late 1500's in Elizabethan England.

4–6 *The Nutcracker*, Martha Swope. New York: Dodd, Mead & Co., 1975. This is a photographic account of the traditional Christmas story of

Tchaikovsky, performed by the New York City Ballet and choreographed by George Balanchine.

4–6 *Putting on a Show*, Melvin Berger. New York: Franklin Watts, 1980. This book, complete with photographs, presents chapters on the various aspects of the theatre including acting, makeup, scenery, props, and so forth.

5–6 *Shakespeare's Theatre*, C. Walter Hodges. New York: Coward, McCann & Geoghegan, 1964. The author starts with the premise that theatre has always been an essential part of life and then describes earliest rituals and other theatrical forms through Shakespeare's day with detail of a performance of *Julius Caesar*.

4 *Sing, Pierrot, Sing: A Picturebook in Mime*, Tomie de Paola. New York: Harcourt Brace Jovanovich, 1983. Drawing from French and Italian folklore, this wordless picturebook features the traditional characters from the commedia del arte—Pierrot, Columbine, and Harlequin—in a tale of love of the highest order. A book to use for storytelling, as a basis of a mime show or shadow play, or just to look at and enjoy.

4–6 *The Story of Bip*, Marcel Marceau. New York: Harper, 1976. This is another book featuring the famous French mimist. In this one he has written and illustrated a story about his best known character, Bip.

4–6 *The Wonderful World of Theatre*, J. B. Priestly. Garden City, NY: Garden City Books, 1959, 1969. This is an informative book with numerous fascinating photos and illustrations, in both black and white and in color, of the history of the theatre. Although brief, it is packed with detail.

15 Story and Poetry Anthologies and Books for Dramatization

ANTHOLOGIES

Throughout the text, numbers in parentheses have referred to these correspondingly numbered anthologies and children's novels.

(1) *All the Silver Pennies*, Blanche Jennings Thompson. New York: Macmillan, 1967.

(2) *Anansi, the Spider Man*, Philip M. Sherlock. New York: Thomas Y. Crowell, 1954.

(3) *Anthology of Children's Literature*, (5th ed.), Edna Johnson, Evelyn R. Sickels, Frances Clarke Sayers, and Carolyn Horovitz. Boston: Houghton Mifflin Company, 1977.

(4) *The Arbuthnot Anthology of Children's Literature* (4th ed.), May Hill Arbuthnot, rev. by Zena Sutherland. Glenview, Ill.: Scott, Foresman, 1976.

(5) *Beyond the Clapping Mountains*, Charles E. Gillham. New York: Macmillan, 1964.

(6) *The Blackbird in the Lilac*, James Reeves. New York: Dutton, 1959.

(7) *Catch a Little Rhyme*, Eve Merriam. New York: Atheneum, 1966.

(8) *Catch Me a Wind*, Patricia Hubbell. New York: Atheneum, 1968.

(9) *Children's Literature for Dramatization: An Anthology,* Geraldine Brain Siks. New York: Harper & Row, Pub., 1964.

(10) *Cinnamon Seed*, John T. Moore. Boston: Houghton Mifflin Company, 1967.

(11) *The Crack in the Wall and Other Terribly Weird Tales*, George Mendoza. New York: Dial Press, 1968.

(12) *The Dancing Kettle and Other Japanese Folk Tales*, Yoshiko Uchida. New York: Harcourt Brace Jovanovich, 1949.

(13) *Eleanor Farjeon's Poems for Children*. Philadelphia: Lippincott, 1951.

(14) *Eric Carle's Story Book; Seven Tales by the Brothers Grimm*. New York: Franklin Watts, 1976.

(15) *Favorite Fairy Tales Told in England*, Virginia Haviland. Boston: Little, Brown, 1959.

(16) *Favorite Fairy Tales Told in Scotland*, Virginia Haviland. Boston: Little, Brown, 1963.

(17) *Favorite Stories Old and New*, selected by Sidonie Matsner Gruenberg. Garden City, N.Y.: Doubleday, 1955.

(18) *Fingers Are Always Bringing Me News*, Mary O'Neill. Garden City, N.Y.: Doubleday, 1969.

(19) *Fire on the Mountain and Other Ethiopian Stories*, Harold Courlander and Wolf Leslau. New York: Holt, Rinehart & Winston, 1959.

(20) *Grandfather Tales*, Richard Chase. Boston: Houghton Mifflin Company, 1948.

(21) *Gwot! Horribly Funny Hairticklers*, George Mendoza. New York: Harper & Row, Pub., 1967.

(22) *The Hat-Shaking Dance and Other Tales from the Gold Coast*, Harold Courlander and Albert Kofi Prempeh. New York: Harcourt Brace Jovanovich, 1957.

(23) *The Hare and the Bear and Other Stories*, Yasue Maiyagawa. New York: Parents' Magazine Press, 1971.

(24) *Just So Stories*, Rudyard Kipling, illustrated by Victor Ambrus. New York: Rand McNally, 1982.

(25) *Let's Marry Said the Cherry*, N. M. Bodeker. Atheneum, 1974.

(26) *A Light in the Attic*, Shel Silverstein. New York: Harper & Row, Pub., 1981.

(27) *Medicine for Melancholy*, Ray Bradbury. Garden City, N.Y.: Doubleday, 1959.

(28) *Mouse Tales,* Arnold Lobel. New York: Harper & Row, Pub., 1972.

(29) *Nobody is Perfick,* Bernard Weber. Boston: Houghton Mifflin Company, 1971.

(30) *Oh, What Nonsense!* selected by William Cole. New York: Viking, 1966.

(31) *Once the Hodja,* Alice Geer Kelsey. New York: Longmans, Green, 1943.

(32) *On City Streets,* Nancy Larrick (ed.). New York: M. Evans and Co., Inc., 1968.

(33) *Piping Down the Valleys Wild,* Nancy Larrick (ed.). New York: Dell Publishing, 1968.

(34) *Reflections on a Gift of Watermelon Pickle*, Stephen Dunning, Edward Lueders, Hugh Smith (eds.). Glenview, Ill.: Scott, Foresman, 1966.

(35) *The Riverside Anthology of Children's Literature*, 6th edition, Judith Saltman (ed.). Boston: Houghton Mifflin, 1985.

(36) *The Sea of Gold and Other Tales from Japan*, Yoshika Uchida. New York: Charles Scribner's, 1965.

(37) *The Sneetches and Other Stories*, Dr. Seuss. New York: Random House, 1961.

(38) *Some Haystacks Don't Even Have Any Needles,* compiled by Stephen Dunning, Edward Lueders, Hugh Smith. Glenview, Ill.: Scott, Foresman, 1969.

(39) *Storytelling,* Ruth Tooze. Englewood Cliffs, N.J.: Prentice-Hall, 1959.

(40) *Stories to Dramatize,* Winifred Ward. New Orleans, LA.: Anchorage Press, 1981.

(41) *Take Sky,* David McCord. Boston: Atlantic-Little, Brown, 1962.

(42) *Tales from the Cheyennes,* Grace Jackson Penney. Boston: Houghton Mifflin Company, 1953.

(43) *Tall Tales from the High Hills*, Ellis Credle. Camden, N.J.: Thom. Nelson, 1957.

(44) *That's Why,* Aileen Fisher. Camden, N.J.: Thom. Nelson, 1946.

(45) *There Is No Rhyme for Silver*, Eve Merriam. New York: Atheneum, 1962.

(46) *The Thing At the Foot of the Bed and Other Scary Tales*, Maria Leach. New York: The World Publishing Company, 1959.

(47) *Thirteen Danish Tales*, Mary C. Hatch. New York: Harcourt Brace Jovanovich, 1947.

(48) *Thunder in the Mountains: Legends of Canada*, Hilda Mary Hooke. Toronto: Oxford University Press, 1947.

(49) *The Tiger and the Rabbit and Other Tales*, Pura Belpre. Philadelphia: Lippincott, 1965.

(50) *The Time-Ago Tales of Jahdu*, Virginia Hamilton. New York: Macmillan, 1969.

(51) *Time for Poetry* (rev. ed.), May Hill Arbuthnot. Glenview, Ill.: Scott, Foresman, 1959.

(52) *The Wandering Moon*, James Reeves. New York: Dutton, 1960.

(53) *Where the Sidewalk Ends*, Shel Silverstein. New York: Harper & Row, Pub., 1974.

(54) *Why the Chimes Rang*, Raymond Macdonald Alden. Indianapolis, Ind.: Bobbs-Merrill, 1954.

(55) *The Wicked Tricks of Tyl Ullenspiegel,* Jay Williams. New York: Four Winds, 1978.

(56) *Windsong*, Carl Sandburg. New York: Harcourt Brace Jovanovich, 1960.

(57) *World Tales for Creative Dramatics and Storytelling*, Burdett S. Fitzgerald. Englewood Cliffs, N.J.: Prentice-Hall, 1962.

(58) *Yertle the Turtle and Other Stories*, Dr. Seuss. New York: Random House, 1958.

BOOKS FOR DRAMATIZATION

The following books are highly recommended for extended dramatization work. They are only a representative sampling of the fine literature available for today's students. Some are older classics that remain as viable today as they were when first printed. Others have been selected for their historical and geographical settings, relationship to other areas of the curriculum, social themes, and their variety of heroes and heroines.

The books are listed alphabetically according to title. Suggested grade levels are indicated to the left of the title.

(59) 4–6 *Alice's Adventures in Wonderland*, Lewis Carroll. New York: The Macmillan Co., 1960. This contains the classic stories of Alice's unusual adventures.

(60) 4 *All Alone*, Claire Huchet Bishop. New York: The Viking Press, 1953. Two boys who are in charge of the herds in the French Alps violate the rule of constant vigil.

(61) 6 *Amos Fortune, Free Man*, Elizabeth Yates. New York: E. P. Dutton, 1950. This is the biography of a slave who struggles for and gains his freedom.

(62) 4–6 . . . *And Now, Miguel,* Joseph Krumgold. New York: Thomas Y. Crowell, 1953. The story of a sheepherding family in New Mexico is presented.

(63) 4–5 *Ben and Me,* Robert Lawson. Boston: Little, Brown and Co., Inc., 1939. This is the ever-popular and amusing story of how a mouse helped Benjamin Franklin with his many inventions and achievements.

(64) 4 *The Borrowers,* Mary Norton. New York: Harcourt Brace Jovanovich, 1953. The adventures of the little people who live under the floorboards of the house and borrow small objects to furnish their home are presented. Sequels are available.

(65) 4–6 *By the Great Horn Spoon!* Sid Fleischman. Boston: Little, Brown and Co., 1963. A young boy and his aunt's butler stow away on a ship headed for California gold in this humorous, historical fiction adventure.

(66) 4 *Charlotte's Web,* E.B. White. New York: Harper and Row, 1952. Wilbur the pig, with the help of his barnyard friends and most particularly Charlotte the spider, develops into a most unique pig.

(67) 4 *Christmas on the Mayflower,* Wilma P. Hayes. New York: Coward, McCann, 1956. A dramatic conflict is presented when the crew of the *Mayflower* wants to return to England before the safety of the Pilgrims in a new land is assured.

(68) 5–6 *Danny the Champion of the World,* Roald Dahl. New York: Alfred A. Knopf, 1975. Danny and his father, a widower, manage a filling station and live in a nearby caravan. Their love and respect of each other is a strong theme throughout the book as well as a marvelous adventure of poaching pheasants, which eventually involves many villagers. It has an English setting.

(69) 4–5 *Ellen Tebbits,* Beverly Cleary. New York: William Morrow, 1951, 1979. Life never seems to be simple for young Ellen, who experiences misunderstanding along with her many other adventures.

(70) 4–6 *Fantastic Mr. Fox,* Roald Dahl. New York: Alfred A. Knopf, 1970. Mr. Fox and his family, along with other burrowing animals, outwit three farmers who are out to destroy him once and for all in this suspenseful, fast-moving tale full of humorous characters.

(71) 6 *The Forgotten Door,* Alexander Key. Philadelphia: The Westminster Press, 1965. In this intriguing story, Jon, a boy from another world, falls through a forgotten door into this world. Because he is different, both he and the family who befriends him must deal with the fears and prejudices of the less tolerant citizens of the community.

(72) 4–6 *From the Mixed-Up Files of Mrs. Basil E. Frankweiler,* Elaine L.

Konigsberg. New York: Atheneum, 1967. Claudia and her brother run away to live for a week in New York City's Metropolitan Museum of Art and make an exciting discovery about a particular statue. This is a modern mystery adventure.

(73) 5–6 *The Great Brain,* John D. Fitzgerald. New York: Dial, 1967. This popular autobiographical account of the author's brother, a loveable schemer, has its setting in the late 1800's in Utah. The sequels are equally appealing.

(74) 4–6 *Harriet the Spy,* Louise Fitzhugh. New York: Harper and Row, 1964. To counteract the loneliness caused by affluent and indifferent parents, Harriet keeps a notebook on her observations of people.

(75) 4–6 *Henry Huggins*, Beverly Cleary. New York: William Morrow and Co., 1950, 1978. The ever-popular antics of a young boy and his dog Ribsy are presented. It is also available in Spanish translation by Argentina Palacios, William Morrow, 1983.

(76) 4–6 *Henry Reed, Inc.*, Keith Robertson. New York: Viking, 1968. A very humorous story of an enterprising boy and his friend, Midge. Sequels are available.

(77) 6 *The High King,* Lloyd Alexander. New York: Holt, Rinehart and Winston, 1968. This last of a five-book chronicle about Prydain, an imaginary realm, can stand independently of the others in the series. Taran, an assistant pig keeper, gathers forces to defeat Arwan, the ruler of the Land of the Dead.

(78) 4–6 *Homer Price*, Robert McCloskey. New York: Viking, 1943. The humorous adventures of a young boy in a small town who manages to capture robbers with the help of his pet skunk and to solve a problem of too many doughnuts.

(79) 4–6 *How to Eat Fried Worms*, Thomas Rockwell. New York: Franklin Watts, 1973. Billy Forrester makes a bet that he can eat fifteen worms in fifteen days for fifty dollars. The plot centers on the many schemes the other bettor uses to keep Billy from being successful.

(80) 5–6 *Johnny Tremain*, Esther Forbes. Boston: Houghton Mifflin, 1943. Johnny, a young silver apprentice in Boston, struggles to maturity during the 1770's in this classical book of historic fiction.

(81) 5–6 *King Arthur and His Knights*, (The Story of), Howard Pyle. New York: Charles Scribner's Sons, 1954. The legendary king of England and the many tales of his equally legendary knights are presented.

(82) 4 *The Little House Series*, Laura Ingalls Wilder. New York: Harper and Row. These several books contain the classic and true stories of an American pioneer family in various Midwest locations. They inspired a long running and popular television series.

(83) 4 *The Mouse and the Motorcycle*, Beverly Cleary. New York: William

Morrow and Co., 1965. A mouse named Ralph has interesting adventures with a toy motorcycle. Sequels of Ralph's adventures are also available.

(84) 4 *Mr. Popper's Penguins*, Richard and Florence Atwater. Boston: Little, Brown and Co., 1938. Still a favorite, this story tells of Mr. Popper who, after writing of his interest in South Pole expeditions, receives a gift of a penguin from Admiral Drake. With a zoo's gift of a mate for the penguin, they increase to twelve. The Poppers train and take the penguins on the theatrical circuit in order to make enough money to care for them.

(85) 6 *Mrs. Frisby and the Rats of NIMH*, Robert C. O'Brien. New York: Atheneum, 1971. Laboratory rats from the National Institute of Mental Health seek to make a better world for themselves.

(86) 5–6 *My Brother Sam Is Dead*, Christopher and James Collier. New York: Four Winds Press, 1974. An American family in Connecticut during the Revolutionary War are on opposing sides—the Tories versus the Patriots. Events before, during, and after the war change their attitudes.

(87) 4–6 *Old Yeller,* Fred Gipson. New York: Harper and Row, 1956. Set in the 1860's in Texas, this story focuses on the comic and heroic behaviors of a mangy dog who strays into a boy's life.

(88) 4–6 *The Peterkin Papers*, Lucretia Hale. Boston: Houghton Mifflin, 1924. This collection of classical, nonsensical stories of a family and their absurd problems remains as popular today as it was a hundred years ago when it first appeared.

(89) 5–6 *The Phantom Tollbooth*, Norman Juster. New York: Random House, 1961. Milo has many adventures in a fantastical land. He tries to be the mediator between two kings who are having a dispute over the importance of mathematics and language.

(90) 4–6 *Pinocchio, The Adventures of*, C. Collodi. New York: Lothrop, Lee & Shepard, 1983. This is the 100th anniversary edition of the adventures of this famous puppet who longs to be a real boy.

(91) 4–5 *Pippi Longstocking*, Astrid Lindgren. New York: Viking Press, 1950. Pippi, a superhuman girl whose widowed father is off at sea, lives by herself and is independent. Her style of living and her adventures are unorthodox and appealing to children who must follow other rules.

(92) 6 *The Pushcart War*, Jean Merrill. Reading, MA: Addison-Wesley, 1964. In a humorous spoof on the traffic problems in New York City, pushcart vendors, who are being overrun by the Mighty Mammoths (truck drivers), start a war with peashooters.

(93) 5–6 (*The Merry Adventures of*) *Robin Hood,* Howard Pyle. New York:

Charles Scribner's, 1946. The legendary accounts of the outlaw-hero of England are presented.

(94) 4 *The Robot and Rebecca*, Jane Yolen. New York: Alfred A. Knopf, 1980. Rebecca Jason receives a robot for her ninth birthday. With its help she is able to solve a mystery involving twin children and alien creatures. Set in the year 2121.

(95) 5–6 *The Secret Soldier: The Story of Deborah Sampson*, Ann McGovern. New York: Scholastic, 1975. A true story of a young woman who disguised herself as a young man and fought in the Revolutionary War is presented by a well-known historical writer.

(96) 5–6 *Shadow of a Bull*, Maia Wojciechowska. New York: Atheneum, 1964. Everyone expects Manolo to be a great Spanish bullfighter like his father, but he makes his own choice in the end.

(97) 4 *Tales of a Fourth Grade Nothing*, Judy Blume. New York: E.P. Dutton, 1972. Peter is convinced his life is worth nothing with a little brother like Fudge who does everything wrong, including eating Peter's pet turtle.

(98) 4–5 *This Time, Tempe Wick?* Patricia Gauch. New York: Coward, McCann and Geoghegan, Inc., 1974. A true story about Tempe Wick, a girl who lived in New Jersey during the Revolutionary War. Forgotten and disillusioned Pennsylvania soldiers try to rob Tempe of her horse so they can return home, but she outwits them in a clever way.

(99) 5–6 *Treasure Island*, Robert Louis Stevenson. New York: Charles Scribner's, 1981 (reissued). Young Jim Hawkins and the villainous, but appealing, rogue, Long John Silver, sail to a tropic isle and become involved in a climactic battle for treasure.

(100) 6 *Tuck Everlasting*, Natalie Babbitt. New York: Farrar, Straus & Giroux, 1975. The Tuck family discover they are incapable of dying after drinking from a spring in a strange forest. Twelve-year-old Winnie Foster, who has run away from her home, meets Jesse Tuck and falls in love. She plans to reunite with him at age seventeen, but realizes she must decide between mortality and immortality.

(101) 5–6 *Twenty and Ten*, Claire Hulchet Bishop. New York: Viking, 1953. When Nazi soldiers come to a mountain retreat in search of ten Jewish children, twenty fifth-grade French children become involved in hiding them in a cave. It is based on a true story.

(102) 4–6 *The Wheel on the School*, Meindert DeJong. New York: Harper and Row, 1964. The children of Shora, a little fishing village in the Netherlands, involve the whole town in their project to get the storks to return.

(103) 4 *While the Horses Galloped to London*, Mabel Watts. New York: Parents' Magazine Press, 1973. On his carriage ride to London, Sher-

man guards a cooking pot which he uses to outwit the outlaw, Rough Roger.

(104) 4–5 *Wind in the Willows*, Kenneth Grahame. New York: Charles Scribner's Sons, 1935. The charming adventures of Mole, Rat, Badger, and Toad are presented. Toad is assisted by his friends in conquering his craze of motorcars and in gaining back his family estate from the Wild Wood animals who take it over when Toad is imprisoned for driving violations. See also the recent edition with illustrations by Michael Hague. New York: Holt, Rinehart, 1980.

(105) 6 *The Witch of Blackbird Pond*, Elizabeth George Speare. Boston: Houghton Mifflin Co., 1958. After leaving her home in Barbados, Kit Tyler feels out of place in a Puritan community in Connecticut. Her spirited personality arouses suspicion, and she finds herself accused of witchcraft.

(106) 4–6 *The Wizard of Oz*, Frank L. Baum. New York: Macmillan, 1962 (reprint). A Kansas cyclone carries Dorothy and her dog to the Land of Oz where she makes friends with a Scarecrow, a Tinman, and a Lion.

(107) 4–6 *A Wrinkle in Time,* Madeleine L'Engle. New York: Farrar, Straus & Giroux, 1962. Children search for their father who has been in outer space for over a year on a classified mission. Traveling through time they land on the planet Camazotz, which is under the rule of a black force, IT, where their father is a prisoner. Sequels are available.

Glossary

aesthetic discipline   The ability of an artist to focus on the requirements and demands of his or her art form.

character   A person, animal, or entity in a scene, story, or play with distinguishing physical, mental, and attitudinal attributes.

children's theatre   Plays performed, either by children, adults, or a combination of the two, for audiences of children.

choreography   Staged dancing; the arrangement of dances for performance.

climax   The moment in a play of the highest dramatic or emotional intensity.

conflict   An essential ingredient of most plots, in which the central character or characters meet opposition that must be resolved.

concentration   The ability to focus and keep one's attention on one's work, excluding all distractions.

creative drama   An improvisational, non-exhibitional, process-centered form of theatre in which participants are guided by a leader to imagine, enact, and reflect upon human experiences.

cue   The final words or actions of one character which signal the next character to begin his own.

dialogue   The words used by the characters, or improvised by the actors, to communicate thoughts, feelings, and actions.

double casting   Using two people to play the part of a single character.

emotional awareness   Creative drama activities used to heighten understanding of feelings.

evaluation   In creative drama, the appraisal of one's own work and the work of others after engaging in dramatic activities.

freeze   To stand completely still as if for a picture. Also used as a command to students to stop their dramatic enactments.

frozen picture   Name given to activity in which students, usually in groups, create interesting visual scenes to emphasize certain important moments or emotional situations.

imagination   The process of visualizing what is not physically present or has never been experienced.

imitative movement   Activities in which children imitate the characteristic movements of animals, people, objects, and the like.

improvisation   The act of spontaneously inventing characters, action, dialogue, or plot during rehearsal or performance of dramatic materials.

motivation   **a.** An activity or discussion which stimulates and prepares the students for the drama activity or lesson to follow, helping them identify with the characters and situations. **b.** The psychological rationale that contributes to a character's behavior.

pair playing   Any number of players interacting as two different characters in a scene. All couples play at the same time.

pantomime   The performance of dramatic action without words.

playing in role   A technique used by the drama leader during the playing, in which the leader pretends to be a character, appropriate to the situation, for the purpose of heightening and advancing the play.

plot   The storyline of a drama. Plot structure usually includes a beginning, middle, and end with a problem that is resolved in some way by the time the drama is completed.

project or projection   To increase the size of the voice and movement so that it can be seen and heard by everyone in the audience.

properties or props   Set props: all that is added to the scenery on stage such as furniture. Hand props: any article or object used by the actor in the playing of his/her part.

proscenium arch   The opening of a stage through which the audience views the performance.

puppetry   The artful animation of objects, from hands to larger-than-life figures, creating characters for dramatic enactments.

quieting activity   An activity that physically and mentally calms down the students at the end of a drama lesson and prepares them to continue schoolwork in a controlled and relaxed manner.

reader's theatre   Staged readings of dramatic materials.

replaying   Enacting a scene or story again for the purpose of changing roles, adding to, or improving upon the dramatic work.

role playing   Enacting a character other than oneself in any dramatic material.

script   The written lines spoken by the actors.

sensory awareness   Perception of one's environment through the senses. To develop the actor's sensory awareness, activities and experiences are used to focus on and sharpen perceptions.

shadow play   A form of puppetry using flat puppets, actors' hands, or actors' silhouettes presented behind a backlighted screen.

sidecoaching   A technique used by the drama leader during the playing, in which the leader offers verbal suggestions or comments from the sidelines to heighten and advance the playing.

simultaneous playing   Several students, and often the entire class, playing the same character or story at the same time.

skit   A short scene of dialogue or pantomime.

solo or individual playing   Any number of players performing by themselves in their own playing space, all at the same time.

spectacle   The visual staging, such as sets, props, lighting, and costumes, to clarify and enhance the audience's understanding of the plot and characters of a drama.

story dramatization   The making and performance of an informal play from a story.

studying the script   The process of careful reading and rehearsal of interpreting the action and dialogue in a playscript.

triple casting   Using three people to play the part of a single character.

"waiting in the wings"   Expression to describe actor's readiness for entry onto the stage.

warmup   An activity designed to limber up actors' bodies/voices as well as positive mental attitude toward further drama work.

wings   Off-stage space to the left and right of the playing area where actors await their entrances and props and small set pieces are kept until needed.

Theatre Arts for All Children: Making Considerations for Children with Special Needs

A child in a wheelchair participates in a story dramatization. He is aided in moving about the room by a classmate who is double-cast in the same character role. A drama leader tells a story, making sure that her lips and face can be seen by a child wearing a hearing aid. A child with special talents has written a story that a small group of her classmates are dramatizing. And a child with behavior difficulties is making a noticeable effort to restrain his outbursts in order to play a drama activity with his classmates and be a part of the group.

Today's elementary classroom has students with a multitude of different needs. Caring for these needs is mandatory if we are going to provide equal opportunities to all. In conducting drama activities, we look at children's special needs in order to help them participate as fully as possible. However, while there may seem to be certain aspects of drama some children may not be able to participate in fully, children frequently will see ways to solve the problem creatively on their own. Focusing on the children's abilities rather than their inabilities will encourage these attempts.

And even though we generally consider the teacher responsible for identifying the various needs children have and for implementing compensatory learning experiences, the classroom can also become a community of learners who willingly assist each other and help each other succeed. Many goals can be achieved by establishing a "buddy" or support system. A child who speaks a different language, for example, can be aided by the child who is bilingual. The academically gifted, in addition to pursuing their own interests, may be able to assist those who need special tutoring. Children can assist handicapped classmates; in fact, some handicapped children can assist others whose handicaps are different from theirs. All of these experiences can give children a needed sense of responsibility and importance in serving the classroom community.

GENERAL DRAMA TECHNIQUES THAT ARE USEFUL

Two drama techniques that have been used throughout this text should be helpful for a number of special needs. One is *simultaneous or unison playing.* When all children are playing an idea at the same time, they are automatically part of the group. They can also see other children participating and learn from this modeling and demonstrating. Yet there is no undue attention on the children themselves, and they can participate and blend into the activity at their own pace.

A second technique is *multiple-casting of roles,* used most frequently in story dramatization. Almost any role in a story can be double-cast, allowing two children to work together, one supported by the other. Some character parts can use even more than two players. This technique can allow any child to play any part because of the assistance from a partner.

Finally, it is helpful to remember that drama encourages participants to get *outside of themselves.* Much of the stress we feel in our lives is the result of inward focus, and children who have been made aware of their special differences no doubt carry an extra burden. By extending ourselves in the world around us and "losing ourselves" in activities like drama, we experience a therapeutic release. This release can help us put life back into its proper perspective and render us healthier for future tasks.

ADDITIONAL SUGGESTIONS
FOR SPECIFIC SPECIAL NEEDS

Following are some additional suggestions for working in theatre arts with children of varying needs and abilities. They are not all-inclusive but merely intended to encourage your thinking. Eventually you will discover many more options yourself that will fit your own and your classroom's particular needs.

BILINGUAL-BICULTURAL

1. Many drama activities in this resource guide are based on folk literature, a universal literary form. Some folktale plot lines (for example, "Cinderella") have been found to exist in almost every language and culture. Take special note to include stories from your classroom's language and culture heritage. Encourage the children to bring such stories to your attention for drama activities.

2. Movement, pantomime, and nonverbal communication are also universal languages. They can take over when words fail or are inadequate to express needs. Bilingual children will enjoy the focus on pantomime activities particularly.

3. Another universal activity is puppetry. Crafting a puppet, making it move, and giving it a personality can all be done without verbal language. Some children may have knowledge of special kinds of puppets from their country or culture that they can share with the class.

4. Incorporate references to special cultural holidays, customs, and experience in drama activities, from simple sensory activities to more elaborate story dramatizations. Utilize the rich multiethnic resources your students can provide for you and for each other.

5. Many story dramatizations, particularly the circle stories, can be a good vehicle for learning vocabulary. Headbands or name tags can be made for characters (i.e. dog, king, man, and so on) using both the English word and the second-language words.

MENTALLY HANDICAPPED

1. These children will need to deal with concrete experiences as much as possible. Pictures, props, and other aids will be necessary for them to understand information and concepts.

2. Pantomime is also valuable for the slow learner, whose verbal skills may not be advanced enough to engage fully in the dialogue and improvisational activities. Include plenty of pantomime activities in each drama lesson.

3. The graded materials in this text should assist in finding literature these children can handle successfully.

4. The roles these children play in drama activities should not tax them beyond their academic skills; and the same time, they can often surprise us with their concentration and involvement, their careful observation of classmates, and their contentment in participating with their peers in a group activity.

ACADEMICALLY GIFTED AND TALENTED

Academically gifted children, who have high IQ scores, are ahead of their classmates mainly in the use of language. However, there are other talents that children can be gifted in, such as music, athletic abilities, or even interpersonal skills. Therefore children can be gifted or talented in some areas but not in others.

Enriching experiences are usually required for gifted and talented youngsters, who can bypass the kind of drill work other children may need.

1. In drama, gifted children will probably excel in dialogue and improvisation. They will particularly enjoy verbal encounters and debates. They may find it easy to invent all manner of dialogue in story dramatization.

2. Some gifted and talented children may be interested in creating drama materials. They may even wish to develop some of the activities discussed in this text, from narrative pantomimes to sequence games to segmented story activities. Encourage

these activities, perhaps letting them work with the many bibliographic references in this text.

3. Gifted children may also want to try their hand at leading drama activities. They may wish to narrate a narrative pantomime story for the class or for a small group to perform. They may show directorial skills by visualizing interesting ways for their classmates to interpret stories.

4. Gifted children may also be encouraged to try their hand at playwriting, creating puppet shows, or even leading a small group to perform dramas for other classrooms in your school.

5. Other avenues of enrichment for these children may include working with film, television, or appropriate community theatre activities. They may be interested in reading further about theatre and sharing their findings with the rest of the class.

PHYSICAL DISABILITIES

1. A partner can assist in moving a wheelchair or in making an area accessible to the child.

2. These children may be partial to verbal and dialogue activities if they are limited in bodily movement. Be sure to give plenty of opportunity for such activities in each lesson.

3. Remember that nonverbal communication (pantomime) is conveyed by all parts of the body—from body posture to facial expression and from hand gestures to the way we move our feet. Depending on the impairment, focus on pantomime activities that can be done with the children's most mobile parts of the body. Facial expression can be focused on for those whose arms and legs are impaired. Or, gestures can be focused on if the hands and arms are mobile.

4. People in wheelchairs tend not to receive as much supportive touch as other children, probably because the chair itself acts as a barrier. Be alert to this fact and give reassurance and emotional tactile support to these children as often as you do to the rest of the class.

VISUAL IMPAIRMENTS

1. Try to paint word pictures and clear details of what you are talking about. Describe pictures, and props, and tell stories with great detail to create mental pictures for the visually impaired.

2. Recorded music is valuable in aiding the mood or environment you are trying to create.

3. Let visually impaired children explore through touch as much and as often as possible. If you are using props, for example, they will want and need to touch and handle them.

4. Abstract concepts and ideas may not be easily understood by these children. Consider this as you plan a lesson in order to make sure you cover all points clearly.

5. Touch, carefully monitored, can assist in calming, directing, or assisting the child and can give moral support and encouragement.

6. A partner can help explain quietly the points that may be missed.

HEARING IMPAIRED

1. Be sure these children can see your face and particularly your lips if they are trying to lip read. There is no need to exaggerate your speech; in fact, that will distort the sounds they have been trained to observe. Also try not to stand with a window behind you, as this will cast a shadow over your face.
2. Repeat comments made by children whose voices are too soft to be heard easily.
3. Visual cues, pictures, props, gestures, directions on cards, are very helpful for these children. Use them generously.
4. These children generally enjoy and are successful with pantomime activities particularly.
5. A partner can repeat directions or explanations quietly whenever the child needs additional assistance.

SPEECH IMPAIRED

Speech impairments generally include articulation disorders, stuttering, phonation problems, and delayed or limited speech.

1. Generally, the classroom teacher can assist with speech difficulties by providing an open and relaxed atmosphere that encourages rather than inhibits these children in their speech. Since children usually consider drama fun, they tend to forget about their speech difficulties during drama class.
2. Pantomime experiences will be particularly enjoyable for these children.
3. Being able to play with oral activities is useful for the speech impaired youngster. They need opportunities to speak and to hear others engaging in language.
4. Engaging in rhythmic activities, choral-type speaking in unison, and character role-playing often lessens stuttering behaviors.

EMOTIONALLY HANDICAPPED

Emotionally handicapped children may have difficulty controlling themselves, but some may be very quiet and withdrawn.

1. Because these children often have short attention spans, they will need to move frequently from one task to another. Be alert to their responses and to the fact that you may need to cut activity short and go to another for variety's sake.
2. At the same time, extending their periods of concentration on a task is also desirable. Move by slow increments in this goal for maximum success.
3. Movements of larger muscles is often successful. Body movement activities and pantomime should be particularly useful for them.
4. A secure, consistent, and supportive environment is important for these children. They also need to experience success and feel good about themselves. Initially, using a series of short activities that they can feel competent in doing should provide a good foundation to build on.

Finally, it is important to remember that there are more similarities than differences between children with "special" needs and their classmates. We are all human and we all have the need to love and be loved, to communicate, to learn, and to feel successful.

The subject of drama is the subject of life. And because it provides a variety of avenues for all to express their specific talents in unique ways, drama has often been called a great "leveler" of persons. No one is considered any greater or lesser than anyone else in drama. And this is as it should be in life itself.

Prentice-Hall Correlation to the Essential Elements Theatre Arts, Grades 4–6 (Teacher Resource Book)

Creative Drama Resource for Grades 4–6 is designed to aid teachers in guiding older elementary children in creative drama experiences, puppetry, and appreciation of theatrical events.

This book is intended for use either by an elementary school theatre arts specialist or a classroom teacher with limited training in theatre arts. While specialists will be familiar with many of the concepts presented, they should find the structure of the book helpful in curriculum planning. Over 400 selections of children's literature are suggested and over 20 sample lesson plans are presented. Along with over 100 games and activities, these should augment the specialists' own collection of drama materials. The classroom teacher with limited formal training in theatre arts should find the book readable and easy to follow. Each chapter builds on the previous one (specifically Chapters 3–12), and each chapter begins with easier activities that progress to the moredifficult. Thus, the teacher can learn along with the students the skills to be mastered.

Creative Drama Resource Book 4–6 is based, in principle, on a successful college text by the same author. However, for this resource book, the format has been simplified and designed for easier reading and reference. It has been considerably expanded with new chapters, new materials, and updated resources. Over 20 sample lesson plans have been included to help teachers experience success and to assist them in designing their own materials.

ESSENTIAL ELEMENTS

Teacher resource books for Grades 4–6 shall include material on:

1. Expressive use of the body and voice
   1.1 develop body awareness and spatial perception using: rhythmic and imitative movement

   sensory awareness

   pantomime

   1.2 express concepts using interpretive movement

   1.3 create original dialogue

   1.4 recall sensory and emotional experiences and utilize sensory and emotional recall in characterizations

2. Creative drama
   2.1 dramatize literary selections and original stories using: shadow play

CORRELATION

See particularly activities in Chapter 3, "Getting Started," pp. 34–45. Imitative movement is encouraged throughout most creative drama activities and in the Resource Book progresses in skill-building particularly through Chapter 4, "Using More Space," pp. 46–58, Chapter 5, "Narrative Pantomime with Children's Literature," pp. 59–79, Chapter 6, "Further Uses of Narrative Pantomime," pp. 80–97.

See particularly 39–41; 42–44; 49–55 (selected activities).

34–45; 49–55; 59–79; 80–97; 98–113; 142–159. In addition, pantomime activities are included in all sample lesson plans and story dramatizations. See, for example, pp. 168–189; 192–214; and 223–232.

9; 62; 80–97; 98–113. In addition, all sections labeled "pantomime" may be considered.

62; 69; 122–141; 151–152; 155–156; 159; 161–162; Dialogue in story dramatization lesson plans can be found on pp. 171; 173; 177–178; 182; 189; 192; 194; 198; 199; 201; 202–203; 204–205; 206; 207–208; 208–209; 211–212; 213; 214. Dialogue activities in Chapter 12, "Extended Drama Lesson Planning," can be found on pp. 224–225; 227–228; 231–232. Dialogue with puppets is covered on pp. 248–250.

16–17; 38–44; 49–55 (selected activities). Activities to encourage this include all those under "pantomime," including Story Dramatization and Extended Lesson Planning.

65–66 (selected stories); 73–79 (selected stories); 252–258.

ESSENTIAL ELEMENTS	CORRELATION
pantomime	37; 59–79; 80–97; 110–113; 142–159. See also "action" sections for lesson plans in Chapter 10 "Story Dramatization: Circle Stories," pp. 168–189 and "pantomime" sections for lesson plans in Chapter 11 "Story Dramatization: Segmented Stories," pp. 192–214. Note pantomime sections also in lesson plans in Chapter 12, "Extended Drama Lesson Planning," on pp. 226–227, and 229–230.
imitative dialogue	69; 114–122. Simple dialogue is encouraged in Chapter 10, "Story Dramatization: Circle Stories," under sections labeled "dialogue" on pp. 168–189.
improvisation	Improvisation in pantomime skits is found on pp. 110–113. Verbal improvisation exercises may be found on pp. 122–141. Further improvisational activities labeled either "pantomime" or "verbal" are found in Chapter 11 "Story Dramatization: Segmented Stories," pp. 192–220 and in Chapter 12, "Extended Drama Lesson Planning," pp. 223–232.
characterization	Pantomime of various characters in stories is particularly covered in Chapter 5, "Narrative Pantomime with Children's Literature," pp. 59–79. Verbal characterization is emphasized particularly in activities found on pp. 126, 127–131, 134. Both pantomime and verbal activities emphasizing particular characters in story dramatization are found in sample lesson plans in Chapter 11, "Story Dramatization: Segmented Stories," pp. 192–214. See further examples of activities in Chapter 12, "Extended Drama Lesson Planning," pp. 223–232.
puppetry	72–79 (selected stories); 80–81; 251; 255–25.
situation role-playing	This is covered in all the stories in Chapter 5, "Narrative Pantomime with Children's Literature," 59–79; Chapter 6, "Further Uses of Narrative Pantomime, 80–97; Chapter 10, "Story Dramatization: Circle Stories," pp. 160–189; Chapter 11, "Story Dramatization: Segmented Stories," 190–220; and Chapter 12, "Extended Drama Lesson Planning," 221–240.

ESSENTIAL ELEMENTS

3. Aesthetic growth through appreciation of theatrical events
   3.1 view theatrical events emphasizing:
   player-audience relationship

   audience etiquette
   recognition of similarities and differences between television, film, and live theatre
   3.2 participate in group planning for story dramatization incorporating:
   analysis of character behavior
   recognition of dramatic conflicts

   prediction of plot resolutions
   suggestions for alternative courses of action

CORRELATION

Chapter 14, "Going to the Theatre," pp. 263–271

264–266
263 ff.

16–17; 143; 147–152
40; 88; 110–112; 135–141; 143; 147–152

110–112; 135–141; 143; 147–159
110–112; 135–141; 143; 147–159

ADDITIONAL FEATURES OF *CREATIVE DRAMA RESOURCE BOOK FOR GRADES FOUR THROUGH SIX* (with page references)

1. Rationale for studying theatre arts in the elementary curriculum
2. Theatre vocabulary
3. Background information needed to teach the specified theatrical concepts and skills
4. Background information that explains the creative drama process and teaching strategies for presenting the instructional material
5. Suggestions for effective theatre arts class organization and management
6. A clearly defined scope and sequence of student learning objectives for theatre arts in Grades 1–6

7. Imaginative experiences and activities for achieving objectives, appropriate for students of varying

1–9

7–8; 68–72; 263–268; 281–283
1–9; 12–13; 40; 42–43; 49; 263–268

12–30; 33–34; 46–49; 59–64; 66; 68–72; 87–88; 98–100; 110; 114–115; 117–119; 122–123; 127; 128–129; 131–132; 142–147; 147–152; 160–167; 190–191; 221–222

12–30; 33–35; 44–45; 46–55; 98–100; 145–147; 162–165; 165–167; 190–191

Chapters 3–12 of *Creative Drama Resource Book 4-6* carefully progress from simpler to more complex activities. See "Scope and Sequence of Student Learning Objectives for Theatre Arts: Kindergarten Through Grade 6."

35–44; 49–55; 64–66; 67–68; 72–79; 81–87; 100–113; 114–131; 132–141; 142–143; 168–189; 192–214; 221–232; 243–245; 246–251.

ESSENTIAL ELEMENTS

ability, sequenced according to complexity for the designated category (Grades 1–3 or Grades 4–6)

8. Quality literature appropriate for the concepts and activities being presented

9. Instructional strategies and procedures for adapting instruction to accommodate students with varied interests, abilities, and special needs

10. Suggestions for correlating creative drama experiences with instruction in such subjects as English language arts, other languages, social studies; art; music; and physical education

11. Model lessons with suggestions as to how the teacher might extend the concepts and create various other lessons

CORRELATION

Grade levels are given for all entries in annotated bibliographies of children's literature recommended for drama activities.
35; 37; 44–45; 64–66; 67–68; 72–79; 81–87; 116; 119–121; 125–126; 168–189; 192–220; 223–229; 255–258; 261; 269–271; 272–280

See "Theatre Arts for All Children." See also pages: 12–24; 24–30; 46–49; 59–64; 66; 68–72; 98–100; 110–113; 131; 135–136; 144–147; 147–152; 160–167; 190–191; 221–222; 243–251; 252–255; 258–259

8–9; 40; 41–42; 43–44; 59–79; 80–97; 100–113; 115–122; 124–131; 132–135; 142–143; 148; 153–159; 168–189; 192–220; 221–240: 255–258; 261

55–58; 60–79; 89–97; 165–189; 190–220; 221–240

Lesson plans, alphabetized by title, include:

Bartholomew and the Oobleck (circle story), 168–171

Boston Tea Party (creative story building), 157–159

Bremen Town Musicians 1, (circle story), 183–186

Bremen Town Musicians 2, (segmented story), 192–194

"Cookin' for Paul Bunyan," 89–91

"The Doughnuts" (segmented story), 195–196

Duffy and the Devil (segmented story), 197–199

The Emperor's New Clothes (segmented story), 200–203

Going Camping (narrative pantomime), 92–94

"The Golden Goose," 172–173

Greek Mythology (extended lesson), 229–232

Johnny Tremain (segmented story), 204–206

"The King's Tower" (circle story), 174–176

The Legend of the Bluebonnet (circle story), 177–178

"The Legend of the Moor's Legacy" (narrative pantomime), 95–97

Scope and Sequence of Student Learning Objectives for Theatre Arts: Kindergarten through Grade 6

Since drama is a new subject area for many readers, the materials in this text have been arranged to help you learn in a step-by-step fashion. As you move through the book, teaching the activities, the children will also be acquiring skills in a sequence. At the same time, each chapter follows a sequence. This feature allows you to begin with particular topics chapters that appeal to you or ones you feel more comfortable with. For example, you might choose to begin with verbal activities in Chapter 9, story dramatization in Chapter 10, or even puppetry in Chapter 13. You should still be able to follow the sequence within each chapter with the help of the cross references to other chapters.

Thus, the arrangement of the text should allow you some flexibility in your teaching. With the help of the activities and the *general* scope and sequence presented, you should be able to develop the methods and procedures that work best for you and that you feel comfortable with. (Just as we allow latitude for children's individual differences and needs, so too should we allow teacher's individual styles.)

BEFORE YOU LOOK AT THE SCOPE AND SEQUENCE CHART

In the opening of Chapter 2, three major goals have been identified for drama. These include drama goals, personal development goals, and additional curricular goals.

Drama goals are outlined specifically in the Scope and Sequence Chart presented below. **Personal development goals** generally refer to interpersonal relationship skills that are required for drama and for social awareness. These would include such objectives as: developing confidence and trust in self and others; showing respect for the feelings and attitudes of others developing imagination and creativity; and working productively in groups. Many of these goals and objectives are already part of your teaching concerns, so it should not be necessary to enumerate these in detail.

Additional curricular goals will be derived from the content material you choose to add to a drama activity. A pantomime of various kinds of transportation, for example, would incorporate the drama goals of developing pantomime skills and the social studies goal of identifying various forms of transportation. Thus, the curricular objectives will be determined by you as you become aware of the various ways to use drama as an educational medium.

In some drama activities, you may emphasize one, two, or perhaps all three of these major goals. And, as already indicated, some of the goals can overlap. For example, "nurturing of creative thinking" could be considered a drama goal, a personal development goal, as well as a goal in any area of the curriculum.

DRAMA VARIABLES

Also in Chapter 2 there are **eight drama activity variables** identified on a continuum chart. Some drama activities, for example, are played at the desk; some are played in pairs and groups; some are closely directed by the teacher; and so forth. It is important to keep in mind that these variables can affect the difficulty of an activity and hence the success the children have with it. For example, a solo narrative pantomime activity in which all the children play the same character at their desks simultaneously is usually easier to do than a narrative pantomime played in small groups utilizing a larger area of space. The more complex the variables, the more complex the activity is for the children to master and the more difficult the activity will be for you to direct.

Although the variables are quite logical and obvious as you undertake drama activities, they are included here so that you can keep them in mind as you consider the Scope and Sequence Chart in the next section.

Drama Activity Variables*

Easier	to more	Advanced
1. Desk area		Larger areas of space
2. Teacher direction		Creative or independent thinking
3. Pantomime		Verbal activities
4. Solo playing		Pair and group playing
5. Run-through playing		In-depth playing for greater involvement
6. Humorous or "light" material		Highly dramatic or "serious" material

*This listing is repeated in Chapter 2.

Easier	to more	Advanced
7. Minimal informational content (curricular)		High data content
8. Unison playing for one's own satisfaction		Playing to share/communicate with observers

SCOPE AND SEQUENCE OF DRAMA GOALS AND OBJECTIVES*

KINDERGARTEN

1. **Develop expressive use of body and voice**
   1.1 Develop body awareness and spatial perception using:
   rhythmic and imitative movement
   move rhythmically and in unison with others through participation in action songs
      and games
   develop coordination through simple activities for self-control
   imitate people and animals (characters)
   explore posture, gesture, and facial expression in simple pantomimes for guessing
   1.2 Imitate sounds
   imitate familiar environment and speech sounds in sound effects activities

2. **Creative Drama**
   2.1 Dramatize limited-action stories and poems using simple pantomime
   dramatize simple narrative pantomime stories and poems
   imitate actions and characteristics of people and animals (characters)
   participate in simple circle story dramatizations

GRADE ONE

1. **Develop expressive use of body and voice**
   1.1 Develop body awareness and spatial perception using:
   rhythmic and imitative movement
   move rhythmically and in unison with others through participation in action songs
      and games
   develop coordination through simple activities for self-control
   imitate people and animals (characters)
   explore posture, gesture, and facial expression in simple pantomimes for guessing
   and sensory awareness
   develop awareness of senses through sensory games
   sharpen ability to use senses through simple sensory pantomimes
   1.2 Imitate sounds
   imitate familiar environment and speech sounds in sound effects activities

2. **Creative Drama**
   2.1 Dramatize limited-action stories and poems using simple pantomime
   dramatize simple narrative pantomime stories and poems
   imitate actions and characteristics of people and animals (characters)
   create imaginary environments in dramatizing stories
   participate in circle story dramatizations

*Note: drama goals in bold type are the essential drama elements required by the state
of Texas. Additional learning objectives appear in regular type.

end puppetry
explore body movement through puppetry
use puppets in narrative pantomime stories and poems

GRADE TWO

1. Develop expressive use of body and voice
    1.1 Develop body awareness and spatial perception using:
    rhythmic and imitative movement
    move rhythmically and in unison with others through participation in action songs
       and games
    develop coordination and control through activities for self-control
    imitate people and animals (characters)
    explore posture, gesture, and facial expression in pantomime for guessing
    sensory awareness
    develop awareness of senses through sensory games
    sharpen ability to use senses through simple sensory pantomimes
    and pantomime
    enact movements of others (animals, people, objects) through pantomime
    create imaginary environments
    explore posture, gesture, and facial expression as a means of communication
    communicate ideas through actions and nonverbal expression
    decode pantomimed actions of stories
    1.2 Imitate sounds and dialogue
    imitate environment and speech sounds through sound effects activities
    explore simple dialogue through puppetry
    participate in simple verbal activities and games

2. Creative Drama
    2.2 Dramatize literary selections using:
    shadow play
    experience nonverbal and verbal language through medium of shadow
       play/puppetry
    interpret narrative pantomime and circle stories through medium of shadow
       play/puppetry
    coordinate shadow play/puppetry materials (e.g., puppets, lights, stage, scenery,
       shadow screen) to produce simple dramatic presentation
    pantomime
    enact movements of others (animals, people, objects) through pantomime
    create imaginary environments suggested by stories
    explore posture, gesture, and facial expression as a means of communication
    communicate ideas through actions and nonverbal expression
    decode pantomimed actions of others
    and imitative dialogue
    recreate dialogue of familiar stories (circle and segmented stories)
    explore simple dialogue through puppets in story dramatization

GRADE THREE

1. Develop expressive use of body and voice
    1.1 Develop body awareness and spatial perception using
    rhythmic and imitative movement

move rhythmically and in unison with others through participation in action songs
and games
develop coordination and control through activities for self-control
imitate people and animals (characters)
explore posture, gesture, and facial expression in pantomimes for guessing
sensory awareness
develop awareness of senses through sensory games
sharpen ability to use senses through simple sensory pantomimes
and pantomime
enact movements of others (animals, people, objects) through pantomime
create imaginary environments
explore posture, gesture, and facial expression as a means of communication
communicate ideas through actions and nonverbal expression
decode pantomimed actions of others
participate in developing simple skits from familiar material

1.2 Imitate sounds and dialogue
imitate environment and speech sounds through sound effects activities
explore simple dialogue through puppetry
participate in simple verbal activities and games
sensory and emotional experiences
pantomime believeable actions by remembering past sensory and emotional
experiences and imagining new ones

2. Creative Drama
2.2 Dramatize literary selections using shadow play
imitate people and animals (characters)
explore posture, gesture, and facial expression in pantomimes for guessing
sensory awareness
develop awareness of senses through sensory games
sharpen ability to use senses through simple sensory pantomimes
and pantomime
enact movements of others (animals, people, objects) through pantomime
create imaginary environments
explore posture, gesture, and facial expression as a means of communication
communicate ideas through actions and nonverbal expression
decode pantomimed actions of others
participate in developing simple skits from familiar material

1.2 express concepts using interpretive movement
express abstract ideas and concepts in narrative pantomime literature and in
pantomimes for guessing

1.3 create original dialogue
participate in verbal activities and games
participate in creating and sharing verbal skits

1.4 recall sensory and emotional experiences
pantomime believable actions by remembering past sensory and emotional
experiences and imagining new ones

2. Creative Drama
2.1 Dramatize literary selections using shadow play
experience nonverbal and verbal language through medium of shadow
play/puppetry

interpret narrative pentomime and circle stories through medium of shadow play/puppetry

coordinate shadow play/puppetry materials (e.g. puppets, lights, stage, scenery, shadow screen) to produce simple dramatic presentation

experience nonverbal and verbal language through medium of shadow play/puppetry

interpret narrative pantomime and circle stories through medium of shadow play/puppetry

coordinate shadow play/puppetry materials (e.g. puppets, lights, stage, scenery, shadow screen) to produce simple dramatic presentation

pantomime

enact movements of others (animals, people, objects) through pantomime

create imaginary environments suggested by stories

explore posture, gesture, and facial expression as a means of communication

communicate ideas through actions and nonverbal expression

decode pantomimed actions of others

and imitative dialogue

recreate dialogue of familiar stories (circle and segmented stories)

explore simple dialogue through puppets in story dramatization

3. **Aesthetic growth through appreciation of theatrical events**
   3.1 **view theatrical events emphasizing**
   player-audience relationship
   understand basic theatrical conventions (e.g. use of curtain, lights, etc.)
   audience etiquette
   understand etiquette rules that make theatrical attendance enjoyable for all
   understand audience rules that are needed to aid the actors in performing

GRADE FOUR

1. **Develop expressive use of body and voice**
   1.1 **Develop body awareness and spatial perception using**
   rhythmic and imitative movement
   move rhythmically and in unison with others through participation in action songs and games
   develop coordination and control through activities for self-control
   pantomime
   enact movements of others (animals, people, objects) through pantomime
   create imaginary environments suggested by stories
   explore posture, gesture, and facial expression as a means of communication
   communicate ideas through actions and nonverbal expression
   decode pantomimed actions of others
   and imitative dialogue
   recreate dialogue of familiar stories (circle and segmented stories)
   explore simple dialogue through puppets in story dramatization
2. **Aesthetic growth through appreciation of theatrical events**
   3.1 **view theatrical events emphasizing**
   player-audience relationship
   understand basic theatrical conventions (e.g. use of curtain, lights, etc.)
   audience etiquette

understand etiquette rules that make theatrical attendance enjoyable for all
understand audience rules that are needed to aid the actors in performing
and recognition of similarities and differences between television, film, and live theatre
understand basics of how films are made as compared with theatre
understand basics of how television shows are made as compared with theatre

3.2 **participate in group planning for story dramatization incorporating analysis of character behavior**
identify story characters' feelings
identify a story character's motivations behind actions
recognition of dramatic conflicts
identify the conflicts or problems in the story that make the plot dramatic
and prediction of plot resolutions
understand the plot structure of beginning, middle, and end
anticipate story endings

GRADE FIVE

1. **Develop expressive use of body and voice**
   1.1 **Develop body awareness and spatial perception using**
      rhythmic and imitative movement
      move rhythmically and in unison with others through participation in action songs and games
      develop coordination and control through activities for self-control
      imitate people and animals (characters)
      explore posture, gesture, and facial expression in pantomimes for guessing
      sensory awareness
      develop awareness of senses through sensory games
      sharpen ability to use senses through simple sensory pantomimes
      and pantomime
      enact movements of others (animals, people, objects) through pantomime
      create imaginary environments
      explore posture, gesture, and facial expression as a means of communication
      communicate ideas through actions and nonverbal expression
      decode pantomimed actions of others
      participate in developing simple skits from familiar material
   1.2 **express concepts using interpretive movement**
      express abstract ideas and concepts in narrative pantomime literature and in pantomimes for guessing
   1.3 **create original dialogue**
      participate in verbal activities and games
      participate in creating and sharing verbal skits
   1.4 **utilize sensory and emotional recall in characterizations**
      pantomime believeable actions by remembering past sensory and emotional experiences and imagining new ones playing a character
2. **Creative Drama**
   2.1 **Dramatize literary selections and original stories using shadow play**

experience nonverbval and verbal language through medium of shadow play/puppetry

interpret narrative pantomime and circle stories through medium of shadow play/puppetry

coordinate shadow play/puppetry materials (e.g. puppets, lights, stage, scenery, shadow screen) to produce simple dramatic presentation

create original stories and skits using shadow play

pantomime

enact movements of others (animals, people, objects) through pantomime

create imaginary environments suggested by stories

explore posture, gesture, and facial expression as a means of communication

communicate ideas through actions and nonverbal expression

decode pantomimed actions of others

imitative dialogue

recreate dialogue of familiar stories (circle and segmented stories)

explore simple dialogue through puppets in story dramatization

improvisation

participate in verbal improvisation games

participate in creating dialogue in scenes, skits, and in segmented story dramatization

characterization

interpret people, animals, or objects, through pantomime and speech, in story dramatization

and puppetry

dramatize narrative pantomime stories, circle stories, and segmented stories with puppets

3. **Aesthetic growth through appreciation of theatrical events**
   3.1 **view theatrical events and emphasizing**
       player-audience relationship
       understand basic theatrical conventions (e.g. use of curtain, lights, etc.)
       audience etiquette
       understand etiquette rules that make theatrical attendance enjoyable for audience
       understand audience rules that are needed to aid the actors in performing
       and recognition of similarities and differences between television, film, and live theatre
       understand basics of how films are made as compared with theatre
       understand basics of how television shows are made as compared with theatre
       and evaluation and aesthetic judgments
       evaluate one's own and classmates' drama work
       evaluate a theatrical performance applying basic aesthetic criteria
   3.2 **participate in group planning for story dramatization incorporating analysis of character behavior**
       identify a story characters' feelings
       identify a story character's motivations behind actions
       recognition of dramatic conflicts
       identify the conflicts or problems in the story that make the plot dramatic
       progress the playing and heighten the tension in building toward the plot climax
       and prediction of plot resolutions
       anticipate story endings

1. Develop expressive use of body and voice
  1.1 Develop body awareness and spatial perception using rhythmic and imitative movement
    move rhythmically and in unison with others through participation in action songs and games
    develop coordination and control through activities for self-control
    imitate people and animals (characters)
    explore posture, gesture, and facial expression in pantomimes for guessing
    sensory awareness
    develop awareness of senses through sensory games
    sharpen ability to use senses through simple sensory pantomimes
    and pantomime
    enact movements of others (animals, people, objects) through pantomime
    create imaginary environments
    explore posture, gesture, and facial expression as a means of communication
    communicate ideas through actions and nonverbal expression
    decode pantomimed actions of others
    participate in developing simple skits from familiar material
  1.2 express concepts using interpretive movement
    express abstract ideas and concepts in narrative pantomime literature and in pantomimes for guessing
  1.3 create original dialogue
    participate in verbal activities and games
    participate in creating and sharing verbal skits
  1.4 utilize sensory and emotional recall in characterizations
    pantomime believeable actions by remembering past sensory and emotional experiences and imagining new ones playing a character

2. Creative Drama
  2.1 Dramatize literary selections and original stories using shadow play
    experience nonverbal and verbal language through medium of shadow play/puppetry
    interpret narrative pantomime and circle stories through medium of shadow play/puppetry
    coorindate shadow play/puppetry materials (e.g. puppets, lights, stage, scenery, shadow screen) to produce simple dramatic presentation
    create original stories and skits using shadow play
    pantomime
    enact movements of others (animals, people, objects) through pantomime
    create imaginary environments suggested by stories
    explore posture, gesture, and facial expression as a means of communication
    communicate ideas through actions and nonverbal expression
    decode pantomimed actions of others
    imitative dialogue
    recreate dialogue of familiar stories (circle and segmented stories)
    explore simple dialogue through puppets in story dramatization
    improvisation
    participate in verbal improvisation games

participate in creating dialogue in scenes, skits, and in segmented story dramatization

characterization

interpret people, animals, or objects, through pantomime and speech, in story
dramatization

and puppetry

dramatize narrative pantomime stories, circle stories, and segmented stories with
puppets

and situation role-playing

create character roles in skits, scenes, stories and specified situations

3. **Aesthetic growth through appreciation of theatrical events**
   3.1 **view theatrical events emphasizing**
   player-audience relationship
   understand basic theatrical conventions (e.g. use of curtain, lights, etc.)
   audience etiquette
   understand etiquette rules that make theatrical attendance enjoyable for audience
   understand audience rules that are needed to aid the actors in performing
   **and recognition of similarities and differences between television, film, and live
   theatre**
   understand basics of how films are made as compared with theatre
   understand basics of how television shows are made as compared with theatre
   and evaluation and aesthetic judgments
   evaluate one's own and classmates' drama work
   evaluate a theatrical performance applying basic aesthetic criteria
   3.2 **participate in group planning for story dramatization incorporating analysis of
   character behavior**
   identify a story characters' feelings
   identify a story character's motivations behind actions
   recognition of dramatic conflicts
   identify the conflicts or problems in the story that make the plot dramatic
   progress the playing and heighten the tension in building toward the plot climax
   and prediction of plot resolutions
   anticipate story endings
   and suggestions for alternative courses of action
   demonstrate ability to create new characters, situations, and varieties of plot development and resolution in dramatizing stories

Subject Index

Title Index of Books, Stories, and Poems

Note: An asterisk (*) next to page numbers indicates that a lesson plan of that title can be found on those pages.